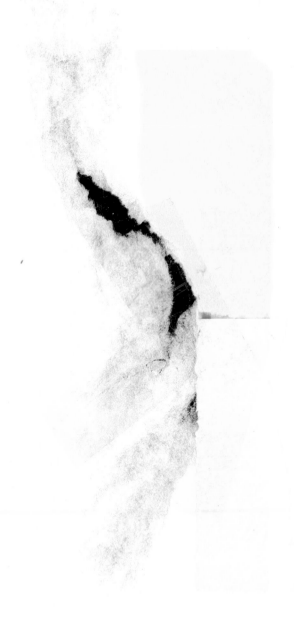

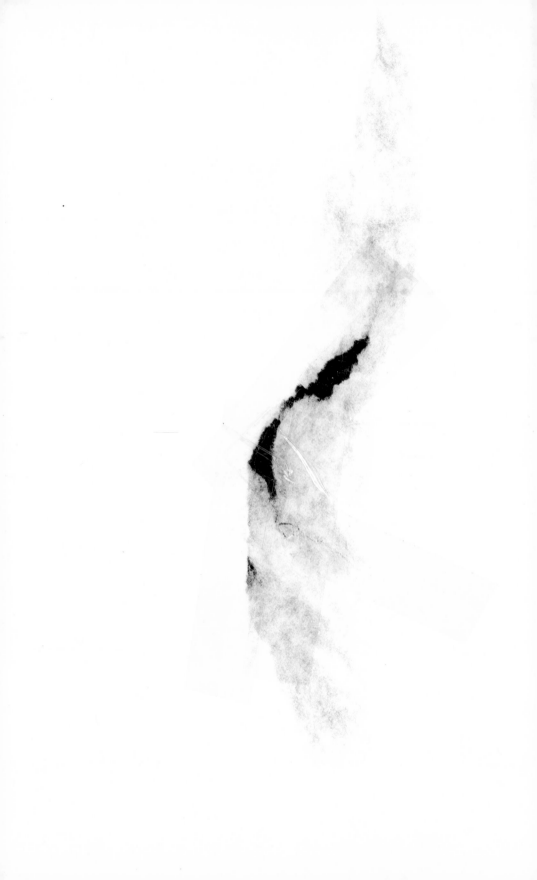

Welcome to the Circus of Baseball

A STORY OF THE PERFECT SUMMER AT THE PERFECT BALLPARK AT THE PERFECT TIME

RYAN McGEE

DOUBLEDAY · NEW YORK

www.doubleday.com

DOUBLEDAY and the portrayal of an anchor with a dolphin are
registered trademarks of Penguin Random House LLC.

Page 259 constitutes an extension of this copyright page.

Jacket images: McCormick Field by Sam Fischer /
Asheville Tourists; mascot used by permission of Asheville Tourists
Jacket design by Michael J. Windsor

Library of Congress Cataloging-in-Publication Data
Names: McGee, Ryan, author.
Title: Welcome to the circus of baseball : a story of the perfect summer
at the perfect ballpark at the perfect time / by Ryan McGee.
Description: First Edition. | New York : Doubleday, [2023]
Identifiers: LCCN 2022030173 | ISBN 9780385548403 (hardcover) |
ISBN 9780385548427 (ebook)
Subjects: LCSH: McGee, Ryan. | Sportswriters—United States—
Anecdotes. | Summer employment—North Carolina—Asheville. |
Asheville Tourists (Baseball team)—History. | McCormick Field (Asheville, N.C.)—
History. | Minor league baseball—North Carolina—Asheville—History.
Classification: LCC GV742.42 .M446 2023 |
DDC 070.4/49796—dc23/eng/20221013
LC record available at https://lccn.loc.gov/2022030173

MANUFACTURED IN THE UNITED STATES OF AMERICA

1 3 5 7 9 10 8 6 4 2

First Edition

Dedicated to all those out there grinding and smiling
at minor-league ballparks every summer

When you get to Asheville
Write me if you will
Tell me how you're doing
How it's treating you.

—"Asheville," from the musical *Bright Star*

Don't tell me about the labor pains.
Just show me the baby.

—Ron McKee, GM,
Asheville Tourists Baseball Club

CONTENTS

CONTENTS

LET'S START WITH A BANG

"**O**h man, I think that sumbitch is actually dead!"

It was a hair-dryer-in-the-face-hot Sunday afternoon at McCormick Field, home of the Asheville Tourists of the South Atlantic League, the proud but not great Class A affiliate of the Colorado Rockies, the first full step of every ballplayer's cleat-wearing march toward the big leagues. On this day in 1994, amid a summer when those big leagues were constantly on the cusp of shutting down their season over money, McCormick Field was the perfect antidote for everyone's MLB illness. It was everything that is right about baseball. A perfectly picturesque all-American throwback minor-league ballpark, just as it was when it was christened in 1924 and just as it still is today. A grandstand packed with patrons, buzzed in the box seats on cold beer and peanuts, and none of it had cost them more than a few bucks. A baseball band-box carved into a Blue Ridge mountainside, laced with the unmistakable scent of western North Carolina honeysuckle blooms. A circle of gray concrete, green vines, and a kaleidoscope of advertising billboards, all wrapped around a diamond of a ballfield that for nearly a century has been tread upon by the Cooperstown-bound cleats of Ty Cobb, Babe Ruth, and Willie Stargell, as well

1

as thousands of minor leaguers whose names and unfulfilled big-league dreams have been lost to time.

In 1924, in the ballpark's first official professional game, Cobb's notoriously sharp cleats churned the dirt around McCormick Field's second base, sprinting around the bag after he slapped a home run. In 1948, Jackie Robinson patrolled that same dirt, in town with the barnstorming Brooklyn Dodgers. Now, seventy summers after Cobb and nearly forty-six years to that exact day after Robinson's visit, surrounded by minor leaguers of 1994, I was convinced that the very same spot of earth where the Georgia Peach and No. 42 had once roamed had just become a crime scene.

The shouter was right. Yes, that sumbitch really did look dead.

Looking back now, I am embarrassed at my surprise. After all, the man who lay motionless where the now-scorched infield dirt met the now-blown-back edge of the outfield grass was known as Captain Dynamite and his Exploding Coffin of Death.

I was a recent college graduate making $100 a week (cash) working in the Asheville Tourists' front office. We had a summertime calendar packed with game day entertainers, everything from an Elvis impersonator ("Elvis Himselvis") and a Blues Brothers–themed comedy act to appearances from Ronald McDonald and Billy Bird, the mascot of the Class AAA Louisville Redbirds. Billy was a much more affordable option than the most famous feathered mascot in all of sports, the San Diego Chicken.

Every performer commanded an appearance fee, covering an extremely wide financial scale. Most asked for several thousand dollars for one evening's work at the ballyard. It was worth it. Every scheduled performance, whether it be a brand-name Chicken or a AAA Billy, brought an instant boost to that night's ticket sales. But there were seventy-one home games in a Minor League Baseball season, and every team had only so much money to spend on pregame acts.

In other words, not every night can feature Elvis Himselvis or the Blues Brothers. Sometimes you must book Captain Dynamite and his Exploding Coffin of Death. I believe his fee was $500 (also cash).

Among the endless tasks that can be found on the to-do list of a minor-league ball club's young, fresh-legged $100 employees is aiding those game day entertainers, helping out with whatever they might need. That could mean lending a hand to carry equipment to the field or sneaking them a postshow six-pack from the beer cooler. When the good Captain rolled up to the ballpark in a well-rusted station wagon, he made it known that he required no such aid. In a superpolite, almost hushed tone, the overtanned fire hydrant of a man smiled and explained that he had brought his own road crew. He pointed to a hard-around-the-edges woman, a living Andrew Wyeth image that I assumed to be his wife, and a half-dozen unbathed children. I supposed they were his grandchildren. Captain Dynamite was seventy-eight years of age but looked at least thirty years older than that.

Like redneck clockwork, the little Dynamites each grabbed a panel of foam board from the back of the Family Truckster and carried it through the stadium service entrance toward the playing field. There, they constructed a rudimentary rectangular box atop the dirt just behind second base.

Spoiler alert: The "Coffin" wasn't a coffin at all. It was a homemade foam faux sarcophagus that had been painted black, but not well enough in a few spots to hide the "3M Insulation" logos. As for the "of Death" part of the setup, well, that looked pretty damn real. At least it certainly felt real as the Captain began carefully stuffing the box with old-school explosives, bright red sticks with long fuses that looked as if they had been stolen directly from the ACME stash of Wile E. Coyote. They even had "TNT" printed on them. After packing the Coffin with the Death, our hero proceeded to pull a dark green jumpsuit over his jeans and dirty

T-shirt, complete with well-worn all-caps "CAPTAIN DYNA-MITE" embroidered across his back, along with the smoke-stained orange cloth image of an explosion. He then yanked a heavily scarred motorcycle helmet over his head, climbed into the foam board casket, and lay down among the explosives like a hillbilly Dracula as the lid was sealed above him. His crew shuffled down to the end of the wire, settling in alongside the first baseline, where Wile E.'s T-handled detonator machine was standing by.

I was watching all this unfold from the steps of the home dugout, only 150 feet or so from the coffin. I purposely stood a little lower than earth line, should that dugout suddenly need to become a fallout shelter. One by one, the Asheville Tourists ballplayers filled the space around me, mouths agape, as the countdown from the press box reverberated throughout McCormick Field and the surrounding neighborhood.

"Ten . . . nine . . . eight . . . seven . . ."

Anyone who had watched television over the previous few decades likely recognized the seat-rattling bass tone of the public-address announcer. Not the name but certainly the voice. It was broadcasting pioneer Sam Zurich, now a retiree living in the North Carolina mountains. For years he voiced promos and commercials for CBS television and local stations across the Carolinas. Sam had seen it all. He was the model of an unflappable broadcasting professional. But as he looked down from his press box perch to the coffin below, even Sam's rock-solid tone carried a hint of "Exactly what in the world are we counting down to here?"

"Six . . . five . . . four . . ."

All 1,100 fans in attendance were on their feet. I felt a tap on my shoulder. It was Tourists righty pitcher John Thomson. He was on his way to a ten-year big-league career. But not yet. Today he was a twenty-year-old prospect half-jokingly handing out batting helmets to those of us in the dugout. "Just in case," he explained in his Mississippi accent. "Some of that guy's body parts might come flying in here."

"Three . . . two . . . one . . ."

BOOM.

The concussion from the explosion was so forceful that the tiny ballpark could barely contain it. The ground was shaken with such power that a plastic cup from the box seats had been blown in from above, dropped from the hand of a temporarily incapacitated baseball fan, and splashed Pepsi all over the floor of the dugout. A flock of startled birds launched from the trees that towered behind the outfield fence. In the distance, car alarms could be heard from every parking lot around McCormick Field, whistles and chimes triggered by the blast. Everyone in the building reflexively raised their hands to their faces, covering their ears, eyes, or both.

When my eyes finally reopened and focused on the field, all I could see was a giant rising cloud of white smoke and falling debris of red infield dirt. That dirt was mixed with hundreds of pieces of black, silver, and pink foam, all dancing back to the ground like snow. The debris field was large. My initial reaction was, *This is going to take forever to clean up.* My second thought was formed as the smoke lifted and the Captain finally came into view, lying facedown in the dirt, not moving so much as one finger as the Family Dynamite scrambled toward him. I never spoke my reaction aloud. I didn't have to. One of the ballplayers said it for me.

"Oh man, I think that sumbitch is actually dead!"

Prior to the performance we had been told that the Captain was in the middle of what amounted to his farewell tour. After four decades, several thousand explosions on everything from county fairgrounds to drag strips, and at least two arrests on charges of improper storage of explosives, Patrick O'Brien was grooming his replacement. Lady Dynamite was already making a simultaneous circuit of summertime ballpark stops, a much younger and much more spangly female version of the act, complete with an Evel Knievel–style cape covering her shoulders and a thong-anchored bodysuit of her own design that covered nothing. But right now, we were thinking that her predecessor's farewell tour was over. Best we could tell, he had just said farewell to life.

Captain Dynamite's crew shook him and screamed at him, all while the remnants of his Coffin of Death settled onto the infield around them. The weathered woman leaned into his helmeted face. I couldn't tell if perhaps she'd stuck smelling salts under his nose or if maybe she had slapped him. Whatever she did, it worked. Captain Dynamite's limbs stiffened, he sat up, and with the assistance of his family/crew, he rose to stand atop wobbly knees and waved to the audience, our jaws collectively unhinged.

Take that, Death.

My coworkers and I ran onto the field to start picking up the debris. I jogged by a stunned Captain Dynamite as he left the field, his arms draped over his companions' shoulders for support as a small trail of blood trickled down one cheek. "Great job!" I said, giving him a thumbs-up. He looked at me and smiled wearily. Clearly, he had no idea what I'd just said. She barked into his ear, "He says you did a great job!" Captain Dynamite replied, but his hushed tone was long gone, his ears no doubt ringing like the bells of St. Paul's.

"THANK YOU VERY MUCH!"

I think he tried to wink at me, but that's when I realized that one of his eyes was glass. I also think he tried to give me a return thumbs-up, but that's when I discovered that he was two fingers short of a full set. Scooting along behind the couple was one of the children, a boy of perhaps seven years of age, who looked me right in the eye as he dragged a roll of wire behind him and said, "My daddy done blowed himself up."

As the Dynamites loaded back into their station wagon with the Captain's five hundred bucks, we hurriedly ran off the field, dragging trash bags that we had just stuffed with a thousand Coffin of Death remnants. As we stepped off the diamond, the home-team Asheville Tourists, in their sparkling pinstriped home whites, trotted by us to take up their positions and take on the Hickory Crawdads. Another shout echoed throughout McCormick Field. It came from behind home plate.

"Play ball!"

WELCOME TO THE CIRCUS
OF BASEBALL

I t was a cold mid-December Friday morning. I was hurtling southbound on I-85 somewhere between Clemson, South Carolina, and Atlanta and I was panicking. It was that most helpless kind of panic when everything is so silent around you that it only intensifies your dismay. Your brain sounds like a blender in your skull, and you can feel a hot pulse pounding through the side of your neck.

My anxiety was a sign of the times. My times as well as America's. I was six months out of college and without full-time employment. My parents were well past the point of being happy to have me back in the house. I'd been handed my diploma and pushed out into the middle of a recession recovery. And, okay, if I'm being honest, I was being too picky. I didn't want any job. I wanted a cool job. Now, with maybe, possibly, hopefully a chance to land said awesome gig—a job in professional baseball—I was in the process of having a mid-interstate panic attack.

Why was I so panicked? Because the skies were pouring an umbrella-useless icy rain, my brand-new Pontiac Grand Am was skating down the highway like a Zamboni, and I was running late. Why was I late? Because that morning I had crashed that brand-new Pontiac Grand Am, bending the right front corner, and now I feared that crumpled sheet metal was rubbing the tire beneath it like a cheese grater as I raced along the interstate. All this while I was also trying to decide: Should I lose even more minutes off the clock by pulling over at the next pay phone to call ahead with my excuse for being late, or should I wait and plead my case in person after I had already been late? Yes, a pay phone. It was 1993.

How had I ended up in this predicament? Because I'd spent the night in Clemson on the sofa of my high school crush, whom I was once again trying to convince to love me, even though I knew it was never going to happen. Just like in high school. I'd overslept on that couch of sadness and in my hurry to get on the road for Atlanta had immediately slammed my new car into the trunk of a much older car that was backing out of a parking space in the apartment complex of the girl who was never going to love me.

It had already been one of the worst days of my young life, and it wasn't yet eleven a.m.

My destination was the Atlanta Marriott Marquis, host of the 1993 edition of the Baseball Winter Meetings, the annual December gathering of the wheelers and dealers who keep America's Pastime running. For decades, the Winter Meetings had been the bunkhouse stampede of sports job fairs. There were no rules. Just a horde of baby-faced college graduates like myself, invading baseball's biggest off-season business convention to hound front-office executives for jobs. A tidal wave of overeager twentysomethings endlessly walking the halls of the host hotel, desperately trying not to look desperate as they stalked those executives, résumés in hand and crazed looks in their eyes.

But this year, for the first time ever, that hunting and gathering process was being organized and corporatized, managed by a brand-new group called Sports Jobs Incorporated. Or maybe it was Jobs in Sports Incorporated or Work in Baseball Inc. Whatever. I forget the exact name now, but I certainly knew it at the time when I'd scribbled it onto the payee line of the $150 check that I'd mailed in with my registration form. The same form that had informed me that I absolutely had to be signed in at the Marriott Marquis by noon on Friday, December 10, no ifs, ands, or buts. *But* there was *no* question *if* I was going to make it by then. I wasn't.

In the trunk of my just-battered Grand Am was my own box of résumés, a hot-off-the-Kinko's-press two pages of illustrious life accomplishments (*"Part-time high school football correspondent, Monroe Enquirer-Journal"*), paired with a cassette tape. On that Memorex was a one-hour compilation of what I had determined to be my best broadcasting moments from the just-finished fall football season. Scratchy recordings made in poorly lit municipal stadiums of my Friday nights and Saturday afternoons spent as the play-by-play voice of the Forest Hills High School Yellow Jackets of Marshville, North Carolina (*"Welcome to the hometown of Randy Travis, country music's finest!"*) and NCAA Division II's Wingate University (*"Go Bulldogs!"*). I had also thrown in a few minutes of my only baseball experience on a microphone, a not-great recording of me doing one game of public-address announcing at my alma mater, the University of Tennessee, calling out lineups and official scoring to the dozens in attendance for a midweek daytime game at the Volunteers' home ballpark, Lindsey Nelson Stadium.

When I listen to that tape now, I hear a kid trying to sound like a man, a youthful Southern-fried voice pushed from way too deep in the back of my throat through the low-def filter of either a college ballpark PA system, a rural AM radio tower (WIXE 1190 AM, *"Wixie in Dixie!"*), or local cable access Channel 69, my voice used as the background audio for the want ads of the Union County Community Calendar (*"Yard sale this Saturday at the Blevins' house over on Magnolia Street!"*).

But when I compiled that tape back then, I was convinced that on it was the sound of the next Red Barber, Mel Allen, or the namesake of my public-address location, Lindsey Nelson. Those Southern-raised gentlemen all managed to "overcome" their accents by charming their way into the ears and hearts of baseball-loving Americans. They had ascended from Columbus, Mississippi; Birmingham, Alabama; and Pulaski, Tennessee, to work in the press boxes of Ebbets Field, Yankee Stadium, and Candlestick Park. If those guys could find their ways from those hometowns to the Baseball Hall of Fame, then certainly I could get to Cooperstown from my own birthplace of Rockingham, North Carolina, right?

I was convinced that my first steps along the path they had trailblazed were to begin now, in an Atlanta ballroom. My plan was to launch my career as a legendary baseball play-by-play man by leveraging whatever resources my $150 fee paid to Baseball Jobs of America Inc. (or whatever it was) to wow the general manager of some Minor League Baseball team with my wit, skill, and can't-miss broadcasting potential. Who cared which of the 173 MiLB teams it might be? I wasn't greedy.

Forget that earlier that fall I had already mailed that same résumé and cassette tape to one hundred of those teams, hand-scribbling their addresses and names that I had painstakingly procured from the *1993 Baseball America Directory* and likely gaining a bout of glue poisoning from licking the stamps for all those manila envelopes. From those hundred letters, I had received precisely one response. It was from the gregarious Curt Bloom, voice of the Class AA Birmingham Barons, who said he figured (correctly) that I had already faced a ton of rejection and/or apathy, but to keep my chin up and get my butt to the Winter Meetings in December, airchecks in hand, just as he had done a few years earlier to get his big baseball break.

Also forget that I had started that same autumn by totally blowing a shot at my other dream job. The week after college graduation, I'd scored an interview with ESPN for an entry-level production assistant (PA) position. PAs answered the phones, ran teleprompter, and cut highlights for the likes of *Baseball Tonight* and *SportsCenter*. I'd flown myself to Bristol, Connecticut, and was ushered into the office of Al Jaffe, an original 1979 employee of the Worldwide Leader in Sports and the man who was responsible for hiring everyone. Like, everyone, for real, from production assistants to anchors. To my unprepared surprise, it was less a job interview and more a sports quiz, with questions carefully selected by Jaffe to lean away from any natural regional knowledge. For a Southerner, that meant "Who do you think is the favorite to win this year's Vezina Trophy?" I didn't know what that was, so I assumed it was a hockey question. I made a joke that unless he had any questions about the 1980 USA "Miracle on Ice" team, I wasn't going to be able to answer any hockey questions. I even tried to make a folksy joke about manure. "Hey, the only hockey we see in North Carolina is horse hockey we just stepped in." I might as well have jumped up onto his desk and started clogging while whistling the theme from *The Andy Griffith Show*. When he asked me what I ultimately wanted to do for a career, I told him that I dreamed of becoming a play-by-play man. He responded coldly, "You need to know that's not what this job and this career path in production is about."

The interview went so poorly that when it mercifully ended and Jaffe pointed toward his door, I asked him how I would know if I'd gotten the job. He explained that he interviewed kids like me all the time and kept us ranked based on how we'd performed in our interviews. When a PA position came open, he'd start at the top of those rankings and make calls offering the job, working his way down the list until someone said yes. He never got past the first couple of names. Then he warned me that the names stayed on his list for only one year. Jaffe looked at his desk calendar and said that if I hadn't heard from him by one year from that day, by August 19, 1994, I could safely assume ESPN had chosen to go in another direction and so should I. He then demonstratively flipped a couple of pages of paper before what I assumed was finally writing down my name. I wasn't merely not at the top of any post-interview power rankings. I was barely on the clipboard. That night at the Radisson across the street from ESPN HQ, I slipped into the swimming pool so that no one could see me crying.

That fall, living back home with my parents in Monroe, North Carolina, I covered high school games for the local newspaper, where I'd sit atop the grandstand, far from anyone else, "broadcasting" play-by-play into a cassette recorder, simply for the practice and to have something on tape in case anyone wanted to hear it. That led to the radio gig at WIXE in Dixie. There I worked alongside fabled local sportscaster James "Foxx" Reddish. The Foxx was a subwoofer-voiced man who weighed at least three hundred pounds and would fling himself up onto the roof of the press box by swinging like a pendulum from the fire escape ladder until he built up enough momentum to go full Simone Biles. Foxx was a fantastic storyteller and during timeouts would regale me with tales from his time as the voice of the Monroe Pirates, a Class A Western Carolinas League baseball team who'd played a season at the same aluminum stadium where we now called small college football games. The Foxx also repeated what Curt Bloom had told me, that my best chance at landing a baseball gig was to get to Atlanta that December and, in his words, "sell yourself harder than an Avon Lady of the Night." I still don't know exactly what that meant. I just knew I needed to attend the Winter Meetings.

So, that's how I ended up on a pay phone alongside I-85 in the pouring rain, scrounging up enough quarters from beneath the seats of my wrecked Pontiac to call ahead to Atlanta and let the people at the Get a Baseball Job Inc. sign-in desk know that I was going to be late. I thought that perhaps if I shared the story of my twice-brokenhearted trip (girl and wreck), they would take pity on me and allow me to check in late instead of throwing my nametag into the trash along with my baseball hopes and dreams.

"Hello, Sports Baseball Jobs Incorporated, how may I help you?"

"Yes, my name is Ryan McGee. . . ."

"I can't hear you."

"Sorry, I'm on a rest stop pay phone right off the highway and . . ."

"Who is this?!"

"MY NAME IS RYAN MCGEE AND I AM RUNNING LATE BECAUSE I WAS IN A CAR ACCIDENT THIS MORNING AND I AM RUNNING LATE AND I WANTED TO SEE IF I COULD CHECK IN OVER THE PHONE NOW OR LATER TODAY IN PERSON BECAUSE I AM RUNNING LATE! THE REGISTRATION FORM SAID I COULDN'T BE THERE LATER THAN NOON AND I AM RUNNING LATE."

"Yeah, okay, whatever, Ron, that's fine. Just get here when you can."

Click.

An hour and a half later, a solid forty-five minutes past the check-in deadline, I sprinted into a side ballroom off the cavernous lobby of the Marriott Marquis, pointed there by a sign on an easel that read "Baseball Job Fair." As I approached the sign-in table, the shoulders of my navy sport coat and the cuffs of my Dockers khakis were both saturated with cold rainwater. I also wore a very slick semi-silk 1990s necktie, featuring a high-concept design involving a collage of golden baseballs. I was very proud of that necktie. Out of breath, I ran to the table, and there was my nametag and arrival packet, along with at least fifty others'. Apparently, a lot of people were having days just as bad as mine.

I gathered up my lungs, clipped my nametag to my blazer, and stepped into the next room. It was like looking into a hall of mirrors. Dark-haired twentysomething college graduates as far as the eye could see, all wearing navy sport coats, Dockers, and their own funky, slick baseball neckties they were no doubt very proud of. One wall of the ballroom was lined with a dozen rolling bulletin boards, adorned with rows of brown manila envelopes. Each envelope had a number, which represented a job opening, and a sheet of paper containing a list of times and empty rows. Every single one of those envelopes represented a chance.

A sales position with the Arkansas Travelers . . . an assistant grounds crew opening with the El Paso Diablos . . . a concessions manager gig with the Beloit Snappers. Some had a salary posted in the description. Some. The majority had a salary "range" listed, and the diminutive size of those financial figures made all too obvious the importance of the next phrase written: "plus commission." I was deflated by the fact that there were very few radio jobs posted. The overwhelming majority of listings were for internships, and the going pay rate for those foot-in-the-door gigs was $100 per week. Undeterred, we the Dudes in Dockers began furiously stuffing those envelopes with our résumés, and those of us looking for broadcasting jobs delicately rubber-banded those papers around our cassette tapes.

Then we waited.

"MCGEE!"

The shout came from a pack of Dockers Dudes standing around a table across the room. It was a college pal, the great Carlton Adcock of Bristol, Tennessee. We'd become friends as students at the University of Tennessee because we'd operated in a shared circle of students with part-time jobs in the athletic department. Carlton is one of the all-time great guys. His smile, laugh, and perpetual good-time attitude that generates that smile and laugh have always been like kudzu. They spread so fast they can't be stopped. "Infectious" has become an overused word, but not when it comes to describing my friend Carlton. That dude is infectious, and in the best possible way. Remember that lone baseball announcing job that I had during college, the one at Lindsey Nelson Stadium that I recorded and included on the tapes I was now dropping into those manila envelopes in Atlanta? It was Carlton who got me that gig. I never asked for it. He just knew that I dreamed of being on a microphone talking about baseball. He knew because he's always been a great listener. He even does this thing with his head where he tilts it to the side, locks eyes with you, and nods while you talk. That rare, real listener. So, when he was working in the press box at Tennessee as a student and the regular public-address guy asked for a day off, Carlton Adcock's first reaction was to tell his coworkers, "Don't worry, I've got a guy who would be perfect for this," and he called me.

"Dude, are we stuck in a khakis factory right now or what?" he said as he shook my hand, letting loose a signature Carlton Adcock laugh and causing me to do the same. He introduced me to another fellow recent Tennessee graduate, Mark Seaman. I didn't know Mark, but I'd heard about him through some other friends. More than a few times I had heard that he too was a good guy. The three of us compared notes on our Winter Meetings experiences. It was easy to feel a little less overwhelmed by it all when I learned that I wasn't alone. We were all overwhelmed. We also quickly realized that the three of us had dropped our résumés into a lot of the same envelopes. Neither one of them wanted to be broadcasters, but once I'd discovered how few radio jobs were listed, I'd decided to throw my name into some of the internship listings, too.

"Wait," Carlton said, pointing to the door. "Here comes someone who looks official."

Every now and then, a team employee would indeed enter the room. They were easy to spot, seeing as how they were usually the only person over the age of twenty-five. Every adult entrance would send a nervous hush sweeping over our side of the room, where we all just stood there not knowing what to do with ourselves. The grown-up would take down one of the overstuffed envelopes and leave. A few hours later, that same person would return and rehang the envelope, now with the names of the worthiest applicants scribbled next to the time slots along with a location. Until the Winter Meetings were over at the close of the weekend, job interviews could be seen taking place scattered throughout every corner of the Marriott Marquis.

"8:00 AM, JIMMY LARSON, ROOM 435" or "1:15 PM, IVAN JABLONSKY, MAGNOLIA CONFERENCE ROOM" or "4:45 PM, KELLY JOHNSON, HOTEL BAR."

Whenever someone entered the room to repost an envelope with appointment listings, they were surrounded like Tippi Hedren in Alfred Hitchcock's *The Birds*. It was the sports version of the classic high school drama department scene, when the theater teacher posts the cast list for the big spring musical and everyone who auditioned swarms to the wall to see who got what part and who got left out. Every envelope posted brought claps of joy, groans of disappointment, and lots of swear words either way. Those noises only got louder as the Winter Meetings entered the second and then third and final day, as potential job opportunities started running out and the wall of manila envelopes dwindled to only a few scattered notices across the vastness of the bulletin boards. The ranks of the Dudes in Dockers would thin out, too, as people either accepted jobs and triumphantly left for home to pack for the upcoming baseball season or became so frustrated at their lack of scheduled interviews that they angrily decided to cut and run.

"Man, I've applied for thirty jobs, and I've had zero interviews," one guy said, eyes red and fists clinched, as we sat on a bench outside the ballroom. He was so incensed that he was venting to me, a total stranger, about how he was going to find someone, anyone, from Baseball Jobs Are Great Inc. and demand his $150 back. "Sorry to get so worked up, dude. It's just, I so do not want to go back home and work for my dad's accounting firm. Because accounting sucks. And because he told me this baseball thing was going to be a waste of time."

Thankfully, I'd never lacked for parental support. My family loved baseball. Dad loved the Yankees; brother Sam loved the Orioles; and I loved the Red Sox. Our longtime family hobby was "collecting" ballparks together, spending many a summer day driving to towns throughout North and South Carolina to attend minor-league games and check another stadium off the list. My love for Minor League Baseball began when I was a little guy and we lived in Shelby, North Carolina, a town of fifteen thousand people tucked into the foothills of the Appalachians, and yes, home to a professional baseball team, the rookie-level Shelby Reds and then Pirates. They played at the local high school in tiny Shelby Veterans Stadium. Most nights it was me, my father, brother, and mother, sitting among a crowd of dozens, made up mostly of player girlfriends, parents, and baseball scouts. We went to spaghetti dinner meet and greets hosted by the "Shelby Pirates Boosters" and arrived during batting practice on game nights to talk to the players at the grandstand fence. Then we would pore over the big-league box scores in *The Shelby Daily Star* to see if any of those players we'd chatted up at the chicken-wire fence had finally made it to what players toiling in the minors have always called "The Show."

The summer I remember best was that of the 1979 Shelby Pirates. A total of thirty-one players spent at least some time in Shelby that season, and only three of them went on from there to the majors, all as bench players with only full-time season shared between them. But in Shelby, they had been our superheroes. I loved a catcher out of San Diego State named Pat Rubino. He'd been super nice to me at the ballpark early in the season, he'd hit sixteen home runs that summer, and, more importantly, I thought his name sounded cool. Rubino never made it any higher than the Western Carolinas League.

My little brother, Sam, developed a great relationship with a Puerto Rican first baseman named Eddie Vargas. He had broad shoulders and an even broader smile, and he was a masher. He hit thirty-one homers in 126 games, including one four-bagger that was straight out of Hollywood, when he'd promised brother Sam during pregame that he would hit one out for him and immediately did just that. My brother was five years old. Eddie played pro ball for fifteen years, including two in the big leagues with Pittsburgh. A decade after his called shot in Shelby, Vargas was playing for the Class AA Chattanooga Lookouts and my brother, now fifteen, shouted down to him from the stands in Greenville, South Carolina. Eddie immediately replied, "Sam!"

See? Superheroes.

Growing up in the Carolinas, there were so many minor-league ballparks to visit, in seemingly every town across each state. Throughout the 1980s we McGees drove to the classic old textile mill town wooden grandstands such as Duncan Park, home of the Spartanburg Phillies, and Sims Legion Field, home of the Gastonia Rangers, as well as the shiny new made-for-MLB-expansion digs of the Class AAA Charlotte Knights. Whenever a new team would move into a town, we would figure out a way to go see them, even if it was hours away. We watched a teenager named Chipper Jones hit bombs for the Macon Braves against the Myrtle Beach Hurricanes, ricocheting off the aluminum stands of Coastal Carolina College. We drove to Durham Athletic Park to watch Ron Gant and David Justice play for the Durham Bulls on the same field and during the same time that Kevin Costner and Susan Sarandon were in town to shoot *Bull Durham*.

Our favorite ballpark of them all was the one where Costner's character, Crash Davis, hit the final homer of his fictional career, the dinger that set the minor-league career home run record. It was McCormick Field, home of the Asheville Tourists. Dad loved the place because the old creaky wooden bandbox grandstand reminded him of the textile-mill-league parks where he grew up watching and playing ball in eastern North Carolina. Mom loved it because it was tucked into the side of the mountain that lined Asheville's Biltmore Village, where the Vanderbilt family had once roamed as they built the American castle known as Biltmore Estate. My brother loved it because he, a tremendous high school infielder, imagined blasting a long ball over the short right-field fence. I loved McCormick Field because it was America's oldest minor-league ballpark, once the playground of Cobb, Ruth, and Jackie Robinson. Living baseball history located just a couple of hours from our driveway.

During the 1980s, no fewer than nineteen towns and cities across the Carolinas were home to a Minor League Baseball team, ranging from the rookie rosters of the Western Carolinas and Appalachian Leagues up the ladder to the Class A South Atlantic League, Carolina League, and AA showcases of the Southern League. If you threw in the teams located just over the Virginia, Tennessee, and Georgia state lines, the number of ballparks to visit doubled. By the time I was a high school senior, we had visited more than twenty minor-league stadiums, giddily spending our late-night drives back home reviewing everything from the ballpark itself to the quality of the hot dogs to the creativity of the promotional contests, guests, and giveaways. We'd seen Max Patkin, aka the Clown Prince of Baseball, gyrate up and down the baselines while spewing geysers of water from his cartoonish face. We'd eaten popcorn out of cardboard containers that after the food was gone could be refashioned into a megaphone. We'd stood in line for commemorative mini bats and cheap corporate-logoed ball caps, and collected so many plastic soda tumblers from so many teams that my mother had to issue a McGee family minor-league stadium cup moratorium. Nary a lunch was served in our house that didn't feature the logo of the Durham Bulls, Greensboro Hornets, or Greenville Braves. I once won an entire room's worth of baseball-themed wallpaper for throwing a ball through a tire at a Spartanburg Phillies game.

That's what made the sting even more acute as the hours and days ticked by at those Winter Meetings in Atlanta. One by one, those teams that my family had driven so far to see, from the Fayetteville Generals and the Augusta Pirates to the Burlington Indians and the Knoxville Smokies, every one of those places and teams that I loved so much had looked over my résumé and responded with a resounding NOPE.

It lifted my spirits a little when I made the decision to stop sitting on those benches outside the ballroom with the other Dudes in Dockers, all of us loitering there looking like a better-dressed but just-as-sad version of the people in those old photos you see from the Great Depression, hanging around outside the Acme Employment Company waiting for a truck to come by with work. Instead, I got up and walked the aisles of the adjacent baseball industry trade show. It was hardball Disneyland. Booth after booth of all the items and characters that my family had paid to own and see, all on display in the same place at the same time and all hoping, like me, to catch the eye of a team executive.

There was Morganna the Kissing Bandit, the busty blonde who became famous in the 1970s and '80s for jumping fences and sprinting across ballfields in the middle of games to place pecks on the surprised lips of Cal Ripken Jr., Nolan Ryan, and their fellow MLB All-Stars. Her first bolt onto a ballfield was in 1971 at Cincinnati's Riverfront Stadium. When a friend dared her to dash out and make out with Pete Rose, the seventeen-year-old exotic dancer did just that, running past former Asheville Tourists manager Sparky Anderson to do it. A stunned Rose said to her, "You crazy f—ing broad!" He called the next day to apologize for his language, in theory because he was a gentleman. The reality is that he wanted to see her—all 60-23-39 of her—again. In Atlanta, Morganna Roberts told that story again and again from her booth, only four years after Rose was banned from baseball for gambling on games during his tenure as Reds manager. "I tell people that my career started with a bet, but Pete's ended with one."

Now she would gladly do some on-field—and perfectly legal—smooching at someone's minor-league ballpark for a price, or perhaps as a favor should that ballpark agree to sell her new Kissing Bandit Peanuts in their concession stands, oven-roasted goobers served in chrome-foiled bags adorned with giant pink kissy lips. Across the aisle from Morganna was a row of magicians. Next to them was BirdZerk! (always spelled with the exclamation point), a multicolored neon cockatoo-ish mascot that advertised itself as "the new bird on the block." There were all sorts of assorted furry and feathered creatures gyrating around the convention hall, all vying for our attention and dollars. At one point I saw some sort of unicorn thing crash into what I think was supposed to be a Jedi from *Star Wars,* but as an unlicensed knockoff he looked more like an old, angry monk with a blue foam sword. After their collision, he gave the other a shove, and they had to be separated by their handlers. From inside the unicorn's rainbow-horned head, I heard a muffled shout that I believe was "Screw you, Fake Skywalker!" I laughed, not yet realizing that I'd just had my own Yoda-ish vision of the future, which would come later that summer in the form of a mascot battle of blockbuster proportions.

Running up and down the aisle between us all was a pack of border collies, leaping into the air to catch Frisbees being thrown from some booth elsewhere in the convention hall. "Welcome!" a man in a ringmaster's uniform blared into a megaphone, attempting to draw attention to his booth that sold, well, megaphones. "To the circus of baseball!"

Human and canine alike, they all hocked their talents amid a sensory overload of smells and sounds. Food service vendors popped new flavors of popcorn (cheeseburger flavored?), while ice cream vendors touted the space-age process of manufacturing liquid nitrogen-flash-frozen "Dippin' Dots" aka THE ICE CREAM OF THE FUTURE! There were displays of crazy-shaped tickets, available now. There were displays of computerized systems with which one could more efficiently sell those tickets, also available now. There were baseball cards and baseball cups and foam baseball bats and baseball air fresheners filled with baseball potpourri that could make your car smell like a baseball field, and I knew that was available now because a salesperson hung one of those baseballs around my neck, and my face smelled like rose-infused infield grass for the next week.

All the above was set to the simultaneous soundtracks of new ballpark organs, for-hire ballpark organists, for-hire national anthem singers, Elvis impersonators, and jazz bands. The biggest crowd to be found at any booth was packed five deep to see and hear the latest in ballpark technology, a personal computer that was filled with sound effects and music. No more scrambling through a box of cassette tapes in the press box to play the *Jeopardy!* theme when a coach was taking too long talking to his pitcher at the mound, "Singin' in the Rain" when bad weather blew in, or "Three Blind Mice" aimed at the umpires after a bad call. Flabbergasted baseball people were lined up, blissfully giggling as they pointed-and-clicked through tunes and tones on one computer while illuminating balls and strikes counts via a digital scoreboard on the other.

I watched them click away for a while. Then I paused to once again gawk at BirdZerk! As I did, Max Patkin walked by, caught a look at the fanciful fowl, rubbed his eyes like he was washing a set of windows, and shouted aloud to no one and everyone, "GOT-DAMN, everybody! The 1960s have finally caught up with me!"

The Clown Prince of Baseball was seventy-three years old and here in Atlanta to book appearances for his forty-ninth and what would end up becoming his penultimate season on the road. As he roamed the aisles of the trade show, he did so not in his signature baggy wool uniform with a "?" instead of a number, but rather in a suit with no tie and sporting a shirt that was unbuttoned entirely too low, with a collar that was popped entirely too high. Anyone who has seen *Bull Durham* would have recognized Patkin's outfit immediately. It was the same one he sported in the film as he asked Susan Sarandon to dance in a Durham honky-tonk. I learned that day in Atlanta that his loosey-goosey dancing style in the movie was no exaggeration. Even now, selling his act and not performing it, Patkin moved around the room like liquid rubber, shaking hands as if his palms were covered in grease and strolling about the Marriott Marquis with a gait that made it look as though his feet were ice skates. But Max was tired. More than a few times over the course of the three days, I saw him sitting on a hotel bench or lobby chair, stroking his kneecaps or rubbing his feet when he thought no one was looking.

On the second day of the Winter Meetings, with still no interviews booked, I was walking back from the trade show to check the wall of job envelopes when I ran into a former neighbor from Raleigh, North Carolina, a Matterhorn of a man and entrepreneur named Steve Bryant, who'd recently invested in the ownership of a Class AA team in Columbus, Georgia, and moved them to the booming outskirts of North Carolina's capital city. The Carolina Mudcats were one of the most popular mascots in Minor League Baseball, with a cartoon logo of a lazy catfish's face sticking through a big red *C* that had become a national mail-order sensation among sports fans. The minors were in the early stages of what the *Baseball America* newspaper referred to as "Logo Mania." Teams were increasingly following the lead of the Mudcats, shedding the traditional mascots of their parent big-league ball clubs and replacing them, often via a public naming contest, and then hiring graphic designers to try to come up with the next MiLB buzz mascot and the resulting merchandise windfall that came with it.

The classics—Durham Bulls, Chattanooga Lookouts, Toledo Mudhens—had been around for ages and required no modern image punch-up. But dozens more teams were implementing extreme cartoon-mascot makeovers. Some were truly great. Many were truly awful. In Iowa, the Cedar Rapids Reds and Quad Cities Angels had just become the Cedar Rapids Kernels and Quad Cities River Bandits. In Indiana, the South Bend White Sox were now the South Bend Silver Hawks. In South Carolina, the Columbia Mets were transformed into the Capital City Bombers.

Mr. Bryant said that he didn't have any open positions on his staff, but he invited me to attend an awards luncheon with him, and right that minute. A colleague had canceled, so he had an extra ticket. I couldn't say yes fast enough. The Sports Employment for You Inc. $150 fee didn't even include a basket of crackers, let alone a luncheon. Entering that ballroom made me feel like I was finally in the club, the ball club. There were a couple of hundred people in there, and I was the only Dude in Dockers to be found, the only attendee sporting a "Don't You Want a Job in Baseball Inc." nametag. At our table it was team owner Bryant; Dan Rajkowski, general manager of a brand-new Class A franchise in North Carolina, the Hickory Crawdads; Larry Ward, the longtime radio voice of the Chattanooga Lookouts; and a couple of salespeople from a couple of other teams. They all were nice enough, but prefaced lunch by assuring me that they also had no jobs to fill. Great. Then . . . no way . . . for real . . . Max Patkin sat down at our table. "Hey, what are you assholes doing?! Eating lunch?!"

For an hour, I said nothing. I simply pushed my chicken cordon bleu around the plate and listened. What I heard was a conversation about baseball at a crossroads. They talked about the sudden minor-league buying spree, as corporate groups and investors were beginning to buy out small-town MiLB franchise owners, but it was yet to be seen if they were interested in keeping the sport tied to its roots or ripping those roots from the ground in search of bigger bottom lines. It was explained to me that normally there would be executives and even players from Major League Baseball teams in attendance at the Winter Meetings, but this year they all had skipped out because of worsening labor issues between the MLB team owners and its players union. Everyone at the table talked matter-of-factly about the possibility of there being no big-league baseball in the summer of 1994. What would that mean for them? Would they be able to play? Would their affiliated MLB clubs still send them players? If they did play, would the public be so angry at baseball in general that they stayed away from the minors too, or would that irritation instead stay focused on the millionaire big leaguers and billionaire owners, thus sending disgruntled fans to minor-league games in search of a purer, less money-hungry version of America's Pastime?

They also talked about what I had seen at the trade show. Goofy dancing birds, space-age ice cream dots, point-and-click sound effects. Were they all crucial pieces to remaining relevant in a future that seemed inevitably more competitive to earn families' limited entertainment dollars? Or was it all too much too soon, an unnecessary departure from the mom-and-pop old-school atmosphere that had always been the hallmark of the Minor League Baseball experience? This part of the discussion was the only time during the lunch that Max Patkin said nothing.

"You are catching our business at a helluva time, Ryan," Bryant said to me as we left the ballroom and reentered the hotel lobby. "It is fun. It will always be fun. We are in this business to have fun. But make no mistake about it, buddy, it is still a business. Now go get yourself a job."

Oh yeah, a job! I speed-walked my way back to the ballroom of bulletin boards. This was probably my twentieth trip into that room over the course of the first two days, and after not seeing my name on a single envelope, I was growing accustomed to the disappointment. Hey, if I went home still unemployed, at least I could tell my family I had lunch with the Clown Prince of Baseball.

I walked along, scanning the envelopes, and zeroing in on the dozen or so jobs I had applied for that morning. Richmond Braves . . . no. Edmonton Trappers . . . no. Wichita Wranglers . . . no. Nashville Sounds . . . no. Boise Hawks . . . no . . . no . . . no . . . no . . . no . . . no . . . New Britain Red Sox . . . n . . . wait . . . yes. YES?

It was true. The Class AA Eastern League affiliate of my beloved Boston Red Sox had slotted me for an interview at three p.m. that afternoon in a hallway outside the ballroom, not too long from then. What's more, it was a radio gig. I saw Carlton out of the corner of my excited eye and ran across the room to tell him the news. "That's awesome, man," he replied. "But you're gonna have to haul ass to get from there at three to where we have to be at three thirty."

Where did we have to be at three thirty?

"You didn't see? The Asheville Tourists scheduled you, me, and Mark Seaman for an interview at the same time, on the bench right outside the elevators on the fifth floor. It's for an internship. One hundred bucks a week, son. We're gonna be rich."

I walked briskly to the spot designated for my three p.m. interview, and I waited, squirming on the bench, standing, then sitting back down to squirm some more. A few minutes later, a pleasant-looking man with glasses and a dark mustache approached. He looked like he could've been my slightly older brother. "Ryan? My name is Jim Lucas. I'm the voice of the New Britain Red Sox."

My jaw got loose. I knew exactly who Jim Lucas was. He was one half of the most famous radio duo in all the minor leagues. I'd read about play-by-play man Lucas and his color commentator partner, Don Wardlow, in *Baseball America* and *The Sporting News* and had seen multiple TV news stories about them. Now, this is the part where you're wondering why in the world the radio booth from the New Britain Red Sox, a mid-level team who played their games in a converted high school football stadium on the outskirts of Hartford, would have received so much national attention.

It's because Wardlow was born with no eyes. Yes, he was a blind baseball radio color commentator.

I had so many questions for Jim Lucas. Wardlow was not there. He was back in Connecticut at the house that the two college friends shared alongside his trusty seeing-eye dog, a black Lab named Gizmo. Lucas explained that Wardlow was already ingesting hundreds of pages of stats and information into a machine that would translate all that data into the stacks of braille pages that he carried with him into the press boxes of the Eastern League. I wanted to ask how that worked. I wanted to ask how they met. I wanted to ask, how in the world did Wardlow have any idea what was happening on a ballfield that he could not see?

Instead, Lucas explained what they would need from me, should we agree that I was the guy for the job. He said he loved my demo cassette. Yeah, it was mostly football, but he liked how I went out of my way to describe the scene around the game and not just the action itself. That made my day. He and Wardlow were both from New Jersey, but thought my Southern accent was endearing and believed that the people of central Connecticut would think so, too. This position would include hosting the pregame show from the studio at the radio station that carried the New Britain Red Sox games, running the audio board for their broadcast, and then cutting up audio highlights for the postgame scoreboard show that they also hosted.

Then Lucas explained that the job paid no money. None. I would have to get myself to Connecticut, and whatever income I made would come from the ads that I sold for the shows that I hosted. That was their deal, too. They were so eager to broadcast the sport they loved that they essentially did it for free. During the 1993 season, that financial model had netted the pair a total of about $5,000 between them. I would live in the spare bedroom. Jim Lucas wasn't selling fortune and fame, and he knew it. He was selling baseball and fun. "We will go to Red Sox spring training in Florida in March and learn about the players in minor-league camp," he said, knowing I was a Sox fan. Then he added with a laugh, "It's good to go sit in the warm sunshine for a month, because when we get back to New Britain, we won't see any of that for a while."

Lucas was so amazingly nice, and his story was so incredibly heartfelt, that I was genuinely starstruck. But when he looked at his watch, we both knew that our chat was over. He had another candidate to interview for the job, and I had to hustle upstairs, lest I be late again and blow my only other chance at these Winter Meetings. "I'm going to talk to Don about you tonight, but I think this is great," Lucas said. "You think about us tonight too, and if it's the right fit for you. We won't make a decision until I get home and discuss it with Don, but let's make sure we talk tomorrow before everyone leaves town."

I took a quick ride up to the fifth floor and breathlessly bounded off the elevator at precisely three thirty, practically tripping over Carlton and Mark Seaman, who were sitting on a bench and listening to the man who stood before them. He was a smooth-voiced dude who looked to be in his early thirties, with a big toothy smile, a blond mustache, and a crew cut. He was wearing an Asheville Tourists pullover jacket and turned to greet me with an extended hand. "And this must be Ryan McGee, the final member of our Tennessee Trio. All we're lacking now is Johnny Cash."

His name was Gary Saunders, about to begin his second season as the assistant general manager of the Tourists. From the lilt in Gary's voice, I had a hunch that he might be a Virginian, and as he made small talk with the three of us seated a little too tight for comfort on the same bench, I learned that my suspicions were right. He talked about his time as a student at Virginia Tech and turned to me specifically when he explained that he had been a communications major and had himself done some baseball on the radio. He talked and he talked. He hit on everything from his first job in baseball, with the St. Louis Cardinals organization two years earlier, to how much he loved all the new gadgets and gizmos downstairs at the trade show. He used that very word, "gizmo." I started to blurt out, "Hey, the guy who just interviewed me for a radio job in Connecticut has a blind radio partner who has a seeing-eye dog named Gizmo!" I wisely restrained myself. When Gary looked down at his watch, we all realized that he was stalling. The boss man was running late.

"Guys, while we wait on our general manager, let me explain what our situation is. We have three internships available for the upcoming season. The job pays one hundred dollars a week, and the three interns will do a lot of everything. And I do mean everything. Front office, ticket sales, concessions, retail, pulling the tarp when it rains, everything."

I knew the Asheville Tourists didn't do any sort of radio broadcast. I asked Gary Saunders if there would be any opportunity to start something up in the future. He told me that he hoped so and had already been lobbying his boss to take the radio plunge, but "our GM has been doing things his way for a long time, and that's understandable because the Asheville Tourists are a great organization and he's the reason for that, but sometimes it's our job as the younger guys to push him on new ideas."

In three sentences, Saunders had summed up the entire conversation I'd heard during the luncheon earlier that day. He had also foreshadowed a tug-of-war that would in many ways dominate nearly the next year of my life. But for now, he was focused on the task at hand. The three of us right in front of him. "Guys, we really liked your résumés. All three of you." I looked at Carlton.

He nodded. We were having the same mathematical thought. Three positions. Three dudes with solid résumés. This was done. We were totally getting job offers, like right here and now!

Then there was a ding. It was the elevator. When the doors to that lift opened, what happened next is hard to describe. Have you ever been in New York City or Chicago in the dead of winter, peacefully sitting in a coffee shop or a pizza joint, when suddenly someone opens the door and a gale-force arctic wind blows in off the street, all at once filling the room with tremendous air pressure but also sucking that frozen air of your lungs to the point that you can't make a sound, let alone speak?

That's exactly what happened when Ron McKee, general manager, co-owner, and force of Minor League Baseball nature exploded off that Marriott Marquis elevator and started stalking directly toward us. All three of us Dudes in Dockers reflexively leaped up off our hallway bench. "Hail to the Chief" might as well have been playing. Or AC/DC's "Thunderstruck."

Ron had a cherubic face but a devil's laugh. He was fifty-one years old and nearly as round as he was tall, with catcher's mitt hands that looked like he could have ripped those elevator doors apart if he'd wanted to. Hell, maybe he had. There aren't a lot of people you meet in this life with the natural ability to instantly take over any room simply by walking into it, especially at an ego-packed event like the Winter Meetings. But Ron McKee was most certainly one of those people. He blew past Gary Saunders, never asking what his right-hand man had or hadn't already explained to us. He came to a stop with a stomp and clapped his hands together with a lobby-rattling boom to get our attention.

"Guys, here's the deal. We like all three of you. We have three intern positions, but we've already hired a guy to fill one of them. So, this is simple. It's the three of you for two spots. You seem like smart guys, so instead of us figuring out which two of you are getting the jobs, we're leaving it up to you. Let us know what you decided to do by tomorrow morning."

And just like that, Ron McKee was gone. I suppose he turned around and got back onto the elevator. Or perhaps he kept walking down the hallway and went to his hotel room. But in my young, shell-shocked mind, I swear I remember thinking that there was an explosion of flame and smoke, and he sailed skyward into the rafters of the Marriott Marquis like Batman.

"So . . . that was Ron," Gary Saunders said with his trademark grin and a raised eyebrow. "Good luck, guys."

Left alone, we three immediately agreed that one of the spots should go to Carlton. This was the only job offer he'd received, and his hometown of Bristol, Tennessee, was only an hour and a half away from Asheville. That left the other spot to be decided between Mark and me. Seaman told us that he had an entry-level offer on the table from the Knoxville Smokies, the hometown team of our shared college alma mater. I told them about my conversation with the New Britain Red Sox, but while I felt great about the interview, it hadn't been an official offer yet. Mark looked at me and said, "If you don't take the Tourists job, I will. I really want it. But it's up to you."

That night, crashing in the guest room of a cousin in the Atlanta suburbs, I slept precisely zero minutes. I weighed the assurance of being on the radio in New Britain versus the possibility of maybe a conversation about perhaps one day being on radio in Asheville. Maybe. I weighed the guaranteed income of $100 per week in Asheville versus the possibility of perhaps maybe we'll see if there might be any money at all in New Britain. That would happen only if I was good at sales, which I'd never really done and when I had tried, I'd been significantly terrible at. Then I weighed locations. Asheville was a place I knew, two and a half hours from my parents and two hours from the college where I'd just graduated.

I was only somewhat aware of New Britain's place on the map because I'd driven by that exit en route to my plane crash of an interview at ESPN in nearby Bristol, Connecticut.

In the end, at around five thirty a.m., as the sun was rising over Atlanta, the one voice in my head that I couldn't shake kept shouting the same sentence over and over. *Man, I love McCormick Field SO MUCH.* When I walked back into the Marriott that morning, I ran into Steve Bryant and told him that I was going to take an internship with the Tourists. "This is the easiest decision anyone at these meetings is going to make," he said to me. "One summer with Ron McKee is like going to Minor League Baseball Harvard."

The conversation with Mark Seaman two hours later was a hard one because Mark was pretty pissed. The talk with Jim Lucas right after that was even worse because Jim was so incredibly nice, even offering up that if I ever found myself in New Britain to let him know, and I could sit in for an inning on the microphone. But as I drove back up I-85 that afternoon, I was smiling all the way home to North Carolina. I had indeed found a Job in Baseball Inc. I was going to be a Tourist. It was time to pack for a baseball season in Asheville.

After I got my car fixed.

"TAKE OFF YOUR SHOES, FOR YOU ARE STANDING ON HALLOWED GROUND."

It was our first day of work as Asheville Tourists interns, and Carlton Adcock and I had arrived early. It was very cold. It was very still. We walked into the ballpark beneath its signature archway, the main entrance located down the right-field line. A brand-new round aluminum sign sporting the logo of the Colorado Rockies was being installed by that entrance. A new big-league affiliate was bringing new big-time excitement to Asheville. But no one was more excited than the two of us were at this moment. Instead of taking the stairs to the left and into the office, we bolted up the steps to our right, the ones that rose to meet the grass just past first base, where we could see the field. We just had to see the field.

To me, the mark of a truly great sporting venue has never been what it sounds like or how it feels when the stands are packed. That's easy. Even the most generic cookie-cutter stadium or arena feels electric when the game is big, the lights are on, and the crowd is amped. The real measure of a ballpark's character is how the place feels when it's empty. When the only noises to be heard are produced by the occasional breeze that slips through the concourse. It rattles the ropes on the empty center-field flagpoles. It pushes a stray plastic cup around beneath the feet of the box seats. And if you listen closely enough, that wind carries on it the whispers of the ghosts. The athletes who played between the lines, their toes in the dirt where only those who compete are allowed to roam.

During my career in sports media, I've heard their voices at Indianapolis Motor Speedway and Darlington Raceway. I've heard them at Lambeau Field and the Rose Bowl. I've heard them at old Boston Garden and Augusta National. And on the morning of Thursday, March 3, 1994, I heard them at McCormick Field. Cobb, Gehrig, Dizzy Dean, Hank Greenberg, Jackie Robinson, Roy Campanella, Willie Stargell. From the Hall of Famers to a thousand minor leaguers whose names no one remembers. I swear, they were all there that morning to welcome us into the little mountain ballpark that they'd helped build.

Because that ballpark is quite literally wedged into the side of a mountain, there's never been a lot of space to spare. But what Tourists fans have given up in terms of elbow room and amenities they have been rewarded double with the gift of intimacy, a chance to feel like you are almost in the game itself. Patrons and the playing field are separated by inches, with nothing between them but a thigh-high wall, the same barely-barrier that Carlton and I were leaning against, where fans can stand so close to the action that someone could lean over and scoop up a handful of warning track dirt if they really wanted to.

I had done that once, on the morning after the Tourists' 1991 season finale. I was driving through Asheville on my way to college, and I stopped in at McCormick Field because the night before had been their season finale and the last game played in the original wooden bandbox version of the ballpark, chunks of it still as they were when the showplace opened in 1924. I walked into the open gate, snatched up a handful of dirt, and was shocked to find a couple of commemorative tickets on that same ground. I grabbed those, too. Demolition and construction equipment was already in the parking lot. A guy in a hard hat explained to me that the stadium was being replaced, but that the playing field itself would be the same. "I know a lot of people are sad about this," the foreman said to me. "But we ain't touching that field. And if you've used any of these 1924 stadium bathrooms recently, then you know it's way past time for something new."

Now, two and a half years later, Carlton and I were marveling at that construction crew's handiwork. It was indeed the same classic playing field, but now wrapped in a freshly painted, boomerang-shaped concrete facility, with a much more creative use of the limited space and indeed much better plumbing. Which is to say the toilets now flushed, and the faucets no longer moaned like a much worse version of those ghosts.

As we stood there, I thought of a story I'd often read about Babe Ruth, at the very spot where we now gawked. On April 7, 1931, the Great Bambino entered the original park in those same footsteps, getting his first gander at then-seven-year-old McCormick Field. The Colossus of Clout, in town with the New York Yankees as they barnstormed back north from spring training, took a deep breath and a drag off the scent of the honeysuckle vines that covered the hillside beyond the little railing that separated the outfield grass from the slopes above it. The Sultan of Swat is said to have exclaimed, "My, my, what a ballpark! What a beautiful place to play. Delightful. Damned delightful place!" Then he and Lou Gehrig blasted back-to-back homers into that honeysuckle, the Iron Horse sending a ball into deep center, Ruth launching an arching blast that easily sailed over McCormick's three-hundred-foot right-field fence and nearly into the elevated neighborhood of homes overlooking that corner of the stadium. New York newspapers wrote that two thousand fans were inside the ballpark, but another fifteen thousand had packed the streets and hillsides around it, many of them scrambling up the hill to search for Ruth's catapulted baseball. The same hill where Carlton had just parked his pickup truck and we had walked down to start our new jobs.

We just stood there for a minute overlooking the field, shivering but smiling as we took in the visions around us. The red and blue seats. The redbrick backstop. The quilt work of outfield billboard ads, from peanuts and Pepsi to a cowboy Marlboro Man who rose like a giant from among the outfield trees, always at the ready to rope a steer and burn a heater.

I recalled the Ruth story, admittedly the second-best Babe-in-Asheville tale (I'll tell you the best one later). The honeysuckle was still there, a lot of it hidden behind the towering thirty-six-foot right-field wall, second only in height to Boston's fabled Green Monster, that now stood watch over the Babe's hill, but the vine's blooms were still weeks away from waking up for springtime. We, however, were plenty awake. Carlton slapped me on the shoulder. "What do you think, McGee? It's like they said in *Bull Durham*, we're going to the ballpark and we're getting paid to do it. A whole hundred bucks a week, son!"

We started laughing and bounded up the stairs into the office. Our excitement was multiplied as soon as we crossed the threshold into the small front lobby. Carlton slapped me on the arm again, pointing to a shadowbox frame that hung just inside the door. It was the Tourists jersey that Crash Davis wore when he hit his final homer at the end of the movie, autographed by Kevin Costner. To this day, I hope that I didn't squeal aloud in delight, because I most certainly did in my mind. But no sooner had we hit that lobby than our gleeful moods came to a halt like a distracted face smacking into a sliding glass door.

"What do you two want?"

The woman sitting behind the front desk looked up from the ledger she was filling out, but never raised her head all the way. She let her eyes do the work, cutting over the top of her glasses to make sure we had a clear vision of their tone. Until that moment

I had no idea someone could give you the WTH side-eye when their eyes were pointed directly at you.

"Um . . . hey . . . we're the new interns. I'm Ryan McGee and this is Carlton Adcock."

She stood up. She was rail thin and five feet tall, maybe. But she still terrified us. Until she smiled. "Well, duh. Of course, you're the new interns. I mean, look at you. Hi, I'm Jane."

Jane Lentz was—still is—as dyed-in-the-tar-heel a North Carolinian as a North Carolinian could possibly be. When Tourists games were being played, she spent her time in the catacombs of the ballpark running the concessions business, At-Bat Food Services. This time of year, the off-season, she kept the Asheville Tourists front office running smoother than the engines that powered the NASCAR Winston Cup stock cars that she loved so much. Her Pontiac had a personalized Richard Petty vanity plate. She raised a pack of Scottish terriers in a home that she constantly kept rocking to the catalog of the Rolling Stones. She was a UNC Asheville graduate with a degree in psychology and, as we had learned after precisely one minute on the job, a doctorate in sarcasm. I had no way of knowing it yet, but I'd just been greeted by one of my favorite people I would ever meet.

"There's still time to quit and go home." Jane paused for maybe one second. "Okay, too late." She gave us a "don't worry, I'm just messing with you" grin, turned her head slightly, and spoke up in the direction of the office behind her and into the short hallway to her left. "Hey y'all, the new interns are here!"

One by one, the full-time front-office employees of the Asheville Tourists, a proud professional sports franchise with roots reaching back more than a century, filed into the room until the entirety of the staff filled the reception area.

All six of them.

We'd already met Jane. The first to join her with us was R. J. Martino, account representative, whose desk was also in the lobby across from Jane because they were out of offices. One year earlier he had been in our shoes, a first-year intern with another South Atlantic League team, the Hagerstown Suns. R.J. was from New York. R.J. was engaged. R.J. was good-looking. He drove a Jeep Wrangler, was built like a middle linebacker, laughed like a Goodfella, was obsessed with the New York Yankees, and wore a smile so bright he might have very well have stolen it off his solar mascot in Hagerstown. He was also on the cusp of becoming a great salesman. What I'm saying here is that R. J. Martino was cool as hell.

Then there was Gary Saunders, our flat-topped friend from the Winter Meetings who had already shared his life story with us as he killed time waiting on the boss in the Atlanta Marriott Marquis lobby. So we already knew he was from Virginia, that this was his second season as the team's assistant GM and his third in minor-league ball, and that he had a smooth-as-a-river-rock voice befitting a man who, like me, had dreamed of a career in the broadcasting booth.

Behind Gary was another Saunders, his wife, Eileen. She moved into the room like a dancer, with big, warm eyes that always promised she was genuinely listening to whatever you were saying to her. Eileen's position was a new addition to the Tourists frontoffice roster, director of merchandising. After six years in department store retail management, she was now charged with *putting* a charge into the Tourists' pedestrian merch sales. The overhauling of McCormick Field two years earlier had created a lot of regional buzz around the team, but its apparel and souvenir offerings were still as creaky and dated as the wooden bleachers from 1924. It was no longer enough to simply stock red-and-blue ball caps adorned with the same white *A* logo that had been in use since the 1960s, or stiff polyester golf shirts and faux-leather batting gloves. In 1994's hyperactive mascot-crazed Minor League Baseball universe, packed with Mudcats, Crawdads, and Quakes, creativity was the key to survival. Eileen and Gary had spent all winter creating ideas and avenues that they believed would push Asheville into the middle of the national MiLB merchandising game, the biggest of which was commissioning a local artist to help design a new mascot and logo.

Ted E. Tourist was a bear ("Ted E." Say it aloud. Get it?), because Asheville is located in the mountains, where there are indeed lots of bears, including a couple that had been caught digging through the McCormick Field dumpsters after a homestand following the scent of stale hot dogs and nachos. Ted was also introduced as "everyone's favorite world traveler" because, well, he was a Tourist. When artist Steve Millard delivered his rendering to the team, Ted E. the big fat smiling ursine sightseer came complete with sunglasses, a camera hung around his neck, a Hawaiian vacation shirt, and a suitcase covered with stickers from all the destinations he'd visited along the way. It was a concept originally dreamed up by Ron, who took one of his kids' teddy bears and fitted it with a toddler's vacation shirt and tiny sunglasses taken from a Barbie doll. Millard took that teddy and turned it into art.

The Tourists had used a bear mascot for years, but I am being kind if I describe him as creepy. His cartoon likeness in the Tourist game programs of the early nineties was a smiling, roundish cub, also with a suitcase and a camera. But the real-life mascot that roamed the rows of McCormick—he had no name, they just called him "Tourist Mascot"—looked like he had been kidnapped from a pack of Times Square Elmo knockoffs and had his giant Muppet eyes ripped off. The suit was red, dingy, and droopy. I will say this, though—that bear could dance his furry butt off. My family went to a game in 1990, and I have no idea who was inside the suit, but he came straight from *Soul Train*. That bear climbed atop the dugout and started popping and locking and doing the Running Man so intensely that you could see his human legs and arms sticking out from beneath his suit, and no one cared about the exposure because the moves that were causing it were so smooth. But he was still janky.

Ted E. Tourist was not janky or creepy. He was cute, and that cuteness was going to be everywhere in the summer of 1994. He would be embroidered on the team's new caps, sewn onto the sleeves of their new uniforms, and printed on T-shirts, sweatshirts, stickers, pennants, and whatever else could be sold in the retail store that Elaine had just redesigned, located on the ground floor of the McCormick Field office, just inside the stadium entrance. The new apparel was cleverly branded Bear Wear. There was even a limited-edition series of Asheville Tourists white wine with Ted E. sketched onto the bottle. Gary had done a deal with a local grocery store chain and Nabisco to keep Ted's suitcase stocked with cookies that he could hand out to the kids. It was all so very exciting. It was all so very nineties. But it was all so very risky. You see, as light and breezy as Ted E. Tourist was, his rendering was no simple cartoon. It was filled with detail, nuance, pencil strokes . . . and ten different colors. He was two shades each of brown and red along with some blue and white and black with a bat that was brown and a suitcase that was yellow. That meant that my man, er, bear, Ted was expensive to reproduce, whether he be sewn, sculpted, or printed on paper for a game program, front-office stationery, or a Chardonnay label. It was certainly a lot more expensive than a block white *A* on a red-and-blue hat or a dingy red Elmo imposter. We were about to find out if Ted was worth the investment. Little did we know that soon we would also find out about his fighting skills in the impromptu Octagon of Mascots.

Next into the room was the person who would keep track of how much Ted cost, as well as everything else, be it bears or baseballs, and how much it all made or lost. Carolyn McKee's official title was business manager, but I've always believed that was only because "Accountant/Bookkeeper/Book Cooker/Team Mom/

Actual Mom/Peacekeeper/Secret Keeper/Hotel Booker/Ticket Manager/MLB Affiliate Handler/Person Who Keeps the GM in Line" was too much to fit onto one business card. Yes, she was Ron's wife. For her, as a mother of four and the wife of who she was married to, the challenge of dealing with baseball players, executives, and certainly baseball interns wasn't much of a challenge at all. When people walked into Carolyn's office, they knew they would be greeted by a mother's warmth. They also knew that if they had screwed something up, they could be greeted by a mother of a temper.

Finally, from out of the main office just off the lobby, a familiar tornado suddenly blew into the room, the same force of nature that had ripped the doors off the elevator in Atlanta. "HEY, LOOK!" the boss man blustered, striding toward me and Carlton with a hand extended. "THEY SHOWED UP!"

Ron McKee was in his fifteenth season as Asheville Tourists general manager. By now he was as much a part of the fabric of western North Carolina as bluegrass music and fall foliage. And here's the least surprising fact that you will read in this book: before Ron took over at McCormick Field, he was a car salesman. Ron was a baby boomer, born in 1945 just down the mountain in Shelby, North Carolina, but was raised in Asheville. He loved sports and as a kid had served as a batboy at McCormick Field, scooping up cracked bats and foul balls produced by some of the city's most legendary teams and players. He met Carolyn in high school and after graduation was recruited into sales because, in his words, "Not everyone I have met likes me, but that was only because I've always been too honest. And if a guy that you know is always too honest about everything tells you that you should buy something, then hell, even if you don't like the guy, you're still gonna have to really seriously consider buying what that guy is selling."

Ron sold a lot of cars, even during the late 1970s when no one in America was selling much of anything to anyone. So, in the winter of 1980, when the struggling Asheville Tourists needed someone to resell them to the community, they called on their old batboy to see if he might want the gig. The scene that he later described to me, when he walked back into McCormick Field for the first time in years, always reminded me of Patrick Swayze in *Road House,* the first time that Dalton the bouncer walked in and looked around to assess the climate of the juke joint he'd just been hired to clean up. McCormick Field was totally the Double Deuce. The fifty-six-year-old ballpark was pocked with X-shaped wood patches that were holding the place together. The outfield was filled with patches too, of dirt with nary a blade of grass to be grown. There were a lot of drunks and a lot of cigarette smoke, and those smoky drunks were in a lot of fights, sometimes with each other and sometimes even with the players, who could no longer take being catcalled by those smoky drunks. Every f-bomb was heard loud and clear on the playing field during nights when there were only a hundred people in the stands. Of those who were there, there were practically zero kids in the crowd. Zero. At a Minor League Baseball game. Can you imagine?

Ron reluctantly took the job. It would be his last moment of hesitation when it came to running the Asheville Tourists. He spent the summer of 1980 dragging those drunks out of the stands, sometimes literally. He hired local police officers to help him do that, seeking out Ted E. Tourist–ish friendly-but-large men who could be at once very welcoming to the good patrons and very dangerous to the bad ones. McKee assured families that they could come back to the ballpark again by establishing designated alcohol- and tobacco-free sections of the stadium, unheard-of at the time. A quote from Ron that ran in the local papers became the mission statement that he preached for decades: "When people walk into McCormick Field, I want them to feel like they are walking into my living room, and it is my job to welcome them and make them feel at home. Like part of the family."

That included his own family. He hired Carolyn to keep the books and put his four kids to work doing everything from tearing tickets to serving food to the fans in the box seats closest to the field. The luxury of having a box seat waitress was also a needed distraction, so that fans didn't have time to realize that they had paid extra to sit close to the field . . . but that seat was either a wooden chair that looked like it had been stolen from someone's grandmother's front porch or a metal folding chair taken from a church bingo hall.

The third of the McKee kids and the closest to my age, Catherine, told me stories of spending preteen nights sidled up to her dad in the ballpark office until the sun came up on Opening Day, cranking out copies on the Xerox machine, and stuffing game programs with starting lineups and scorecards. Then she reminded me that while my hundred bucks a week might have seemed like next to nothing, for a lot of her work she had been paid an actual nothing. But she also never failed to smile when she told me about it.

The Asheville Tourists were a literal mom-and-pop organization, and as the 1980s rolled along, the stream of night-ruining drunks dried up. The giggles and energy of kids returned. Heck, everyone returned. By mid-decade, the team was drawing more than one hundred thousand fans per season, more than double what attendance had been before Ron took over.

He worked especially hard to look after the longtime Tourists fans, the folks who, like him, had been there for the glory days of the 1960s, had ridden out the beer-soaked decline of the '70s, and now were there with him to watch the fun return. Many had purchased stock in the team and had the framed certificates to prove it. Sure, it was a largely ceremonial promotion conjured up by the team's operating committee to raise capital funding when times were bleak, but the feeling of having ownership in the ball club was real. When season-ticket sales started picking up with the rising popularity, Ron made sure those McCormick Field veterans weren't relegated to the worst seats when the stands were packed. That created a small but intensely devout army of Ron McKee loyalists, made up of longtime locals as well as plenty of baseball-loving "Reverse Snowbirds" who moved to Florida from the Northeast in search of milder winters, but fled the Sunshine State in the summer because it was too hot and chose the North Carolina mountains to stay coolish. It was a legion that would serve him well whenever he felt squeezed by politicians or any others who dared question his motives and moves. I'd find that out all too well during the '94 season.

Ron created "Shirt Off Your Back Night," in which at the conclusion of the game, Tourists players would pull their game-worn jerseys off and give them directly to some lucky fans. The man that the *Asheville Citizen-Times* described as the "P. T. Barnum of Baseball" always took credit for the phrase "The Greatest Show on Dirt" and always claimed that Hollywood director (and former minor-league ballplayer) Ron Shelton had stolen it to use in *Bull Durham* after shooting his scenes at McCormick Field and seeing it painted over the door.

Ron saved enough money to bring in the Famous San Diego Chicken, including one home game that drew more than seven thousand fans to a stadium that seats only four thousand. The Chicken entered the stadium via helicopter, hanging out of the open side door and waving with his feathery orange wings. But landing a Huey in a little ballpark that's wrapped by a mountainside of towering trees, powerlines, and swirling winds is not easy. That caused the Famous Chicken's chopper to suddenly lurch as it made its approach. "At that moment all I could see was the headline the next day all over the world with my picture next to it," Ron recalled to me. " 'Asheville minor league team kills fans using falling Famous Chicken!' " Everyone survived. Whew.

But Ron's most enduring contribution to baseball was an idea that came to him while trying to solve the eternally confounding minor-league challenge of luring fans to the ballpark for midweek games. His solution was to offer cheap drinks. Soda, beer, whatever you wanted—it would be served in a very large cup, and it would cost only a dollar. He called it "Thirsty Thursday," and unlike his other phrases, he had this one trademarked. That was decades ago, and to this day if you are in any MiLB park on any Thursday in any corner of this nation, from Spokane to Sarasota, then you are more than likely imbibing on the cheap because of Ron McKee. On March 3, 1994, I saw the framed Thirsty Thursday trademark agreement hanging on the wall of the McCormick Field office. It still does. It should. My back used to hurt so badly from all the kegs I had to sling around on Thirsty Thursdays. It still does. It should, too.

"Boys, come on in my office, we have a lot to go over," Ron said with a yank of his thumb toward the door behind him. The room itself wasn't big, but for McCormick Field it might as well have been the Oval Office. What we could see were the framed photos of Tourists teams of the past, the coveted Bob Freitas Award, given to the most outstanding Minor League Baseball organization each season, and a TV that was tuned to the Weather Channel. We would come to learn that TV was always tuned to the Weather Channel, to keep an eye on the one aspect of the job over which even the great Ron McKee had zero control. Weather.

What we could not see was what was inside Ron's desk, especially the big locked drawer to his left. I later learned that it contained only three items. A bottle of moonshine—not the commercialized water they sell in liquor stores, but the real stuff as cooked from real corn by real bootleggers in the nearby Smoky Mountains—a stack of nudie magazines, and a loaded pistol. It was an inventory that foreshadowed what he was about to tell us.

"Boys, we have a good time here, but this isn't all about the good time all the time. It's also a helluva lot of hard work. But if you hang in there, I promise it will be worth it. The Colorado

Rockies will let us know what players they are sending us pretty soon. Those guys will be here in five weeks. Their trainer is already in the clubhouse. The third intern is from Asheville, and he will be here to join you guys next week. Now, go talk to Gary about what to do next."

We said, "Yes, sir," jumped up, and headed for the door.

"Guys . . ."

We stopped and turned around.

"Remember, this is hard work, but it beats the shit out of selling cars. I did that for a long time. This is better than that."

We said, "Yes, sir," and headed for the door again.

"Guys . . ."

We stopped and turned around again.

"Remember this too, and this is the most important thing. You remember this and we are going to get along great. . . ."

We waited.

"This is not a democracy. This is a dictatorship."

We said, "Yes, sir," again and headed for the door again. This time we made it out. In Gary's office, he handed us a sheet of legal paper titled "Game Day Duties" with five columns. There was one each for him, R.J., Jane, and then us interns. He explained that once the season started, we three interns (me, Carlton, and TBD) had three positions that we would rotate through on a monthly basis. Office intern, ticket intern, and concession intern. Each gig had its own prescribed duties, listed here:

Office Intern: 1. Stuff programs & scout packages 2. Stats to manager 3. Lucky numbers for program drawings 4. Get pass list from clubhouse 5. Set up prize boxes 6. Drawing winners & notify souvenir shop 7. Work customer relations 8. Bat room distribution for players (in spare time) 9. Set up program seller's booth 10. **TARP**

Ticket Intern: 1. Assist souvenir shop 2. Parking lot cones out by 3 PM or 11 AM, get cars out of the way 3. Deliver baseballs to umpires 4. Work guest relations during game 5. Set up press box 6. Set up speed pitch 7. Run ticket booth 10 AM–4 PM 8. **TARP**

Concession Intern: 1. Do whatever Jane says 2. **TARP**

"We have seventy-one home games, plus the postseason if we make it and a couple of exhibitions," Gary explained. "That sounds like a lot. But once we get rolling and you get used to your game day routines, it will fly by. Now, first things first, let's show you around the ballpark and show you how things work around here."

McCormick Field was empty. The Rockies were still in Tucson for spring training, though the threat of a Major League players strike was still looming. Regardless, there was a lot to do to get ready for the arrival of the team in five weeks, and then the fans in the stands one week after that. I had no idea how to do any of it. Opening Day was forty-one days away.

Now, if this book were a movie (and considering that I've already referenced *Bull Durham, The Birds, Batman, Goodfellas,* and *Road House,* you should now be aware that I really love movies), this is the part where we would cut to the montage of me and Carlton getting a crash course in the mechanics of the manual labor involved in keeping up the duties of a minor-league intern. You can already see it in your head, can't you? And hey, what's that you hear? Why, that's the opening handclaps of John Fogerty's "Centerfield"!

Clap clap
clap-clap-clap
Clap clap
clap-clap

There I am, totally overdressed in a collared shirt and khakis because, silly me, I thought that on my first day of work I would be sitting in orientation meetings and filling out tax paperwork. Instead, I'm taking off running in my leather shoes from the muddy warning track, sprinting alongside Carlton in our matching Dockers, dashing across the playing field as we push a twenty-foot-long corrugated-aluminum tarp roll. I trip and fall, but scramble back to my overdressed feet and catch back up, completely unaware that I now have green and red stains on the knees of my britches and a blade of grass stuck in my teeth.

(Guitar riff) *Duh-dah-dah-duh*
Duh-dah-duh
Duh-dah-diggity-duh

There's me and Carlton, under the watchful eye of Jane, in the beer cooler under the first baseline grandstand. Forget that it's already like forty-five degrees out. She wants to make sure we can tap a keg properly. Carlton does it like a pro. Snap, click, twist, pump, shooosh, the suds launch through the tube, vanishing into the wall and flowing into the taproom concession stand next door.

My turn. Snap, cl . . . cl . . . okay, finally, click, twi . . . twi . . . TWIST . . . p . . . p . . . dammit . . . p . . . p . . . pump . . . and boom, a Bud Light geyser erupts from the keg with so much force that it knocks my glasses off.

Well, I beat the drum
and hold the phone
The sun came out today

There's us again, carrying giant awkward boxes filled with thirty-two-ounce plastic cups upon which are printed the 1994 Asheville Tourists schedule. There are dozens of them, and they were unexpectedly delivered weeks early, and we have nowhere else to store them but in the visitors' clubhouse, which is all the way down the third baseline, a solid quarter mile from where they were dropped off by the shipping service. We carry them one . . . two . . . three . . . thirty . . . past the hand-painted mountain-scape-backgrounded "ASHEVILLE TOURISTS" mural that takes up an entire wall inside the concrete slab building. Yes, the same painting that you can see behind Kevin Costner in that lonely clubhouse as his baseball career comes to an end in *Bull Durham*.

We're born again,
there's new grass on the field
A-roundin' third,
I'm headed for home . . .

Carlton is on the radar gun, measuring my weaker-than-expected throws in the concourse Speed Pitch contest we've just set up. I might have just torn a rotator cuff.

It's a brown-eyed handsome man
Anyone can understand the way I feel . . .

We're both in the clubhouse, loading the washing machine with white towels and—circle wipe—as we pull them from the clothes dryer, they are pink. We agitatedly dig through the rags and find that we've accidentally mixed a jersey into the wash, which we ran at way too hot a temperature, and not only has the red from the "Tourists" lettering bled into the towels, but the jersey is now small enough to fit a Ken doll.

Oh, put me in, Coach,
I'm ready to play today
Put me in, Coach,

I'm ready to play today
Look at me, I can be,
Centerfield

My friend Carlton Adcock and I are sitting in the home dug-out, exhausted, drenched in wintertime sweat and sharing half of a leftover Gatorade that we found in the back of the clubhouse refrigerator. I have an ice pack on my Speed Pitch–ripped shoulder. The blade of grass is still in my teeth. He looks at me and says, "Dude, how are we gonna do this for the next seven months? Also, how are we gonna make four sixty a month rent making four hundred a month?" I shrug and say, "Aw hell, I have no idea!" We laugh. The shot freezes.

(Big guitar finish)
Bah-daaah
Bah-daaah
Bah-dah bah-dah bah-dah bah-dah
B-b-b-b-bah-dah-dah-daaaaaah

That night we attended a dinner of the Asheville Tourists Pinch Hitters Club at the local Quincy's Steakhouse. It reminded me so much of those Shelby Pirates Boosters spaghetti dinners that Dad took us to when I was a kid. It was a room full of those people whom I told you about earlier, the longtime season-ticket holders and Reverse Snowbirds that Ron McKee had been so wise to take care of over the years. They were the team's true fan club, a small but proud congregation of gray-haired baseball lovers who knew my Babe Ruth "What a great ballpark!" tale and dozens more McCormick Field stories I'd yet to learn. We sat with a man named Ray Baldwin, who lived near the McKees in nearby Arden, North Carolina. The Asheville native said that McCormick Field was where he had found solace after the death of his beloved wife,

Rose, nine years earlier. Ray said that since the 1987 season opener he had missed only eleven games. Eleven. Games. Out of 994.

The leader of the Pinch Hitters was Bob Terrell, longtime writer for the *Asheville Citizen-Times* and the author of a book that was for sale in the ballpark's souvenir store and gift shops all around western North Carolina titled *McCormick Field: Field of Reality.* He always said that other places might be satisfied being called a *Field of Dreams,* but that McCormick was the field where dreams became real. Mr. Terrell was exactly the man you have pictured in your mind right now. His hair was shock white. His voice dripped with absolute belief. He was an amazing writer, and he talked in the exact same style that he wrote, which is to say with a flourish.

Near the close of the dinner, Terrell stood up to address the room. Then Carlton and I realized that he wasn't addressing the room at all. He was directly addressing the two of us, a couple of hundred-bucks-a-week interns who'd just had a Sisyphus of a first day of work.

"Gentlemen, have you read your Bible?"

We nodded, as if to say, *Sure, sir. We are familiar with the work.*

"When Moses climbs Mount Sinai to speak to God, an angel tells him, 'Take off your shoes, for you are standing on hallowed ground.' When you take the steps onto McCormick Field tomorrow, young men, take off your shoes, for to us you are on hallowed ground. Lou Gehrig hit a home run there. Willie Stargell has roamed its basepaths. Thomas Wolfe once wrote that he liked to sit in the stands and smell the aroma of the timber and hear the thump of the bat against the ball. Realize where you are, and understand what it is that we so dearly love."

Suddenly, there was a tinkling of glasses. The members of the Pinch Hitters Club were clanging their silverware against their goblets of sweet tea, so much so that a symphony of *tink-tink-tink-tink* rose until it filled the room. Every person with whom we made eye contact nodded, raised their glass, and in a few cases, wept.

Around ten p.m. that night, we got into Carlton's pickup and drove back to our $460-a-month apartment. We were totally quiet. Now, part of the reason for our silence was that the only apartment we could afford was in a retirement community, and all our neighbors were very old and very asleep, and we didn't want to wake anyone up. We were also too tired to talk. It was fourteen and a half hours after we'd reported for our first day on the job. We were worn slap out. But the main source of our speechlessness was what Mr. Terrell had said to us in his toast. And the weeping.

It was time for another movie moment. A conversation taken straight from one of the previous year's biggest Hollywood hits, *Tombstone*, the conversation after everyone has just watched Wyatt Earp walk into a river, staring down death and the barrel of the bad guy's guns to impossibly save the day.

"Hey, McGee," Carlton said around midnight as we unpacked boxes in our bedrooms. We had *SportsCenter* on the TV in the den. They were talking about Michael Jordan making his spring training debut with the Chicago White Sox the next day. "How about that dinner, man? You ever see anything like that?"

"Hell, man, I've never even heard of anything like that."

Hallowed ground. When the sun came up in a few hours, we weren't going back to work at a ballpark. We were going back to work on hallowed ground.

LET'S GIVE IT UP FOR YOUR ASHEVILLE TOURISTS!

"**H**ey, McGee, look at this damn guy. . . ."

By now you've likely noticed that I keep referring to three Asheville Tourists interns, but thus far you've only met two, myself and the great Carlton Adcock. The arrival of the man who indeed closed out our Tennessee Trio didn't happen until a couple of weeks later, and lawd, what an entrance it was. But we had to wait, so I'm going to make you wait for a moment, too.

While it was just us, Carlton and I had settled into a nice March preseason routine. We arrived at the ballpark each morning, received our assignments, and went to work. We never had any idea what we might doing on any given day. To some, that uncertainty would drive them batty. To us, variety equaled awesome.

We made copies of sponsor contracts. We sorted tickets. We helped Elaine set up the Bear Wear displays in the store. We rode around town asking every gas station attendant and restaurant hostess if they wouldn't mind putting a stack of Asheville Tourists pocket schedules by the front door of their business. Most said yes, though one guy at a barbershop did reach for his gun.

One time Gary took me on a sales call. He was always so smooth when he was selling, whether it be a meeting with a longtime advertiser or a cold call on a hunch. He created a fantastic, decades-long career in the business of sports largely due to his ability to keep the person across the table at ease. My favorite of those moments was when he took me with him to the Continental House of Pancakes, an independently owned Asheville breakfast institution that was located right around the corner from a franchise of the billion-dollar global brand, the International House of Pancakes. Gary, always the master of asking just the right question at the right time, addressed the owner and potential client: "I can't even imagine the work that it takes to start a place like this and be as successful as you have been. Looking back, what was the most difficult part of it all?" The restaurateur took a long time to think. He rubbed his chin. Then his eyes sparkled with realization. Without even one iota of irony or humor, he looked at us and said, "Coming up with the name."

One day, we were sent out into the mountains to Canton, North Carolina, a beautiful place, but one of America's truly stinkiest towns. We were given an address that didn't make a lot of sense, and all we were told was, "You're picking up a shirt." That didn't make any sense, either. But, quick reminder, this wasn't a democracy. So we asked no questions and made the twenty-minute drive out west into a town that is best described as Appalachian Blade Runner. The Pigeon River, the same river whose waters bathed little Dolly Parton and has filled the tanks of many a moonshine still, cut through a town of four thousand residents, all of whom were engulfed in humongous marvels of engineering. Conveyor belts, steam pipes, skyscraper smokestack towers, they all hissed and ground and churned from every corner of the village. Since the first decade of the twentieth century, when the local baseball team was known as the Asheville Moonshiners and McCormick Field had yet to be imagined, the Champion Coated Paper Company mill had produced millions of tons of paper products, and the process that made those materials also created a mighty sulfuric smell. There, amid all that industrialness, we knocked on an unmarked door and were greeted by a man who looked like he had been lost inside the Champion Mill ductwork his entire life.

"Here you go," he said with a disarming smile, but squinting as if he hadn't seen the sun since Eisenhower was in office. "I hope it fits him good."

The man handed us an XXXXL red short-sleeved, button-down garment that was adorned with the images of giant white flowers and closed the door. I looked down into my hands. It was a Hawaiian shirt. In Canton? So . . . that guy was a tailor? Or maybe a screen printer? Both? And . . . wait . . . okay . . . this shirt was too big for a human. So . . . hang on . . . we figured it out. "Dude," Carlton said to me. "This is for the damn bear." It was indeed for Ted E. Tourist. Hopefully, Ted liked popcorn, because the big white spots all over his shirt looked a lot more like they came from Orville Redenbacher than from Honolulu. This also now explained the next stop we'd been assigned to make on the way back to the ballpark, visiting a local travel agency to see if they had any old-school destination stickers. They would be for Ted's suitcase.

Back at the ballpark, the empty silence of early March started giving way to a steady flow of visitors as April approached. Some were stopping in to buy tickets, and those who did almost always asked the same question: "When is Michael Jordan playing here?" Yes, sports fans, this was that summer. The greatest basketball player who ever lived walked away from the court in the fall of 1993, and then, on February 7, 1994, the former Chicago Bull announced that he was going to try to become a member of the Chicago White Sox. Every one of MJ's spring training at-bats was the biggest story in baseball, a circus that provided a welcome distraction from all the speculation surrounding a potential MLB player strike. The Jordan Effect even reached us sitting in the winter-chilled ticket booth at McCormick Field. Whenever someone asked, we would inform them that the Sally League's White Sox affiliate, the Hickory Crawdads, would be in town for four games in mid-June and another five scattered throughout August. We never mentioned that there was a good smell's chance in Canton that the ChiSox were going to start the baseball career of His Airness all the way down here with us in Class A ball. We just sold them the tickets. Those nine games, based purely on the off chance that Jordan might be in town, had already neared sell-out status by the end of March.

No matter where we were working in the ballpark, we often found ourselves being serenaded, and always by the same song, "The Star-Spangled Banner." I wish that every human being could find something in their work that brings them the kind of joy that R. J. Martino found in being the staff member charged with field-ing calls and visits to the front office from people seeking to sing the national anthem before Tourists games. As soon as you saw him in the morning, you would know that he had auditioners lined up for later that day. He glowed. There were church choirs and Girl Scout troops and barbershop quartets. Because it was Asheville, a town that has always been a melting pot of hippies, hipsters, and hillbillies, would-be anthem performers were as likely to show up with a sitar as with a guitar. Keep in mind this was also 1994, the age of Garth Brooks and Boyz II Men. That led to a lot of yodel-ing country singers in overpressed rodeo shirts and at least that many groups of young people draped in stonewash and cardigans trying way too hard to harmonize their way through remixed runs of "Aaaaaand the ROCK-itz last uh-glare unhunhnhnhnhnh . . ."

Whenever R.J. scheduled an audition that he knew was going to be a hot one, he would give us a heads-up. He would lead the performer out onto the field, and we would instantly pop up from all corners of the ballpark to sit with him in the stands like judges on a TV talent competition. When they were good, they were very good. The man who ended up as our go-to was one of those surprise walk-ins, a saxophone player with an extensive background as a jazz studio musician. He informed us that he'd be around all summer. Good thing. Because R.J. had seventy-one open dates on the calendar, and there weren't enough Barth Grooks and Men II Boyz in Asheville to fill that calendar.

My personal favorite was a woman who claimed to be classically trained and showed up dressed to prove it, in a bright gold sequin-covered ball gown that was made for Carnegie Hall on a Friday night, but this was lunchtime at a minor-league ballpark on a Tuesday. When she stood at home plate and addressed the microphone, the sun suddenly broke through the treetops at just the right angle to hit her like a spotlight. Instantaneously, she became a giant disco ball, throwing off hundreds of shimmering, jiggling spots of light into every corner of McCormick Field, from the box seats to the billboards. But hey, there was no doubt she'd be able to sing, right? Then, instead of starting with "Oh say, can you see . . ." she broke into a series of vocal warm-up exercises that sounded like a cross between the chimes used to communicate with the aliens in *Close Encounter of the Third Kind* and the air horn of an eighteen-wheeler. But hey, there was no doubt she was now warmed up, right? This was going to be amazing! And it was, just not for the reasons that Madam Sequin believed. In all fairness, the first ten minutes of it were pretty good. It was the next ten minutes that went south. When it finally ended with the appropriate crescendo and crash, we all worked hard not to laugh. I pinched my own arm to prevent a smile. I thought we had done a great job of making her believe that she had crushed it. We clapped. She smiled. Then it was quiet. That's when we could hear the dogs from the porches of the homes surrounding the ballpark, howling.

R.J. escorted her to the gate and said he would be in touch. Then we noticed that Ron had come out of his office and was standing on what I would come to call his "Vatican Porch," a balcony-like outdoor area that was right off the main office door, overlooking the ballpark from right field. He had heard the entire performance. I suppose the entire city of Asheville had heard it. Even if they hadn't, they most definitely heard Ron's reaction. "Bad news, guys! Season's been canceled!" he shouted down to us. "It has to be over! The damn fat lady has already sung!"

I don't think that's precisely when the third intern rolled up in front of the ballpark, but in my mind that's how it happened. The prima donna's giant Cadillac pulling away and then the vacated parking spot being immediately occupied by a Corvette that skidded into place like it was entering the pits at the 24 Hours of Le Mans. I also don't know if Led Zeppelin's "When the Levee Breaks" was actually bass-pounding its way through the Stingray's windows or if that's just how I like to remember it. I do know that when the door of that sports car flew open and the occupant rose out of the driver's seat like he was levitating, that was most definitely the tune that I heard in my mind. He was tall, his hair was perfect. He looked like Patrick Swayze. "Hey, McGee, look at this damn guy. . . ." When Carlton said it to me under his breath, it wasn't a dig. It was a compliment.

"Hey, guys," he said as he removed his sunglasses and offered up a handshake in one fluid motion. "I'm Stephen Whitt. Go Vols."

All we'd known about Stephen Whitt was that he was a fellow recent University of Tennessee graduate and that he'd grown up in nearby Candler, North Carolina, the last outpost one sees traveling west from Asheville and into the Great Smoky Mountains. He was joining us late because he had to finish up some school stuff, and he immediately apologized for that. We really wanted to hate him, but he was too awesome. In fact, we were already kind of mad at him because of something that had happened due to his absence during most of March. When it was time to take the staff photos for the game programs that would be sold all season, the front-office crew—Gary, Eileen, Jane, R.J., and Carolyn—had their portraits taken by the local Glamour Shots, the pre-Instagram filtered photography phenomenon whose studios filled shopping malls across 1990s America. Their teased-hair, airbrushed, soft-edged likenesses are forever frozen in time on page twenty of that program. At the bottom of that page is a coupon for a $14.95 makeover and photo session down at the Asheville Mall Glamour Shots. I told you Gary was a good salesman.

We interns weren't in on the Glamour Shots deal (neither was Ron, per his choice), and that was fine with us. But we also would have preferred our personal program imagery to be a little nicer than the milk carton "Have you seen this kid?" shots we ended up with. One morning we were handed a couple of old white golf shirts taken from the souvenir store clearance rack, led into the ballpark concourse, stood in front of a brick wall with the sun in our eyes, and photographed with a disposable camera, all before we even knew what had happened. But not Stephen Whitt. Since he wasn't yet on the job, he wasn't there for the mug-shot session and instead sent in his own photo. It was his official college fraternity portrait, well lit and Hollywood and everything that Glamour Shots wished that it could be. It was easily the best-looking photograph in the 1994 Asheville Tourists game program. When we first saw it, Carlton and I were a little mad. Who the hell sends in their frat shot? Then we met him. Hell, truth is truth, handsome is handsome, and the truth was that Stephen Whitt was handsome. He still might be the smoothest dude I've ever met. That's why when we saw the vanity plate on his Corvette, the nickname by which we would forever call him was born. In big block red lettering it read "S WHITT." I spoke it aloud. "Switt." We immediately changed it up to "Swish." Because my man Stephen Whitt, as slick as he was, that dude was definitely a Swish.

Now our team in the office was finally complete. All we needed was a team to put on the diamond.

The bus that delivered that team rolled in from the Asheville

Regional Airport and pulled up alongside McCormick Field around midnight on April 3. After more than a month of stocking shelves, hosing down concrete, and sitting in the ticket office staring out into space, wondering if any actual baseball was ever going to happen, our excitement was nearly immeasurable. Our ballpark was going to have a ball club. The 1994 Asheville Tourists had arrived. We stood on the curb outside the entrance arch to welcome them, practically vibrating with anticipation.

From that first Pinch Hitters Club dinner until this very moment, our five weeks without the team had been filled with nonstop McCormick Field history and magic. That very day, the 1994 MLB season started, even as the chasm continued to grow in the ongoing big-league labor dispute. Many agreed that Opening Day had happened simply because no one—players or owners—wanted to be responsible for slaying the most sacred of all baseball cows, the "Iron Man" streak of Baltimore Orioles shortstop Cal Ripken Jr. Entering the '94 season, he had appeared in 1,897 consecutive MLB games and was 234—roughly a season and a half—shy of Lou Gehrig's long-thought-unapproachable mark of 2,130.

As sportswriters and baseball fans began looking for connections between the two legends, their searches often led them to Asheville. Gehrig played with the Yankees at McCormick on three different occasions, the first on the bench behind first baseman Wally Pipp, the man whom he would famously replace in the lineup two months later to begin his fourteen-year reign as baseball's Iron Horse. A half-century later, Ripken sat in that same bunker-like dugout as a batboy, laboriously watching pitchers and taking notes on what they threw and when. It was the early 1970s, and the Tourists weren't the Tourists at all. They were the Asheville Orioles, Baltimore's Class AA Southern League affiliate. The team's manager was Cal Ripken Sr., and both of his future big-league sons, Cal Jr. and Billy, were McCormick Field fixtures.

"I loved it there so much," Cal Jr. recalled to me in 2011. I was working on a story for ESPN.com about, of all things, a NASCAR race, but I couldn't resist asking him about his time in Asheville. "I was twelve, thirteen, and fourteen years old. Dad would work us out at the ballpark, and the players would work with us, too. Then we would either stay for the game or go play in our own youth-league games. Those players were my heroes. Al Bumbry and Mike Flanagan, Doug DeCinces, Eddie Murray. Several years later, when I got to Baltimore, all those guys were my teammates. And I absolutely remember the old fans talking about seeing Lou Gehrig play in Asheville. I just thought that was cool. Of course, at the time I had no idea the connection I would have with him later."

That connection was how I found myself giving a couple of late-March tours to sportswriters from New York and Baltimore as they were researching stories on the Iron Men. We'd also had a steady stream of walk-up visitors who were there to see . . . wait . . . the center-field clock from Ebbets Field? Someone had written in a new book about baseball stadiums that the legendary old "OFFICIAL TIME BULOVA" circular timepiece that stood watch over the home of the Brooklyn Dodgers for decades had made its way to McCormick Field after the team moved to Los Angeles and their home ballpark of Ebbets Field was razed. It was a story that had been running around since 1959, when the city of Asheville did indeed purchase a clock for the scoreboard that was said to have been saved from Ebbets. The problem was that an identical clock, also pitched as the timepiece from Brooklyn, had also just been mounted in nearby Charlotte . . . and another in Chattanooga . . . and still more in at least a couple of other Southern minor-league parks.

So, the Ebbets-to-McCormick clock tale, as old as time, wasn't true. At least, I don't think it was. There were persistent rumors that perhaps it had been real but was removed during the ballpark renovations of the 1980s and was now located somewhere on Ron

McKee's mountaintop property south of the city. When I asked him about it, he said I was wrong. "It's not at my house. It's in my truck. I keep it in there so that I make sure I'm never late to anything." Ron was joking. I think.

Now the 1994 Asheville Tourists were plenty late. But, fueled by a solid month of hallowed ground history and stories of Tourists gone by, to me their midnight arrival amid McCormick's mythology and mysticism felt like destiny, a genuinely enchanted moment. Heck, even when we threw the switch that turned on the ballpark lights just as the team bus arrived, there was a low layer of misty mountain fog sitting atop the playing field. The giant Marlboro Man looked like Moonlight Graham. All we needed was for James Earl Jones to give his "People will come" speech about the romanticism of baseball. Instead, we got a record scratch.

"Dammit, my back is stiff as hell!"

The Tourists stepped out into the shadowy concourse behind the ballpark, not as superhuman gladiators arriving to take stock of the coliseum where they would do battle. No, they unloaded off the bus like someone had spilled a stack of bowling balls. Their morning had started in Arizona, and the day had taken them through two other stops before they finally boarded their flight into the tiny Asheville airport, a plane that had skipped over the Appalachian Mountains like a stone on a river.

"Where in the hell are we?!"

There were twenty-six players in all, twenty-five active and one already on the disabled list. They ranged in size from five foot eight to six foot seven and from 160 pounds to 240. The twenty-one players from the continental United States hailed from cities scattered across a baker's dozen of different states, from California and Illinois to Connecticut and Louisiana. Of the five Latino players, two came from the territory of Puerto Rico, two from the Dominican Republic, and one from Venezuela. The oldest player, Texan catcher Jason Smith, was all of twenty-three. The youngest,

Puerto Rican outfielder Edgard Velasquez, was eighteen, or at least that's what his paperwork said. No matter what their age or where they were raised, everyone was tired and stiff.

"Okay, guys, that was a lot for one day, so make sure to take a moment and stretch out!" Amid the groans, grunts, and yawns, the instructions came from Marc Gustafson. Gus was the team trainer and the only member of the roster who had been with us throughout much of our March prep work. He was a Colorado native, a Colorado State Ram, and he was immediately drawn to us interns because he himself had held down the same gig with the Class AAA Denver Zephyrs, who played their games at Mile High Stadium, home of the NFL's Denver Broncos. The Zephyrs no longer existed because in 1993 they were replaced by Denver's new expansion MLB team, Gustafson's employer and our parent club, the Colorado Rockies.

"Gus! Where is the icy hot muscle rub stuff?!"

In case you don't know, and in my experience most don't, this is how the relationship works between an MLB club and its MiLB affiliates. The big-league organization scouts, signs, trains, evaluates, and pays the players. Depending upon how they perform during spring training and during the season, those players are assigned to a rung along the minor-league ladder with the hope of ascending to what they refer to as The Show. The big club also provides the coaches, trainers, and in some cases, equipment. For example, the Rockies supplied bats, but we were responsible for distributing them, trading one-for-one whenever a player turned in a stick that was cracked or that he believed had lost its ability to connect with baseballs. If the count ever got off, the Rockies let us know about it hurriedly and angrily. As for those baseballs, we paid for them, delivering three dozen new balls to the umpires prior to each game and making sure the team had plenty of not-so-new balls to bang around in batting practice. In short, the parent club worried about the baseball-related stuff, while the minor-league organization—us—was responsible for providing the best possible work environment through stadium upkeep and game operations, but also by arranging travel accommodations, distributing meal money, and doing whatever was needed to help the players settle into their new town. The best that I could tell, only one of our players had ever so much as visited Asheville until the night they arrived as Tourists.

"For real, where the hell are we? This is Tennessee, right?"

In 1994, the Rockies had six minor-league affiliates, including the Tourists. The "Road to the Rockies" began in Arizona, where the Chandler Rockies were a "rookie ball"–level member of the summer-only "short season" Arizona League. Chandler's roster was filled mostly with kids who had just been signed in the MLB draft, most coming straight out of high school. Next were the Bend Rockies in Oregon, also a short-season team as members of the Northwest League. The Central Valley Rockies of Visalia, California, were part of the High Class A California League. The New Haven Ravens, who played at Yale, were in the Class AA Eastern League, just below the Class AAA Colorado Springs Sky Sox of the Pacific Coast League. They all hopefully funneled talent to the Colorado Rockies in Denver.

Colorado liked having a team in Asheville because of the altitude. No, McCormick Field wasn't a literal mile high like the home of the Rockies, but it did sit 2,134 feet above sea level. The Tourists were the third rung on the organizational ladder, sandwiched between Bend and Central Valley, proud members of the South Atlantic League, a confederation of ball clubs that had existed in some form or another since 1904. We were Low Class A, which meant that we were also most players' first experience with a full-time 142-game professional-length schedule. We weren't simply the level of baseball where guys were figuring out tweaks to their swing or how to add pitches to their arsenal. We weren't even just the level where former college players were working on the transition from metal bats to wood. No, we were the level where most of the guys were living away from home for the first time. Where they would learn how to balance a checkbook. Where they would have to learn how to cook for themselves. And for five of the guys on our roster, they would be doing all the above while also learning how to speak and read English.

Our players were made up of three groups of guys. The ones right out of high school, the ones right out of college, and the ones right out of the Caribbean. That's how they'd ridden on the bus that night. That's how they were gathering outside that bus right now. That's pretty much how they'd operate all season long, from the dugout to the clubhouse to their living quarters.

Tonight, they would haul their baseball gear into that clubhouse and pick out a locker. Of all the improvements made when McCormick Field was rebuilt, everyone was proudest of the spacious, rectangular home clubhouse. They should have been. For a minor-league team, especially Class A, a space like this was unheard-of. Most MiLB locker rooms were crammed beneath an immovable grandstand, and they felt like it. They were small, shaped weird, and seemingly designed to keep any team from having any meeting larger than a few guys leaning up against a laundry cart. That had been the case in the old McCormick clubhouse, a stand-alone cinder-block labyrinth of rooms that had been added on like Legos over the course of decades. That building, down the third baseline, was still there. But now it was the musky domain of the visiting teams.

The five Spanish-speaking Tourists immediately moved into the lockers located in the same corner, the one closest to the door that led into the parking lot. The college guys took over the opposite corner, the one closest to the door that led to the dugout. Everyone else grabbed a spot wherever they could. We stood back and watched it all as if we were tuning into a voyeuristic reality TV show, sizing up personalities and social status based on their body language and how they reacted to one another. I noticed that Velasquez immediately started decorating his locker with photos of Roberto Clemente. I wanted to tell him that Puerto Rico's all-time baseball titan had played at McCormick Field several times in the 1960s, when the Tourists were affiliated with Pittsburgh and the Pirates would come to Asheville every spring to play an exhibition game, but I decided that could wait.

I also noticed that everyone in the room kind of worked around one player particularly. Jamey Wright was a slick-armed, six-and-a-half-feet-tall right-handed pitcher out of Oklahoma City, who threw a full catalog of nasty breaking balls. He was our version of *Bull Durham*'s Nuke LaLoosh. Wright wasn't as flaky as the Tim Robbins character, though he did wear the same Oklahoma Sooners T-shirt every single day he reported to the ballpark. For decades. Like Ebby Calvin LaLoosh, Jamey Alan Wright was a "Bonus Baby," and everywhere he went in the baseball world everyone knew it, especially here in this clubhouse. He was drafted by the Rockies straight out of Westmore High School, the twenty-eighth overall selection of the 1993 MLB draft and the recipient of a then-astronomical $395,000 signing bonus, plus paid college tuition to assuage any trepidation over his decision to bypass school and head straight for the pros. *Baseball America,* the weekly bible of the hardball world, had named Wright the fourth-best prospect in the entire Colorado farm system. The Rockies franchise was fresh, cool, and—with a new ballpark coming and homers being blasted through the thin Rocky Mountain air—already considered a beacon for the bright future of baseball. Jamey Wright was being framed up as one of the most important pieces of that future. He was nineteen. He was very likable, but he was also very conscious of how others viewed him.

Standing across the room and observing, our initial impression was that everyone was keeping their distance from Wright, careful to tread lightly around the Bonus Baby. Most in that clubhouse were making around $600 a month in take-home pay. But that actually wasn't the reason for the distance. Wright wasn't being treated with kid gloves. He was just a kid with a glove.

"I was shy, man. That clubhouse was full of college guys, big personalities, and they came off the top rope talking shit from the very first minute," Wright recalled to me eighteen years later. "If you wore an ugly shirt on the bus one morning, it was over. They were going to let you have it over that shirt for the next month. Looking back, it wasn't mean, it was hilarious. But I had no response for that yet. I was nineteen. I couldn't get into bars with them yet. I didn't know how to cook anything or how to do my own laundry. Man, I had a lot to figure out. So, the last thing I was going to do was try to go at it with the big personalities right off the bat."

Yes, these guys had worked out together during spring training. Many, including Wright and Velasquez, had been together on the Rockies' rookie team the previous summer. But all that was fractured and scattered, especially where they'd just arrived from. At spring training, they were mixed in with a couple of hundred other ballplayers working out on a half-dozen fields. Now they would be teammates for the next five and a half months. Not just playing together but living together. I thought back to my first week of college, when I'd been assigned a roommate I couldn't stand. Dude never threw his trash away and every night at one a.m. would wake me up scooping tuna out of a can and spreading it out on oranges like finger sandwiches. I also had to share a community shower and toilet with a hundred strangers, all with a hundred different smells. Then we spent an entire year eating and sleeping in the same place, every single day. We saw each other naked all the time. It was strange.

This scene in the Asheville clubhouse was way stranger because these guys were essentially strangers . . . and now they lived together . . . and this was their job . . . and they were dependent on those strangers (with whom they now lived) to help them keep their jobs.

"Gentlemen, the bus is rolling out to the hotel shortly. Tomorrow the front office is going to work with you to find an apartment and all of that. But hey, what do you say we walk out and see your new home ballpark!" The speech came from our manager, Tony Torchia, as he walked out into the middle of the room and gently clapped his hands to get everyone's attention. His office was located just off the clubhouse, as was the locker room reserved for himself and his two assistant coaches. Those rooms had clearly sacrificed square footage to make the main space as large as it was. The coaches' quarters were both so tiny that it never felt like you walked into them. It was more like you were putting them on. Torchia's metal desk, upon which sat one phone and that was it, took up nearly every inch of the space between the back wall and the doorway. "When you are a minor-league manager, your door is always open," Torchia said to me as he stuck a few items from his briefcase into a desk drawer. "Because there's never enough room in one of these offices to close it." It was the first of a summer-long series of bits of wit and knowledge that Tony Torchia would share with me.

The 1994 Asheville Tourists filed through the little hallway that led into the home dugout and took the three steps up onto the field. Gary had turned on the lights. That mountain mist was still there. Everyone was completely silent. I looked at Carlton. He nodded and winked. We could feel the team finally soaking in the McCormick magic that we'd been marinating in for the last five weeks. Or so we thought.

I found myself standing next to Randy Edwards, an outfielder from West Covina, California. I smiled at him and said, "Well, you think you can play here?" What I meant was, "Hey, isn't this place beautiful? Isn't it so amazing that this is where you get to work? Wasn't Babe Ruth right when he said it was a damn delightful place? Babe Ruth, who played here, where you play now?!" That's not what Randy Edwards heard. What he heard was, "Well, do you think you can play here?" as a challenge. He turned his head sharply toward me. "I know I can play here. I can play anywhere." He let loose a disgusted scoff and walked away.

It was the first time I realized that even though all these players were basically my age and even though we were all working very literally side by side, there would likely always be a moat between us in the front office and them in the clubhouse. Not all the time (there would be some moments of fun interaction), but I certainly was going to be more careful with my words from here on out. In that way, my relationship with them wasn't much different from most of their relationships with one another. We were going to work together to have a great season, maybe even win a pennant. We were going to be teammates. But we weren't going to be pals.

By the way, Randy Edwards lasted less than three weeks. He was the first player cut from the 1994 Asheville Tourists.

The next day was a frenzy. Gary, R.J., and the McKees drove players around Asheville to meet landlords of apartment complexes with whom they had relationships, punctuated by trips to furniture rental places, grocery stores, and Wal-Mart. Once again, the team naturally divided itself up into the teen/college/Spanish divisions, though only the Spanish speakers made the decision to cram five guys into one place. Torchia went with them. He did that a lot. I even heard tales of Tony Torchia helping his Latin players earn their driver's licenses, quizzing them on the bus to get ready for the written exam, and then driving them to the DMV in his own car to take the driving test. He told me: "I don't speak a lick of Spanish, except for a couple of baseball terms here and there. But I have to help those guys. Call it the dad in me. I think about my two sons, if they were eighteen and thrown into a foreign country trying to chase their dreams. I would hope that someone would help them."

But why was everyone scrambling so on the first day of the gig? Because everyone wanted to get as settled as they possibly could before the season began four days later, hitting the road to face the Greensboro Bats, Charleston (West Virginia) Wheelers, and Hickory Crawdads, before returning for the April 13 home opener, also against Greensboro.

The most crucial item on the day's to-do list was also the task assigned to us interns, helping a photographer corral the players for the big team photo on the field. We were even allowed to be in the photo, proudly wearing our very own "uniform" alongside the players in theirs. We were given two cotton golf shirts, one white and one navy. The white one was very soft. The blue one felt like polyester chain-mail armor. Over our left breast was an embroidered likeness of Ted E. Tourist and the words "Asheville Tourists Baseball Club." Sewn onto the left sleeve was a patch, the official emblem commemorating the 150th season of professional baseball. It was the MLB batter logo but made with gold thread. Underneath it was a block-letter "STAFF." Over the years I have had the chance to wear expensive suits, tuxedos, even NASCAR fire suits, and fighter pilot jumpsuits. But I've never been prouder to wear an article of clothing than the one that had that word sewn onto the sleeve. "STAFF."

For the players, the team photo was merely the pregame, for next came their baseball card pictures. Fleer handled Minor League Baseball cards via its Pro Cards brand. Should any of the youngsters on our team go on to have a Hall of Fame career, then perhaps that pack of Pro Cards would one day be worth something on yet-to-exist eBay. For now, it was worth five bucks in the Bear Wear store.

One by one, our candidates for a greater glory stood at home plate to be eternally immortalized in cardboard. There was Nate Holdren, the massive Michigan Man who played first base and had also laid a few licks in the Rose Bowl as a Wolverine linebacker. He was followed by Doug "Snake" Walls, the only other member of the roster to join Wright on *Baseball America*'s top-ten Rockies prospects list (No. 9) and who earned his nickname because he roomed with a pair of boa constrictors, which is still easier on a roommate than eating tuna on orange slices. Then there was a big-smiled, switch-hitting shortstop who came with a built-in local fan base. Keith Grunewald had just wrapped up an All-ACC stint with the beloved University of North Carolina Tar Heels, and we'd already had some pale blue–wearing folks stop by to get his autograph. They posed one after the other, from John "Juice" Giudice and Mike "Hatty" Hatfield to Mike "Higgy" Higgins and Keith "Barnesy" Barnes. No, I don't know what it is with baseball players and adding a *y* to everyone's name.

Whatever their name, we had to keep a close eye on them all because a few jokey jokesters tried to lie on the questionnaire that sought fun facts to print on the backs of their baseball cards ("C'mon, dude, your dad isn't a space shuttle pilot"), and we also had to double-check every ball-cap lid, batting glove, and bat knob to make sure no one was trying to sneak in any extra adult messages. This was, after all, just a few years removed from former McCormick Field resident Billy Ripken and the most infamous baseball card ever printed, a 1989 Fleer with "F—k Face" written very clearly on the bottom of the bat he posed with. I'm proud to say no one snuck one by us.

I'm also proud to say that, incredibly, everyone was where they were supposed to be when they were supposed to be there, wearing their new uniforms for the first time, sparkling white with blue pinstripes and red-trimmed blue script "Tourists" sewn across the button-down chest, and a Colorado Rockies logo patch on the right sleeve. On the left sleeve was the unmistakable image of Ted E. Tourist. Ted E. was also on their caps. He was on the billboards in the outfield. He was on signs out front reminding folks that the home opener was two weeks away. He was on shirts. He was everywhere . . . except where he was supposed to be at this moment.

Gary Saunders was getting a little irritated. "Can someone check and see if Ted, er, I mean Jack, has called the office?"

Jack was the guy we had hired to don the Ted E. Tourist costume. He was not the kid from recent years who had wowed McCormick Field with his b-boy dance moves atop the home dugout in the shabby Elmo suit. Jack was a trained thespian. Sort of. He was a local actor, a veteran of the Asheville community theatrical stage, and his self-selling point during his job interview was that he had a clear understanding of the surprisingly complicated world of being a sports mascot. He knew the rules of mascot performance and said he had learned by studying the masters of the craft, such as the Famous Chicken, the Phoenix Suns Gorilla, and Mickey Mouse, the Mount Rushmore of fuzzy giant heads. Jack knew that mascots didn't talk. He knew that once the paws and claws were donned, the human inside the felt was to become one with the animal, dinosaur, crustacean, or whatever. He claimed to have had training as a Method actor, those performers who refuse to limit themselves to taking on a role only when the stage (or ballpark) lights were on. Instead, the Method men and women live in the skin (or pelt) of their character all the time. Jack said two summers earlier he had shadowed (okay, stalked) the modern master of Method acting, Oscar winner Daniel Day-Lewis, who had lived in Asheville during the filming of *The Last of the Mohicans,* shot in the mountains that surrounded the city.

Jack knew all that. Frankly, Jack knew too much. But he didn't know how to write "Baseball card photo session, Monday at noon" in his day planner. We still don't know where he was. Perhaps he was in rehearsal with an improv troupe. Or at a bar. Or maybe he was in a self-defense class, preparing for that summer's pinnacle unplanned event, a baseball mascot battle royal. We just knew he wasn't here to have his photo taken.

As the entire team and front office stood around waiting by home plate, an irked Gary turned to us. "Okay, does anyone here have any mascot experience?" I wasn't sure if he was serious, but I raised my hand. My senior year of high school, when an injury befell the classmate who normally portrayed our mascot, I volunteered to slide into the role of the Travelers Rest High School Devildog. He was a bulldog with a bad attitude and a military helmet. During the handful of football games when I acted as the Devildog it was fun, except for the funky aroma produced by the crusted sweat of my predecessors that had taken up permanent residence inside the giant plastic head. Then there were the rednecks at rival high schools who thought it would be fun to throw rocks at that giant head in stadium parking lots. The continuous thuds that rattled my exo-head, the same oversize cranium that rendered me too blind to see where those rocks were coming from, had been traumatic. But it had been several years. I was ready to go back in.

"Okay, McGee," Gary replied. "Suit up."

Like every American kid, I had grown up dreaming of doing exactly what I suddenly found myself doing right then. I was in the clubhouse of a professional baseball team, putting on a uniform and walking up the steps of a dugout to stride onto a diamond and pose for a photographer who would capture the images that would be printed upon my very own baseball card. I just hadn't envisioned those strides happening in scuba flipper–size furry feet while carrying an antique suitcase with my furry hands. To my surprise, the scent inside the head wasn't gross. It smelled like a new car. And no one threw anything at me.

My grin on the inside of that head was nearly as gigantic as the exaggerated smile stitched onto the outside. Ted E. Tourist and I had indeed melded as one, except for the fact that I weighed about half as much as Jack, and the red popcorn-covered, sorry, flower-covered shirt and blue pants hung off my bony body like they were draped on a wire hanger in the Bear Wear store.

"Okay, Ted, sell it!" the photographer said, waving his hand in the air to set my eyeline, as if I had real eyes and could see anything he was doing. I cocked one knee in the air like Captain Morgan and waved with one paw while I wagged the luggage around with the other. So, heck yeah, I sold it. And we sold it in the store.

When the finished product arrived a couple of weeks later, Carlton immediately ripped open the pack, dug out the bear card, and handed it to me with a pen. "Sign it, Ted E. McGee!" When we got back to our retirement community apartment that night, he smacked two images onto the wall of the den, the only décor of any kind in our spartan dwelling. It was the eight-by-ten glossy team photo and my baseball card.

We always had to stay super muted when we returned home from work because everyone living around us went to bed at like six thirty every evening. Have you seen that movie *A Quiet Place,* when Jim from *The Office* and his family have to live their lives in silence so as not to wake the monsters who live around them? It was totally like that. We played our music super quiet. We learned how to laugh in hushed tones. We weren't surrounded by monsters. Quite the opposite. Those sweet old ladies would even fold our laundry for us and bring it to our apartment door if we'd accidentally left it in the community dryer. (Okay, once we figured that out, we "forgot" about our clothes a few more times.) We didn't certainly want to jolt them awake at midnight being twenty-two-year-olds, listening to Danzig's "Mother" turned up to eleven and smashing Coors Light cans against our heads.

So, when Carlton triumphantly pinned my baseball card to our wall, he didn't do it with a hammer and nail. He posted it gently with a thumbtack. Then he turned, pumped his fist, and screamed like a mime.

It is still on my wall today. I have that card framed in my office and always will. As of the writing of this book, the 1994 Asheville Tourists baseball card team set was selling on eBay for $5.95. That's nearly a one-dollar increase over what we were charging for it that summer.

You're welcome, Bonus Baby.

PLAY BALL!

O fficially, McCormick Field's first game was held Thursday, April 3, 1924, when the Detroit Tigers were deposited by train into downtown Asheville at eleven a.m. They lunched with the Rotary Club and then strode up the stone stairway that led them into a mountainside wooden ballpark so brand spanking new that the smell of wet paint and wood resin was almost overwhelming. The four-thousand-seat stadium had cost the city $200,000 to construct, the equivalent of $3.2 million in twenty-first-century dollars, with the goal of attracting the very kind of event that took place on this very day. It was named for Dr. Lewis M. McCormick, who had died less than two years earlier. He was beloved in the community, known as "The Fly Man" because when the bacteriologist had moved to town in 1904, he was appalled at the overwhelming clouds of houseflies that had overtaken Asheville. He pushed for laws that cleaned up the town's horse stables, purified its milk, and recruited children for his "Swat That Fly" campaign. The kids were hired by households to chase and kill the airborne, disease-carrying pests. Within weeks the city had been saved, and the movement went on to sweep the nation.

Now, the brand-new ballpark named in his memory was hosting

a trio of flyball-chasing Baseball Hall of Fame outfielders. The fearsome threesome of Tigers, all Cooperstown bound, consisted of player/manager Ty Cobb, then still regarded by many as the greatest baseball player to ever sharpen his spikes (and man, did he do that), along with Harry Heilmann and Heinie Manush. They were in town to face the Asheville Skylanders, one season before the home team would settle into its love affair with the Tourists moniker (and end years of using rotating nicknames). Fans lined the waist-high wooden railing that lined the outfield behind the three legendary Tigers, though the day curiously fell short of a sell-out. A giant white banner waved in the breeze as it hung from the left-field grandstands, reading "Asheville—Playground of America." That day Manush slugged the ballpark's first homer. Cobb added one, too. But the Skylanders blasted four round-trippers of their own and stunned the team that the previous season had finished second in the American League. Asheville won 18–14, and in the decades since, stories and chapters in books have been written about the game again and again. A framed panoramic photo of the historic day still hangs in the McCormick Field front office. In 1994, we sold dozens of "Opening Day 1924" posters featuring that same photo.

Thing is, it wasn't really McCormick's first game. That happened a week earlier, when the Skylanders defeated the considerably less sexy Weaver College Blue Giants, 13–5, on what was a chilly, wet, when-the-hell-is-spring-gonna-get-here day in front a few dozen people. It was the kind of day that you'd just as soon forget, so the annals of Asheville Tourists history have done just that.

Seventy years later, we had a similar situation. Opening Day 1994 was on April 13 against the Greensboro Bats, a New York Yankees affiliate that featured future two-time World Series–winning outfielder Ricky Ledée. At least, that's what the record shows. The reality is our first game was, like 1924, a full week earlier, on a gross

April 6, 1994. It too was an exhibition against a local college team, UNC Asheville, to help the struggling Bulldogs program raise a little money and to get the inexperienced Tourists some playing time under the lights in front of a crowd, two conditions that a big chunk of the team weren't used to. Recalls Jamey Wright: "The year before, I was playing in high school games in front of no one, and then I was in Rookie League games in Arizona, played in front of even smaller crowds, and they all started at ten in the morning so we could get done before it was a hundred and twenty degrees outside. Playing in front of a couple of thousand people under the lights for six months, I might as well have been playing baseball on Mars."

I don't think the term "soft opening" was even a thing yet, at least it wasn't to me, but that's exactly what this UNC-A game was. And holy geez, I was as bad as the indoctrinated players. I was assigned ticket intern and screwed up something with my math that accidentally sold more seats in one section than that section had in it to sell. I also completely forgot to deliver the three boxes of baseballs to the umpires. I pulled up the venetian blinds on the box office window and was greeted by a pissed-off umpire dressed in nothing but his socks and boxers wondering how I expected them "to play a damn baseball game without any damn baseballs." Earlier, while on the way to help set up the press box, I dropped what I liked to call "Gary's Big Box of Music" and scattered dozens of cassettes and CDs of in-game tunes—you know the ones, like Creedence Clearwater Revival's "Who'll Stop the Rain" for rain delays, and the *Jeopardy!* theme for when the opposing team's meeting at the pitcher's mound went too long—all over the concrete steps. I was down on the concrete with one knee stuck into a spot of spilled mustard and reaching under the bleachers to retrieve an ESPN *Jock Jams* CD when I looked up to see Gary standing over me, grinning. "Is this the day the music died?"

Carlton's April assignment was concessions intern, and he told me later that he didn't pull the boxes of meat out of the freezer as early as he was supposed to, so we'd sold a batch of burgers that were essentially frozen hockey pucks covered in hot, melted cheese. As the office intern, Swish surely screwed something up too, but . . . oh hell, who am I kidding? He was fine. He was Swish.

It was also raining. Not enough to cancel the game, but just enough to make everyone miserable and cause the teams to have to come off the field several times. Anyone who has ever attended or even tuned in to a rainy-day ball game at the highest level of the sport has taken in the true beauty of a fully manned, perfectly orchestrated tarp unfurling. It's like watching a NASCAR pit stop in super-slow motion, set to classical music played by the New York Philharmonic. On this day our effort was more like the Marx Brothers with musical backing from a middle school pep band. We mistimed our very first in-game tarp pull of the season so badly that it became heavy with pools of rainwater, so that the half dozen of us couldn't pull it with enough speed, so the tarp pull turned into more of a tarp drag. The game was called after five innings and a 1–0 score. The college umpire, the one whom I'd seen earlier seething in his Fruit of the Looms, called it a mercy killing.

Witnessing our tarp drag, you would have realized we were severely understaffed. Every Minor League Baseball team hires a huge number of part-timers to cover various game day duties around the ballpark throughout the season. Someone needed to man the ticket window, sell programs in what looked like a wooden lemonade stand located just inside the front gate, run the two concession stands, the snow cone stand, the ice cream stand, and the beer stand, run the grill, operate the Speed Pitch, usher fans to their seats, work as box-seat waitresses, and escort Ted E. Tourist as he roamed the stands to mingle with fans, not to mention a whole lot of other jobs that I can't remember now—and so you know we certainly didn't remember all of them then.

We had posted these jobs in the *Asheville Citizen-Times* in

March and April, as well as posted notices all over town. These days, teams host ballpark job fairs to lure potential applicants. We should have done that. Instead, we welcomed a daily cavalcade of folks who made the national anthem auditioners look like a meeting of Nobel Prize laureates. High school students who couldn't yet work weeknight games because they were still in school. Local college students who could work games now but would be gone during summer because they went home. Many members of Asheville's very large retirement community also answered our want ads, but more than a few of them said they couldn't work evenings because that was simply too late. I wanted to scream, "Come on, old people, don't you know that we are a baseball team and that means most of our games start at night?!" But I didn't. A herd of hillbillies came down out of the mountains to inquire about working in concessions, though more than a few appeared to not have enough teeth to chew the concessions they were applying to sell.

We had no shortage of job candidates. We had a shortage of good job candidates, especially in early April, the start of the baseball season, but a full two months before the start of summer.

"We have a problem," Gary said to Ron as they stood by the front gate watching fans file in for the UNC-A game. "We're short a few hands. Actually, a lot of hands." Indeed, we already looked overwhelmed because there was no one to tear tickets at the turnstile, the first job we needed to have filled, because it was quite literally the first job that needed to be done. So, I did it. And I was terrible at it. There was a big box to catch the perforated part of the ticket that was used to tally the final attendance numbers and help Carolyn balance her books. You handed the rest of the ticket, the part with their seat location on it, back to the fan. Turns out I was super great at throwing the fan part into the box, while handing the fan the part that was supposed to be in the box. Perhaps I should have been concentrating more on tearing and not so much on eavesdropping.

Ron replied to Gary with a shrug. "Don't worry about it. We've got a week before the real games start. It'll work out. It always works out."

During the exhibition game, I overheard Jane voicing the same concern to Ron about her concessions staff. She had a lot of regulars who always returned, but it wasn't enough. Again, he dismissed it with a "It'll work out. It always works out."

After nearly a month and a half on the job, if I am being honest, I was having my doubts about Ron McKee. As overwhelming as he was with his personality, he had been underwhelming due to his lack of presence. We hadn't seen him much. I had heard stories about how he would take care of interns as they worked to get their Asheville foundations established, even allowing some to crash in the guest room of his impressive mountaintop house until they got their own place. But he never offered that to us. We had been up to the house once, to watch the NCAA March Madness final, and by the time we got there, he was already well marinated in amber liquids.

I had always heard about his promotional genius, but all I had seen so far was a grumbling resistance to the idea of Ted E. Tourist, even though he had been the one to come up with the concept, and as best I could tell, his irritation had more to do with the cost of printing the multicolored Ted E. logo than anything else. When I was in the ticket office sorting stacks of paper and rubber bands while I tallied sales with a calculator and pencil, all I could think was, why didn't we have one of those fancy ticketing computer setups like I'd seen them selling at the Winter Meetings trade show? If we'd had one of those machines, I wouldn't have screwed up the sales count for the UNC Asheville exhibition game, right? And as we hoofed Gary's Big Box of Music up and down the steps each night, we openly coveted all those point-and-click sound-effects generators from Atlanta, too.

Ron had been spending the off-season jetting back and forth to

Texas. A lot. That was the home state of the owner of the Asheville Tourists, Peter Carlson "Woody" Kern. In 1994, Woody Kern was the owner of Texas Health Enterprises (THE), operators of more than one hundred nursing homes and a company that produced an annual revenue of more than $200 million. Kern was never not dressed in a baseball cap and jeans, and he liked to wear sunglasses all the time, even when he was meeting with investors or sitting in the endless court depositions tied to the many lawsuits being filed against THE for allegedly poor conditions and patient neglect in its facilities.

Kern lived in Denton, Texas, just north of the Dallas–Fort Worth metroplex, and was on the cusp of purchasing a $3.6-million, 240-acre ranch featuring a twenty-nine-thousand-square-foot, thirty-four-room house, originally built by the man who founded Taco Bell. That was fitting, because as a $100-a-week intern, I ate a hell of a lot of Taco Bell. Woody Kern loved baseball, was a high school teammate of New York Yankees great Thurman Munson, and fed that love by purchasing pieces of Minor League Baseball franchises in five different states, from the Little Falls (New York) Mets and the Newark Orioles to the San Jose Bees. In 1982, just as Ron McKee's McCormick Field resurrection efforts were gaining traction, Kern purchased the Tourists for a bargain basement price of $17,000, plus $25,000 in debt that had to be paid off. His first decision as Tourists owner was also his best one, to keep the McKee family in the front office, promising to leave them alone and let them keep doing whatever it was they had done up to that point to steer the Houston Astros affiliate away from the cliff of ruin. By 1993, the relationship between Ron and Woody had grown to the point that when Kern decided he also wanted to get into Arena Football League ownership, he named Ron McKee general manager of the Fort Worth Calvary. That's why Ron wasn't around much in March 1994. He was commuting to Texas, selling billboard ads, and purchasing uniforms for a football team that would be playing its inaugural season in the Fort Worth Convention Center at the exact same time that the Tourists would be playing at McCormick Field, almost exactly a thousand miles apart.

So, the doubt in my heart about Ron was rooted very deeply in the fact that I wasn't seeing him. He had been the biggest selling point of taking the job, but he hadn't been around. Meanwhile, harking back to those baseball-at-a-crossroads conversations I had heard at the luncheon in Atlanta, chats with my younger-and-cooler coworkers increasingly revolved around "Is this place equipped for the future?" and "Is the old man out of touch?"

It didn't help that every conversation with Ron was an exercise in absolutes. When you'd try to explain something to him, he would inevitably interrupt and say, "Don't tell me about the labor pains. Just show me the baby." During that March, the Southern Conference was holding its college basketball tournament at the Asheville Civic Center. Carlton and I went to Ron and asked if he knew anyone who might have a couple of tickets we could use. He told us to grab a pen and paper and gave us directions to the arena and where we could find a window right by the front entrance. "That's called the box office, and there will be a woman sitting inside that window, and she will sell you all the tickets you want."

He also had a knack of getting out of manual labor at the last minute. The classic move always happened whenever it was time to roll out the tarp. During the season we would have help with that task from game day staff and would even recruit fans from the stands to help us either unfurl or retract the 25,600-square-foot sheet of vinyl from or onto the massive metal tube upon which it was wrapped. But during the off-season, or when the team was on the road or was playing, say, a preseason exhibition against the local college, we were on our own doing the job, with only those of us who worked at the ballpark, at most six or seven people. We didn't have enough bodies. That's how a tarp pull becomes a tarp drag. So, in those situations it had to be all hands on deck.

Ron would always change into a red Tourists "TARP CREW" T-shirt and a pair of old-school polyester snap-button blue shorts, the same ones your least favorite high school gym teacher used to wear. The costume change was a way of letting us know that he was all in, *let's do this.* We would line up shoulder to shoulder, hands on the tarp roll, and begin the three-two-one-push count-down. That's when the shout would come from the Vatican Porch. It was Carolyn. "RONNNNN! YOU HAVE A PHONE CALL!"

"Sorry, fellas," he would say as he left us on the warning track. "Gotta take this one."

Looking back, the "old man" wasn't old at all. He was fifty-one. As for out of touch, the way he'd been going about his job since 1980 had been working pretty dang well thank you very much. After all, we were going to work in a ballpark that was barely two years old, a place for which Ron had gone to political war for a decade to have built. But I was still too young-and-cool to appreciate that like I should have, certainly in April. I mean, holy cow, y'all, how more twentysomething and cocky Gen X could I possibly have been? After a full five weeks on the job, I was looking at Ron McKee and thinking, *I know way more about how all of this should work than this damn guy!*

That's why I thought he was nuts when I went to him and said, "Hey, Ron, I heard what Gary said. He's right. I'm a little worried about us being short-staffed for Opening Day next week. I can't do all I have to do and tear tickets. We really need a guy to tear tickets."

"Don't worry about it," he repeated. "It'll work out. It always works out."

That would have been a hard sell to the Asheville Tourists themselves. The very young ball club left town for a season-opening six-game road trip. They lost all six. The bus pulled back up to the ballpark around midnight having just made the seventy-two-mile drive up the mountain from Hickory, where the Crawdads had just handed the Tourists that sixth loss via a two-run double with two outs in the bottom of the ninth inning. The rambunctious energy that the team had stepped off the bus with nine nights earlier was gone. These guys were frustrated, embarrassed, and silently walked to the small handful of waiting vehicles, crammed into them like clown cars, and headed to the apartments that they'd be sleeping in for the first time.

We were still there that night because we were hustling to get everything set for the next night's "real" home opener, so when we saw the bus pull up, we greeted it to see if the team needed anything. We helped carry some stuff into the clubhouse, but that was it, so we headed back to finish up whatever it was that we'd been doing before they arrived. As I headed for the door, I heard a thick Long Island accent come curling around the corner from the tiny coaches' locker room. "Hey, glasses, come here." I wear glasses, so I figured the voice was talking to me. I poked my head into the door, and there sat three coaches, looking like someone had grabbed one of the rubber mallets we used to tamp down the dirt around home plate and used it to smack them in their collective faces. An 0-6 start will do that to you.

"You guys got all the food and stuff stocked for the season?"

The question came from the same voice that had called me over, a weathered, gray-haired, red-faced man who was sitting on a stool in front of his locker with his pants pulled down around his ankles. It was our pitching coach, Jack Lamabe, and apparently, he had started to change clothes but decided to stop halfway through and chill. I answered his question. "Um, yeah. I think so. Concessions weren't my assignment this month, but my roommate Carlton has been down there, and I think they've gotten it all set up, though they kind of messed up the hamburgers for the game last week and—"

"Hey, man," the hitting coach interrupted me. His name was

Bill McGuire, but no one called him that. They called him Moose. "Jack is trying to ask you if he can have a beer."

I looked at Moose, thirty years old, who just two seasons ago was himself a minor-league player, a former first-round draft pick out of the University of Nebraska who spent eight years as a professional catcher with a brief call-up—"a cup of coffee"—with the Seattle Mariners in 1988 and then again in '89 as teammate to rookie sensation Ken Griffey Jr.

Then I looked at Lamabe, fifty-seven years old but resembling a man twice that age, a righty pitcher who played in the big leagues for seven years. His nickname was Tomatoes, bestowed upon him by Boston Red Sox teammate Dick Radatz because of Lamabe's round and perpetually red face. Some have claimed that the name was inspired by his legendary and unprecedented ability to eat an entire pizza while also gnawing on a plug of Red Man chewing tobacco while washing it all down with a beer. When the Red Sox radio broadcasters started calling Lamabe "The Old Tomato" on the airwaves, it stuck. After his stint in the bigs, he'd coached in college for a decade and was now in his ninth season as a minor-league pitching instructor. Jack had tried selling insurance. He'd worked at the post office. He'd gone back to school and gotten a master's degree. He even signed up for the US Marine Corps reserves. But in the end, he kept coming back to baseball.

"What's that quote, I think Jim Bouton said it," Tomatoes said to me later that summer as we chatted about his life. "You spend your whole life gripping a baseball, and in the end, it turns out that it was the other way around the whole time."

I knew there wasn't supposed to be beer in the clubhouse. They knew that I knew there wasn't supposed to be beer in the clubhouse. Half the team couldn't legally have a beer. Hell, Tony Torchia, the manager who wrote and enforced that very rule, was sitting right there in that same room, staring at me alongside his assistant coaches, all waiting to see how I would react to the request. Torchia stood up, winked at me, and turned toward his tiny office. "I'm going to leave you with this moral dilemma. I saw or heard nothing."

Then Moose spoke up. "Did you know that Jack has a World Series ring? Bring him a beer and maybe he'll show it to you."

It was true. Lamabe loved to tell the story. He recited it to me at least three times that summer, and I never tired of it. It was the 1967 edition of the World Series, still considered one of the greatest Fall Classics ever played. Lamabe's former team, the Red Sox, were in their "Impossible Dream" season, powered by American League MVP Carl Yastrzemski and AL Cy Young Award–winning pitcher Jim Lonborg. Lamabe's current team, the St. Louis Cardinals, were anchored by National League MVP Orlando Cepeda and one of the most intimidating hurlers to ever step onto a pitching mound, Bob Gibson.

Gibson won Games 1 and 4. Lonborg won Games 2 and 5. With a chance to win it all, Tomatoes took the mound in relief in the seventh inning of Game 6 with the score tied 4–4. It was a wacko frame of baseball, with the teams combining for six runs scored and the Cards using four pitchers to face ten Boston hitters. By the time the carousel stopped, Lamabe had been the pitcher of record when the Red Sox took the lead for good and was scored as the game's losing pitcher.

"I was sitting on the bus after the game, just devastated," Lamabe told me for the first time, one midsummer day as we sat and talked in the McCormick Field bullpen, watching Jamey Wright warm up for a start. "Gibby got on the bus, sat down next to me, and said, 'Don't worry about it, Jack. You just won me the World Series MVP. Charline needed a new car anyway.'"

The next night at Fenway Park, Gibson defeated Lonborg by throwing a complete game three-hitter in which he struck out ten Red Sox and even hit a home run for good measure. Charline, his wife, indeed received the new car that was awarded to the World Series MVP. Tomatoes received a World Series ring and one of the greatest stories I've ever been told.

So yes, I walked down to the beer cooler and snuck the man a cold one. What I didn't know was that he already had a backdoor distribution deal in place with Jane for every home game once the real season started. We were to make sure he was stocked, just as everyone was to make sure that they refused to acknowledge that beer's existence. I also didn't know about that pizza/tobacco/beer trick. If I had, I would have insisted that Jack do it for me. Heck, I would have asked him to do it on top of the dugout as pre-game entertainment. I'm betting it would have been better than BirdZerk!

I stuck my head into Torchia's closet office and asked if he needed anything. He winked again and said no thank you. He was at his desk, flipping through a pad filled with the notes that he had jotted down during the bus ride, on every player who'd gotten into the game that night in Hickory. This would be his thirty-first season in the minors, and he was fifty years old. I'm not great at math (see: screwing up those ticket sales for the UNC Asheville game), but that's a mighty big percentage of a man's life spent in a baseball uniform. That's why his skin looked like well-cured leather, all those summer days spent in the sun, coaching players on baseball and teaching those same players how to sign a lease or how to take their driver's license test.

Torchia was drafted by the Dodgers out of Miami Edison High School in 1962 and traded to the Red Sox the following year. He was a first baseman and/or outfielder for nine different teams spread out over five different leagues over the course of thirteen seasons, from the Keokuk (Iowa) Dodgers and Toronto Maple Leafs to the Winston-Salem Red Sox and Toledo Mud Hens. He even won a couple of batting titles, including the 1968 Eastern League (Class AA) with a batting average of .294, one of only a handful of players since 1905 to win a professional hitting crown with a mark under .300. If that's not the most Crash Davis–ish minor-league statistic of all time, I don't know what is.

Seven of those seasons Torchia played agonizingly close to the big leagues, in AAA ball, spending every single day feeling like one big night at the plate or knowing that one big injury to a big leaguer might cause a call-up to Fenway Park. He never got that call. In 1974, he retired as a player and became a coach. The '94 Tourists marked his thirteenth season as an MiLB manager, serving ten years with four teams in the Red Sox farm system, and two seasons managing two teams under the umbrella of the Padres. This was his first and, as it would turn out, only season with the Rockies. He owned three championship rings from three different leagues. He coached Wade Boggs, Oil Can Boyd, Carlos Baerga, and Dave Hollins, some on the way up and some on the way down. Torchia was the man who in 1983 sat in the Pawtucket Red Sox clubhouse with Mark "The Bird" Fidrych, a player who had been baseball's biggest star just seven years earlier, on the cover of *Rolling Stone* and *Sports Illustrated,* with Big Bird no less, and an MLB All-Star. Torchia, in an empty clubhouse in Rhode Island, is the man who told The Bird that it was time to stop hanging on. Fidrych retired the next day.

The one season Torchia did spend in the big leagues was as bullpen coach for the 1985 Boston Red Sox. He hated it. Not at first, when he would excitedly call his wife Nancy and two young sons from American League stadiums. "Can you believe I'm at Yankee Stadium?!" But as the season kept grinding, Torchia couldn't believe what started to happen. He caught himself missing the little stuff. Stuff like raking the baselines at Beehive Field in Bristol, Connecticut. He missed washing the uniforms alongside Nancy in Winston-Salem, North Carolina, which they did for a month because the clubhouse attendant had walked off the job.

"The big-league bullpen coach does zero coaching," he told me late one night after finding out that I'd grown up a Red Sox fan (my first tee-ball team in Shelby, North Carolina, as randomly drawn from a box of ball caps, was the Red Sox). "They were paying me to carry six baseballs down to the bullpen every night and sit on the bench all night while I waited to answer the phone maybe twice. It was not fun."

What Tony Torchia really pined for, while he was stuck in the Fenway Park bullpen, was teaching. In fact, whenever he was back home in South Florida between minor-league seasons, he worked as a substitute teacher. Granted, his love for educating young minds was only a part of the reason he took that job. He also needed the money. The most he was ever paid for any season in the dugout was around $35,000.

"The teaching aspect of it, the coaching, the spending time with young guys who want to get better, that's why I do this," Torchia said to me that spring, when I was tasked with grabbing a couple of quotes for a press release about some incoming new players but ended up getting into a much lengthier conversation about his baseball life. "I love it when a player that I've spent a season with succeeds at the highest level. But the reality is that most of these guys, they won't make it to the Majors. I hope that whatever they end up doing for a living, they think back on their time with me and think, 'Tony really helped me.' That could be a talk when he wanted to quit out of frustration. It could be me showing him how to do laundry. Some days I'm a father confessor, others I'm a babysitter. I have talked to guys about going back to school. I've lent some kids money. I try really hard to help those kids fit into the real world because for most of them, it's their first time in it."

He told me that Nancy had always been bothered by the name Minor League Baseball. She didn't like the connation that what her husband and his teammates were doing was identified by a word whose dictionary definition reads: "1. Lesser, as in size, extent, or importance, or being or noting the lesser of two. 2. Not serious, important. 3. Having low rank, status, position."

"She says that they should change it to 'Necessary Leagues.' I do know that they are necessary to the big leagues. They are necessary to these guys in this clubhouse. They are certainly necessary to me."

As I watched Tomatoes guzzle his beer and Moose do a final check of the clubhouse before heading home, I heard Torchia on the phone. He was reading aloud from that pad of player-by-player evaluation notes, into an answering machine on a desk somewhere in Denver. The next morning, a member of the Colorado Rockies player development staff would listen to that recording as they sipped their coffee, taking their own notes and making decisions that would either further or forever end someone's baseball dreams.

Tony Torchia did this every single night, home or away.

"Next up is Nate Holdren. . . . I realize that he had another oh-for-four night, but I'd like to keep him in that five-spot in the lineup for a little while yet. He hit two balls hard tonight. I think he's still suffering from a little bit of wooden bat transition."

The next day, actual 1994 Opening Day for McCormick Field, was a gift from the ballpark ghosts. The sun was out. The crowd was lively and surprisingly large for a Wednesday night. I didn't screw up any ticket office math. Carlton correctly thawed Jane's burger patties. Gary's Big Box of Music was rocking, R.J.'s new clients were happy, Eileen's Bear Wear was moving off the shelves. And yes, the front gate was manned with a ticket tearer.

It was one of the craziest happenings I've ever witnessed. I had been at my post in the ticket office all day, but now it was five p.m. and I was closing the window to step out and start my pre-game duties. During the week since the UNC-A exhibition, every part-time job in the ballpark had been filled, except one. There was still that nagging absence at the front gate by the turnstiles. I had resigned myself to the fact that I would have to do it, already rehearsing in my mind "short stub in the box, long stub to the fan." But then, as I was drawing the shades, someone knocked on the window. He was probably thirty-five years old. The most normal-looking dude.

"You guys have any jobs available? I've worked as a ticket taker before, and I was kind of hoping maybe you needed one." I thought I was being messed with. I walked him up to the office and introduced him to Gary, who, after closing his dropped-open jaw, told the guy he was hired as soon as he filled out a little paper-work. As they walked down the hallway, Gary looked at me like, "Can you believe this?" It turned out that he was the manager of a local Hooters and was looking for something to do away from the restaurant. I am also 100 percent sure that he was also there to stand at the front gate, where he could see everyone, and scout for potential Hooters waitresses.

An hour later, watching our new ticket tearer greet fans as they marched in, we relayed our *Twilight Zone* story to Ron. All he said was, "I told you guys it always works out."

The whole night worked out. The ceremonial first pitch was thrown by Scott Strausbaugh, a local resident who'd won an Olympic gold medal for canoeing in the 1992 Barcelona Games and wore that medal around his neck as he threw a strike across home plate. The national anthem was performed perfectly by the all-male a cappella Land of the Sky Chorus. The Bonus Baby looked like he was worth every penny as Jamey Wright smoked his way through five innings. He had room to work with thanks to three homers, including an eighth-inning three-run blast from Hatty that proved to be the game winner.

The only aspect of the night that went a little rough went liter-ally a little rough. Remember those awesome shirts we got to wear for work? Turns out that amazingly embroidered Ted E. Tourist over our left breast had a bit of a dark side. The stitching that looked so great on the outside was held together by an intricate crisscross of threading on the inside of the shirt, anchored by a rectangle of thin, coarse plastic. By the time the game had reached the seventh-inning stretch, I realized that the patch sliding back and forth as I'd walked around had rubbed my skin so raw that it felt like my left nipple was going to fall off. I ran into Swish, and he asked, "Hey, man, is this shirt tearing your skin up?" We agreed that we were going to have to use an undershirt all season long. That was fine for now, but that was going to suck in the July and August heat. But we figured we'd rather sweat to death than bleed to death through our nipples.

As the game entered the ninth inning, Ron McKee found me in the concourse breaking down the Speed Pitch net for the night and told me to come with him. We went up to the Vatican Porch and overlooked the field to watch the end of the game, with the good guys leading 8–5. As the Greensboro Bats recorded their second out and the crowd of 2,670 came to their collective feet, Ron pulled his walkie-talkie off his belt like Clint Eastwood with his Colt .45. He held it to his lips, pushed the button, and said to, well, honestly, I didn't know who he was talking to, "This is Ron. Be ready to go. On my mark . . ."

Even from 250 feet away we could hear the crack of the bat. The grounder glided into the glove of Keith Grunewald at shortstop, who flicked the ball into the waiting hands of Holdren at first. The 1994 Asheville Tourists had finally won a baseball game. They rushed the field to celebrate as the crowd erupted. Ron, curiously, was looking away from the field and into the darkness of the hills beyond the outfield wall. Once again, he squeezed the button on his radio.

"Go."

All at once, from the mountain above McCormick Field,

streaks of red, white, and blue flames rocketed into the sky. The fireworks exploded directly over our heads, instantaneously lighting the field, the trees around us, and every single upturned face. The team froze in their cleats to watch from the infield. Everyone was frozen. They were smiling. I looked over at Ron McKee, his glasses reflecting the show that he had just unleashed. He was laughing. Nah, he was guffawing. He caught me looking at him and raised an eyebrow.

"Pretty damn cool, right?"

Yeah, it was. Maybe the coolest thing I had ever seen. That's when I realized that Ron McKee wasn't out of touch. And he was certainly no old man. He was The Man.

"HEYWOOD JABLOWMEE, PLEASE REPORT TO THE PRESS BOX"

O kay, here's something I didn't know until the summer of 1994. Baseballs are expensive. Like, way more costly than I thought they would be. It would stand to reason that the rawhide spheres used by professional baseball organizations would be a little pricier than the bags of balls we all buy down at the local sporting goods store for our rec leagues. But still. I'm telling you. They aren't cheap.

As has already been explained, we the team operators were required to provide the two-man Sally League umpiring crews with three dozen baseballs for each home game. Each box of twelve officially licensed Rawlings MiLB-branded baseballs cost around $150. Seriously. And depending on the number of foul balls and how picky the umpires and pitchers might be about the condition of the primary instrument of their craft, thirty-six baseballs were typically not quite enough to get through a nine-inning game.

A not small part of the job of delivering those baseballs to the men in blue was making them all look new, even the ones that weren't. It was a baseball shell game between Ron and the blue. Especially when we had an experienced crew of umps visit McCormick Field, we knew that the game was on. "Hey, kid, don't leave yet," the veterans always said. "Wait here for one second while we go through these."

The umps would pop open the boxes and give each ball a twice-over examination. They would always toss a couple of worn orbs aside right off the bat. Then, when they started their pregame ritual of rubbing the balls down with mud from a secret riverbank in New Jersey to give them better grip (every professional league does it), even the most clandestine of recycled balls would reveal themselves. The tiniest scuff or scratch would soak up that mud like a paper towel and create a telltale scar. It too would be thrown out of the game-ball mix. The batch of bad baseballs was handed back to us with a smirk and a message. "Tell Ron this wasn't his best effort."

I have heard multiple stories over the years from coaches and players with cash-strapped college and Minor League Baseball teams about the lengths taken to replenish old balls in a way that would make them look like they had just arrived from the factory. Legendary University of Miami head coach Ron Fraser once told me that in the early years of his College Baseball Hall of Fame tenure as the head coach of the Hurricanes, the most common complaint that he received from umpires was that Miami's baseballs smelled like rotten eggs. Fraser was quick to correct them, explaining that no, that was the smell of spoiled milk. He dipped baseballs in milk to make them look whiter.

Jack Lamabe told me about an evening pitching for the Lincoln Chiefs, when several innings into the game he realized that not only were the tips of his fingers drying out, they were also turning white. In the clubhouse that night, he discovered that the team owners had been leaving old baseballs floating in buckets of bleach overnight. He said, "It looked like the world's worst version of bobbing for apples."

White paint, white out, whitewash. Growing up, when I'd heard those stories, I simply thought the baseball people were being cheap. Now I realized that the real issue was that the base-balls those people had to use were much the opposite of cheap.

And that was why Ron McKee employed James the Mountain Man.

The first time I saw James the Mountain Man was during that inaugural homestand of the season. The team was about to begin batting practice, and I was walking out of the office to go set up the press box with Gary. We spotted a very large and heavily bearded man dressed in nothing but denim overalls, making his way through the back gate service entrance with an old burlap sack thrown over his shoulder. I thought someone was breaking into the ballpark, or perhaps they just didn't understand that they needed to buy a ticket and go through the main gate like everyone else. I shouted down, "Sir! You can't go in there!"

Gary gently put his hand on my arm to shut me up. "It's okay." He waved at the man, who waved back. "Hello, James! Happy hunting!"

"Thank ye," James said back, and then he disappeared behind the giant right-field wall. He walked directly into an uncharted jungle of honeysuckle vines, kudzu, and whatever other exotic vegetation could survive in the swampy Dagobah that existed in the tight space between the back of the corrugated-metal fence and the mountain that the ballpark was carved into.

"That was James," Gary said with a sly grin. "He's a real moun-tain man."

Yeah, I had picked up on all that. But what in the world was James the Mountain Man doing? Right on cue, a ball was blasted from the batting cage around home plate and sailed over the thirty-six-foot fence. It bounced off the hill, hit the back of the wall, and pinballed its way back and forth, presumably to the tiny path of flat earth at the bottom of the fence. You could hear it rattling all the way down, like Plinko on *The Price Is Right*. Then came the sounds of someone scuffling around behind that fence, like a hand being dragged along the back of the wall, followed by the soft *ker-thunk* of a heavy object hitting the bottom of a cloth bag.

Yep. James the Mountain Man was there to retrieve baseballs.

His arrangement with Ron was simple. For every clean base-ball that James brought back, he would receive fifty cents. For the slightly dirtier balls, he was paid the slightly smaller sum of a quarter. Plus, there was the added incentive that James could keep whatever he killed. Over the course of the summer, I watched him haul out hundreds of baseballs as well as dozens of animals. Possums, squirrels, rabbits, at least one fox, and more snakes than one could count. There were so many snakes that even James lost track of how many he'd carried out from behind that wall over the years. One night he emerged with a full bag, and when he proudly held it up to show me how many baseballs he'd rescued, it revealed a snake that had to have been three feet long, hanging from his naked biceps. The serpent wasn't wrapped around his arm, it was clamped down onto it, dangling by its fangs that were dug into James's flesh.

"Dammit, James!" I yelled to him in horror. "That snake is bit-ing you!"

James the Mountain Man looked down at his arm, wrapped his other hand in the snake's tail, yanked the reptile from his flesh with an audible pop, spun it around like a whip to snap its neck, and stuffed it into the pocket of his overalls.

"Thank ye."

James was only one of a seemingly infinite number of can't-make-them-up characters who flowed through the ballpark on a nightly basis. Have you ever seen that poster from *The Simp-sons* where they cram every character who was ever on the show into one picture, hundreds of them? That's what it was like at McCormick Field, every night. Some, like James, were perma-nent fixtures. If they missed a game, you immediately worried that something must be wrong. Others were just passing through, from the mountain people who'd made a big trip into town to watch a ball game to tourists stopping by to see the Tourists. No matter who they were, how long they stayed, or what planet they came from, they were all part of the family. Guests in Ron McKee's four-thousand-seat living room, just as he'd promised.

For example, Big Mike. Big Mike was indeed a large man, six-five and probably three hundred pounds, and was as quiet as he was huge. Atop his very tall frame he wore a substantial Afro, like right out of 1977. Big Mike struggled with some mental developmental issues but was a sweet-hearted guy. Like James the Mountain Man, the first time I laid eyes on Big Mike I thought he was trying to sneak into the ballpark without paying, but I recognized him. There was a small car dealership at the bottom of the hill that any visitor to McCormick Field had to drive by as they entered our little parking lot, and anyone who glanced over at that lot would have seen the unmistakably massive frame of Big Mike, washing the cars on that lot over and over. On game nights, Mike would walk up the hill and into the ballpark. He never had a ticket, and he didn't need one. "Mike been coming here for a long time," Carolyn explained to me. "We don't make Mike buy a ticket."

I was told that if Mike really knew someone, he had the ability to talk their ears off, but the most I ever interacted with him was to say, "Hey, Big Mike, how we doing?" and the most I got out of him in return was, "Good." A significant cause for his lack of chattiness was that his mouth was full of food. Always. It was never clear to me if the McKees charged him for concessions or not. Either way, they were going to lose money on Big Mike.

The man ate so much food that every night it was an unspoken part of our job to keep tabs on where Big Mike was and, more importantly, what he was eating. Our code name for Mike was "Jimi," because his haircut looked exactly like rock-and-roll titan Jimi Hendrix.

Click. "Okay, guys, we have a Jimi sighting. He has just emerged

from the first-base stairwell, box in hand. It looks like we're starting off with three . . . no, check that . . . four hot dogs and a
Super-Size Hawaiian Punch."

It was Gary, speaking from the press box over our walkie-
talkies. Our running scorecard of what concessions he consumed
had nothing to do with money lost at the sales windows, and we
certainly weren't making fun of him. We loved Big Mike. We
kept score because we were in amazement. Big Mike made world
eating champion Joey Chestnut look like a Weight Watchers
spokesperson.

Click. "Jimi is now in line at the main concession stand . . .
looking like a Nachos Supreme . . . a box of popcorn . . . and yes,
another Super-Size Hawaiian Punch!"

The most I ever saw Big Mike eat in one night was a box of
four hot dogs, which he ordered every night, a cheeseburger with
fries, nachos, a box of popcorn, a strawberry Dairy Queen sundae,
a bag of Cracker Jacks, and he always had a Super-Size Hawaiian
Punch with each order. All that even though he typically left in
the seventh inning because he didn't want to miss his bus home.

Click. "Ladies and gentlemen, Jimi has left the building."

Gary's reports came from within the admittedly tiny press box
that sat on the top row of the main grandstand. From inside, a
half-dozen people overlooked home plate from the concrete room
that looked an awful lot like a pillbox bunker from Omaha Beach.
Most nights the entirety of the press corps was two people, a writer
from the *Asheville Citizen-Times,* usually a tireless scribe named
Keith Jarrett, and the visiting radio broadcaster. There was a tiny
separate room that acted as a radio booth. All but three of the
fourteen Sally League teams had play-by-play radio announcers, calling the action all alone through a headset that was dialed
through a telephone line into a radio station back home, statically
bringing the action to the people of Savannah, Augusta, or one of
the two Charlestons, in South Carolina or West Virginia. We were

still one of the three teams who weren't doing radio, though Gary and Ron continued to promise me that we'd talk about it.

Some nights there would be a camera from Asheville's lone television station, WLOS, Channel 13, perched in the other tiny room next to the radio booth. The number-two sports guy at that ABC affiliate was Mike Morgan, whom I'd known a little before I got to Asheville, but by summer's end would have become a lifelong friend. As is the routine for pretty much every local TV sports reporter working in a minor-league market, Mike would shoot the first couple of innings until the home team did something big, say a homer or a double play or an entertaining WWE-worthy argument with an umpire, anything that would provide video for a thirty-second clip that could be shown during that night's newscast.

Mike's boss was Stan Pamfilis. Now, even if you've never been to Asheville or don't even know where Asheville is, I promise you already know Stan Pamfilis. Every city has a Stan Pamfilis. Perhaps not a guy with a Pringles-can smile, curly receding hair, and a black mustache that belongs on the face of every bad guy in every TV cop show ever made. Stan had all that. But wherever you grew up, you had *the* sports guy in your town. The dude who everyone wanted to come out and cover their high school games. That was Stan Pamfilis. Stan worked at WLOS for nearly forty years, so long that his trademark crazy head of dark hair became not so dark and way too thin to be too crazy. He was at Channel 13 for so long that when his family went to yard sales or flea markets, they always saw his face for sale, thanks to decades of "Stan Fan" promotional giveaways, his mustache mug printed, cut out of cardboard, and then stapled to wooden sticks to be handed out to a couple of generations of western North Carolina sports enthusiasts so those fans could fan themselves.

It felt like Stan Pamfilis was everywhere in Asheville all the time . . . except McCormick Field. No one was exactly sure when, why, or how the beef between Stan and Ron McKee had started, but the feud was at its white-hot peak temperature during the summer of 1994. Ron never believed the local media did enough to cover the Tourists. He had been livid with the *Asheville Citizen-Times* on the day of our home opener because the story about that night's game was at the bottom of the sports page while half that page was dedicated to the news that the Tour du Pont cycling event, featuring three-time Tour de France winner Greg LeMond and some kid named Lance Armstrong, was coming to Asheville in May. "Bicycles, really?!" I heard him asking of the paper's editor-in-chief over the phone.

We were always working to convince the media to give the Tourists more coverage. We constantly updated and republished our media guide whenever players were sent up, sent down, or cut. Keep in mind that when I say published, I mean copied on the Xerox machine and stapled together. We were always pitching stories like, "Hey, we've got a player named Snake because he owns two boa constrictors!" Or "Hey, we also have a player who sort of played in the Rose Bowl!" That's how I learned the proper way to write a press release, and by summer's end I was volunteering to write them all. We were always super nice to anyone with a notebook or camera, hoping that in turn they would be nice to us and inadvertently help us sell some tickets. Gary was in constant Saunders sales mode whenever someone showed up to do work in his press box. All the while, Mike Morgan promised us that he'd been talking to the boss on our behalf.

Then, one day, for Pepsi WLOS T-Shirt Night, there he was. *Stan Pamfilis!* We excitedly ran up to Ron's office to tell him that, yes, all our politicking and buttering up, it had worked! "Ron, he's here! Ron? Ron, where are you going?"

Ron blew past us and took up his post on the Vatican Porch just in time to watch Stan make the climb up the stairs and into the seating bowl. Stan was there to say hello to the one thousand kids who'd received a Tourists shirt with a big Channel 13 logo on the back. I watched the boss wait until the sportscaster had walked deep into the ballpark. Then he cupped his hands around his mouth, so as to launch his voice into the stadium clamshell with maximum acoustical boost.

"Oh my God! Ladies and gentlemen, the great STAN PAMFI-LIS is here! STAN PAMFILIS actually showed up for a Tourists game! Look! There he is! The great STAN PAMFILIS! Can you believe it? Maybe he'll even sign your T-shirt! Will you do that, STAN PAMFILIS?"

The last time I was driving along the Blue Ridge Parkway, I stopped at an overlook to watch the sunset. The air was hushed, peaceful, and when I closed my eyes and concentrated, I'm pretty sure I could hear Ron's shouting at Stan Pamfilis, still bouncing around the Appalachians decades later. The following season, they had a talk and cleared up whatever it was that had created the tension between them, and Stan was back at the ballpark on a regular basis. But we never saw Stan again in the summer of '94.

Anyway, back to the press box. Joining those members of the media who hadn't been scared off, Gary also kept an eye on a scoreboard operator, the official scorekeeper, and a fourth intern who was added to the mix, but for a limited time only. Thankfully, fitting in was never a problem for the walking good mood that was the honorable Lee Tillery of Statesville, North Carolina, who'd joined us from the sport management program at nearby Western Carolina University. My man Lee was never a candidate for any stress-related illnesses, even when we tried to haze him by sticking him into the beer cooler on a Thirsty Thursday. Most of his time with us, he was in the press box with Gary.

Finally, and most importantly, the anchor of the McCormick Field pillbox was our public-address announcer. Sam Zurich was, like so many living in the Asheville area, a retiree with roots in the Northeastern Corridor. His parents had immigrated from Croatia to New York, where Sam was born in April 1923. He celebrated his first birthday just days after McCormick Field was christened by Ty Cobb's Detroit Tigers. As a little boy, Sam stayed glued to the family radio, so mesmerized by the booming voices of the announcers that he taught himself to mimic their sound in his own speaking voice. The result was a fifty-year career in broadcasting and advertising that made him a huge part of the pioneer days of the radio and television industry. From Columbus, Georgia, to Columbia, South Carolina, to Charlotte and ultimately to national advertising campaigns run out of the *Mad Men*–era agency offices in New York and Connecticut, Sam Zurich's baritone voice was heard throughout the homes of America on radio and television commercials and promotions for years.

Now it was heard by a couple of thousand people every night at McCormick Field. When Sam leaned into the microphone and the words "Now batting, outfielder Tony Dur-mend-zee-ev" rumbled up out of the depths of this throat, it was almost too much for our smattering of bullhorn stadium speakers to handle. What an incredible privilege it was to have a legend like Sam Zurich as the voice of our ballpark. Me being the broadcasting hopeful that I was, I selfishly cornered him at least once every homestand, begging to hear more stories about the early days of the business.

Sam was seventy-one years old, a World War II veteran, and a devoted church and family man. He was old-school, especially when it came to his gig with us. In TV terms, we were his producers, so he trusted us. Gary was almost always by Sam's side, making sure the proper script for that game was good to go and the litany of announcements was running along smoothly. Whatever was put in front of Sam, he would read it, no questions asked. By the end of every game, there would be a pile of cards and papers.

"Ladies and gentlemen, please turn to page twenty-five of your souvenir program. . . . If you have the number one-three-zero-three-eight, congratulations, you have won a free round of golf at the French Broad Golf Center."

"Let's wish a happy sixty-second birthday to Pastor Robert McHenry of the Blessed Be the Savior Free Will Baptist Church of Black Mountain."

"If you are driving a gray Mazda RX-7 with a license-plate number TKZ348, you'd better get out there. Your lights are on . . . and they are getting dimmer."

One game day a couple of us interns were in place for a between-innings on-field fan contest, and we had R. J. Martino with us. Perhaps it was the Dizzy Bat Race, when a pair of fans would place their foreheads on the end of a bat that's barrel was stuck into the ground, rotate ten times around that axis, and then embark on a footrace to a waiting Tourists intern, only to inevitably run sideways and crash into the turf. Or it might have been the Tire Toss, sponsored by a local auto parts store, where a fan would have three chances to throw a baseball through a Goodyear tire that swung from a chain on a metal frame, hoping to win a coupon for what I'm sure was a great deal on a set of new wheels for their Mazda RX-7 with the dead battery.

Whatever it was, we were in one dugout ready to go with the gear, and R.J. had the lucky fans who'd been chosen to participate. We could see Gary, chatting up some folks in the box seats. It was unusual for him to leave the press box midgame, but R.J. explained that the guests were new potential sales clients, so Gary was, as Gary pretty much always was, doing work.

There was still one out to go before the end of the inning when Sam Zurich's voice rolled through the concrete stadium. "Ladies and gentlemen, especially you parents out there, your attention please. We have a little guy here who has lost his father. We are looking for Dad. So, would Heywood Jablowmee please report to the press box."

We looked at R.J. He looked at us. In the dugout, several of the players looked like a row of puppies, their heads cocked with the same inquisitive, confused expression, craning their necks to look toward the press box. R.J. asked us, "What did Sam just say?" As if Sam had heard the question, the telltale click of the stadium public-address microphone keyed open again. This time Sam Zurich really took his time and enunciated, so that everyone in attendance was sure to hear him clearly.

"HEEEY-WOOOOD JAAA-BLOW-MEEEE, PLEASE RE-PORT TO THE PRESS BOX."

Gary Saunders looked like Rocky Balboa racing up those stadium stairs. By the time he got there, the "missing" kid was indeed missing. Sweet, trusting Sam had been the victim of a prank, and none of us had been there to protect him. We were mad. But only a little. Honestly, we were mostly impressed by the mystery kid's efforts. Our radios crackled with Gary's voice. "Guys, the kid is gone. So, let's all keep our eyes peeled around the ballpark for Bart Simpson."

Had Bart or any other ballpark ne'er-do-well needed somewhere to lie low, we all knew the best place for them to do it. Because we'd all hidden out there, too. In the groundskeeping office located down the third baseline, next to the stadium's only old McCormick Field carryover, the cinder-block home-turned-visitors' clubhouse. The original ballpark in 1924 had been underwritten by the city. Our newer version had also been built using public funds, $3 million rustled up by Buncombe County to raze the rotting blue wooden structure and then raise the modern weatherproof concrete-and-metal version of McCormick Field.

Because the ballpark had been built using public moneys, primarily a hotel tax fueled by, fittingly, tourists, the home of the Tourists was operated and maintained by the Buncombe County Parks and Recreation Department. That department employed and provided the ballpark's head groundskeeper, responsible for the playing field and the grounds around the stadium, including a handful of small garden areas. He had a luxurious head of thick, white hair and a two-tone, thin-cut beard that accentuated his very square jawline in a salt-and-pepper black-and-white frame. He wore a smirk that told me all at once he suspected I was probably totally full of crap, but he also liked me. His palms were always red from handling warning track gravel, his boots were always green with grass stains, and his clothes always smelled like SAE-30 lawn-mower oil.

The groundskeeper's name was Grady Gardner. Because of course it was.

Grady had been with the county for a dozen years and had been looking after the grass beneath the cleats of the Tourists for at least half that time. He had successfully navigated the challenge of protecting the playing field during the transition between stadiums in 1992. Now he ran the daily obstacle course that came with splitting the difference between the demands of a Major League Baseball team that wanted certain turf conditions to aid certain types of players (e.g., short grass is fast to run on and slap grounders through, but difficult to keep healthy during hot summer months, while long grass slows everyone and everything down, but is much easier to keep alive) and the always-tight parameters of a government-monitored budget.

To the rest of us, that sounds stressful, right? Not to my man Grady Gardner. Grady didn't really do stress.

"Listen, man, this job is pretty simple," he once explained to me during a visit to his office. I ducked in there a lot. Grady was not old, but he wasn't young, either. He was the father of two daughters, crazy-smart girls, and when I think back now on my conversations with him in that shed or out on the field, it always felt like I was visiting a sort of grass-growing guru. He always had great life advice to share, whether I'd asked for it or not. Some people climb into the clouds to seek worldly wisdom from wise men who live in introspective solitude atop that mountain. I walked down a few stairs to learn from a guy who spent a lot of time alone in a ballpark shed on the side of a mountain.

By the way, I know that right now you are dying to ask me this, so yes, Grady's "office" totally looked like Carl Spackler's hideout in *Caddyshack*, just smaller. There were stacks of bags everywhere. Bags of fertilizer, bags of grass seed, bags of lime, bags of chalk, and bags of Speedy Dry. I can neither confirm nor deny that there was also a bag of northern California sinsemilla hidden in there somewhere. Unlike Bill Murray's character, Grady didn't stock his shed with machetes and dynamite. Well, as far as I knew he didn't. His weapon of choice was the bow and arrow. It was very common to be working on something in the empty ballpark while the team was on a road trip and hear from behind the groundskeeping shed the sound of a "Zzzzzzzzthwap!" over and over, often followed by a "There you go!" or a "Dammit!" It would be Grady, making like Hawkeye and trying to knock the center of a bull's-eye pinned to a wooden post. If you asked, he'd gladly teach you how to do it, too. I tried a couple of times but chose to abruptly end my budding career as a bowhunter when I sent an errant arrow sailing sideways into one of those stacks of bags and dumped about $100 worth of weed killer onto the ground behind the shed. I'm pretty sure nothing has grown on that spot since.

Okay, now back to Grady Gardner's even-keeled explanation of his gig. When you read this, you should have Larry the Cable Guy's voice in your head, with the accent turned down to about an eight and the speed dialed down to a five. "I'm gonna make that field look green and alive. We're gonna water it when it needs water, rake it when it needs to be raked, and cover it when it needs to be covered. Sometimes the baseball guys are gonna come down here and yell at me. Sometimes Buncombe County is gonna come down here and yell at me. If they've already decided that they're gonna yell at me, then they are gonna yell at me no matter what I do or say. So, I just let them finish yelling, say, 'Yes sir, I hear you,' and when they get tired of yelling and leave, I'll go cut the grass."

Unless it was Tuesday night. Then we were on our own. That's because that was line-dancing night down at the local honky-tonk. Grady Gardner would work all day getting the field ready for that night's game, mowing and raking and lining, all with a little more hop to his step than usual. During the pregame, as the teams were introduced, if you walked by the visiting clubhouse, you could hear a lone shower running and see steam rolling out from the vents. Then, as the teams took the field, Grady Gardner would emerge from that clubhouse, wearing shined-up cowboy boots and stonewashed Wranglers. Those jeans had been ironed to the point that a hard, raised crease ran up the front center of both legs, from the top of those sparkling boots all the way up to his chrome belt buckle that was as big as a picture frame. He wore a classic 1990s Garth Brooks–ish permanent-press rodeo shirt, and that long white hair, still wet from the shower, was combed back into a silver swoop. Grady Gardner would strut through the grandstand, his boots a'clomping through the concrete concourse as he headed for the front gate. People would whisper, "Who's the guy that looks like Sam Elliott?"

Waiting outside that gate was Grady Gardner's dance partner. He said she was "just a friend," but we all knew better than that. She was either more than a friend or was working hard to become more than a friend. Every Tuesday we watched her check her very high hair and very red lipstick in the rearview mirror as she waited on our boy to jump in. She drove a white conversion van with tinted bubble windows, with a very large fiberglass wing bolted onto the rear and an even larger air-conditioning unit mounted on the roof. The sides of that passion wagon were adorned with blue pinstripes that ascended into a scene of a blue palm tree swaying in the breezes of an even bluer beach sunset. In a flourish of cursive, of course in blue, the vehicle identified itself as the *Tropical Traveler*.

"Hey, man cannot live on fertilizer alone," Grady Gardner said on the first Tuesday-night game of the year, as he slid into the fine Corinthian leather of the passenger seat. As the van revved its engine, he pointed out the window to the overcast skies above and shouted, "It ain't gonna rain tonight, but it is gonna be misty. So have the Speedy Dry ready, boys!" And with that, his friend hit play on her Brooks & Dunn cassette, and the *Tropical Traveler* departed for parts unknown and an evening of boot scooting.

When the game ended that night, we found that Grady was right. There wasn't rain, certainly not enough to go to the trouble of pulling out the tarp, but as would often happen at a ballpark located in the mountains, there were a lot of low-flying clouds rolling in. It was indeed misty. Ron decided that, yeah, it would be a good idea to spread a little Speedy Dry around the dirt of the infield. That would keep the mound, batter's box, baselines, and infield from becoming too saturated with dew during the night and potentially turning themselves into a tacky mud for the next day's game, a rare four p.m. "Businessman's Special."

So, we pulled a couple of bags of Speedy Dry from Grady's shed, cut one corner off each sack, and spread the stuff in a zigzag motion. It was a fine, powdery substance, S curves of off-white that contrasted starkly against the dark brown of the infield dirt. Carlton, who had stadium ops experience that I did not, explained that the stuff was made of basically any material that was known to be absorbent and could also be crushed into that desired texture of grainy powder. Stuff like clay, wheat, corn, and sand. We raked it around to distribute it more evenly into that dirt, until the entire infield took on a hue of pale tan. We paused, scanned the field, nodded our collective heads, and pleased with our efforts, departed for our apartment around midnight.

Seven hours later, we were back at the ballpark. You never slept much during a homestand, and you barely slept at all whenever you had to make the night game–to–day game turnaround.

Carlton and I rolled into work drearily just as the sun began to rise over the Land of the Sky. As we walked in, we noticed R.J. and Swish standing on the Vatican Porch, hands on hips and staring out at the field. I thought maybe they were admiring the sunrise. Then Steve said, "Hope neither one of you guys is allergic to cats."

There had to have been two dozen cats out on that infield. A chorus of conflicting meows ricocheted off the empty plastic seats. It sounded like a middle school string section tuning their violins. Some of the noises were guttural, almost sexual. Cats rolled around on their backs. Others just lay there. More than a few were relieving themselves, squatting with their spines arched, then using their paws to dig up the infield dirt and cover up what they'd just done to desecrate the ballpark, our hallowed ground.

That's when it came to me. *Any material that was known to be absorbent and could also be crushed into that texture of grainy powder. Stuff like clay, wheat, corn, and sand* . . . "Oh, dammit," I said to the guys. "Speedy Dry is kitty litter!"

We had used way too much of the stuff. Where we'd only needed a dusting, we had committed a dumping. McCormick Field's hallowed infield was now an eighteen-thousand-square-foot litter box, where the alley cats of Asheville were now committing a dumping, too.

It took some work to run all the feral felines off our beloved ballfield. There was running and clapping and whooping. Grady Gardner, who couldn't stop laughing about what we'd done, fired up the lawn mower and burped the engine to scare the last of them away. All but one. He was orange, a bit mangy, and when all the other cats had retreated into the woods, he defiantly climbed the stairs into the seating ring, took up a spot on the top row near the press box, and just stared at us. With the first pitch still several hours away, we decided to leave him be.

That afternoon, I took my lunch and sat out in the stands by myself to eat. Within a few minutes, he was back, watching me from a distance and then eventually strolling over to sit down next to me. He didn't want anything. He just sat there, staring out at the field with me, watching Grady as he cuss-mumbled his way through removing the last of the piles the cats had left buried in his dirt. That afternoon during the game I saw the cat again, perched on a brick fence top near the front gate. The next day, and the day after that, I kept running into the same cat at different spots around the ballpark. I never saw any of those others again, just the orange one.

"What's the story on the cat?" Jane asked me, pointing at it and acknowledging that while she was a big-time dog person, there was something about this cat that intrigued her. I told her I felt the same way. He was growing on me. So, I decided he should have a name.

"I'm going to call him Julio," I told her. She asked why. "I don't know. He looks cool. And Julio is a cool name. Plus, you know, it's like that song, 'Me and Julio Down by the Ballyard.'"

"It's schoolyard," Jane the rock-and-roller corrected me.

"Don't step on this beautiful moment, Jane. He's our new mascot."

"Well, don't tell Ted that."

Oh yeah, Ted. That reminded me of something. Gary needed to have a talk with Ted, and I didn't want to miss that.

ME, NATE HOLCOMB, JEFF SORKOVIAK, BILL
McGUIRE, JAMEY WRIGHT, PAT
McCLINTON, R.J. MARTINO

MARK GUSTAFSSON, GARY SAUNDERS, JACK
LAMABE, RANDY EDWARDS, JOSE NATOS,
BOB LASBURY, JASON SMITH, JOHN THOMSON,
CHRIS NEIER, PEDRO CARRANZA, TONY
TORCHIA, RON McKEE

KEITH BARNES, DOUG WALLS, JAVIER DIAZ,
VINCENTE GARCIA, KEITH GRUNEWALD,
JOHN GIUDICE, NEIL GARRETT

CARLTON ADCOCK, DENNY McADAMS, JACOB VIANO,
MARTIN DELETT, MIKE NICOSIS,
TONY DERRAENDZIEU, EDGARDO VELASQUEZ,

RICK HATFIELD, STEPHEN UNITT

Your 1994 Asheville
Tourists! That's me,
far back row, far left,
brought to you by
Workout Express Ladies
Only Fitness Club.

	Gary	RJ	Office Intern	Ticket Intern	Concession Intern
	Outside Sales	1) Programs & Scout Packages	1) Programs & Scout Packages	1) Asst. Souv. Shop	
		2) Tarp Manager	2) Stats to Manager	2) Cones out by 3 & 11	Jane
		3) Front Gate @ 6-7 p.m.	3) Lucky Numbers – PB & GS	3) Baseballs to Umpires	Food to Umps After Game
		4) Fax score after Game; Call Radio & TV	4) Pass List	4) Work Guest Relations During Game	Golf Cart Maintenance
		5) Dugout Contest	5) Prize Boxes	5) Set up Press Box	
		6) Call in Scores After Game	6) Drawing Winner & Notify Souv. Shop	6) Set up Speed Pitch	
		7) Call in Scores Team on Road	7) Work Customer Relations During Game	9) Ticket Booth 10-4	
			8) Bat Room (spare time)	2- GET CARS OUT OF THE WAY	
			9) Set Up Program Seller	3- 3 DOZEN BALLS FROM BAT ROOM	
	Tarp	Tarp	Tarp	Tarp	Tarp

$1.00 - 3 PITCHES

EITHER FASTEST OF DAY
(SEAT COLUMN)

OR

GUESS YOUR SPEED
(PAINTER'S CAP)
Paris 5

GET THIS STUFF

The game day job duties
list. If it rained, it didn't
matter who you were
or where you were.
"TARP" became your
job. Unless you were
Ron McKee and had yet
another perfectly timed
phone call to take.

My ticket from the Battle of Hickory. That's Minnie Minoso's overserved autograph, which is much easier to read if you put on beer goggles.

A box seat to McCormick Field. The best six bucks you'll ever spend.

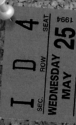

1994 Asheville Tourists

25 Keith Barnes	11 Martin Dewett	23 Neil Garrett	22 Bob Lasbury	20 José Matos	16 Dennis McAdams
31 Pat McClinton	30 Chris Neier	33 Jeff Sobkoviak	27 John Thomson	17 Jacob Viano	28 Doug Walls
21 Jamey Wright	9 Javier Diaz	13 Mike Higgins	26 Jason Smith	3 Danny Figueroa	7 Vincente Garcia
8 Keith Grunewald	34 Nate Holdren	12 Tony Dermendziev	15 Randy Edwards	24 John Giudice	4 Edgard Velasquez

Our program roster insert. Only three of these twenty-four players made it to The Show, including No. 4, Edgard Velasquez, Roberto Clemente's nephew.

Carlton Adcock, Stephen "Swish" Whitt, and me posing with first-pitch thrower and my new crush, Shelley Fabares. "What was it like to kiss Elvis?"

Our entertainment lineup included the Blues Brothers Act; Captain Dynamite; the Colorado Silver Bullets, an all-female baseball team; and Rick Dunham, aka Elvis Himselvis. Uh, thank you, thank you very much.

To: Ryan

Thank You Very Much

"Rick" "Elvis" Dunham

Overalls-wearing assistant GM Gary Saunders made sure we repped the Tourists at every civic event, like the Asheville Rice and Beans Cook-Off. Spoiler alert: We did not win.

CHAPLAIN, GROUNDSKEEPER & INTERNS

J. P. BRANHAM, Chaplain

J. P. Branham is serving his 8th year as team chaplain for the Tourists. J. P. holds a worship service at the ballpark before Sunday home games for the Tourists' players and staff.

GRADY GARDNER, Head Groundskeeper

Grady Gardner is back for another year as Head Groundskeeper. Throughout the summer, you can always find Grady hard at work preparing the field for another home game. Grady is the proud father of two daughters, Jennifer and Joy.

CARLTON ADCOCK, Intern

Carlton is a graduate of the University of Tennessee with a degree in Private/Commercial Recreation. His degree included a special emphasis in Sports Management. Adcock hails from Bristol, Tennessee. He looks forward to a long career in professional baseball. Carlton's hobbies include cooking, softball and watching ESPN. He enjoys the music of Jimmy Buffet and Tom Petty and the Heartbreakers.

RYAN McGEE, Intern

McGee, a native of Monroe, NC, grew up watching Tourists games at the old McCormick Field. Ryan is a recent graduate of the University of Tennessee with a major in Broadcast Communications. His goal is to become a play-by-play announcer with a professional baseball club. McGee likes running and travel. He is a longtime Red Sox fan and lists Ted Williams as one of his heroes.

STEPHEN WHITT, Intern

Whitt rounds out the Tourists' "Tennessee Trio" for the 1994 season. Stephen is also a University of Tennessee graduate with a concentration in Sport Management. This native of nearby Candler, NC, is looking forward to his first season in baseball. Away from the ballpark, Whitt likes outdoor sports, the music of Led Zeppelin, and TV's "Home Improvement."

The infamous interns page of the game program. Carlton and I look like we're at the DMV and Swish looks like he's in GQ.

TOURISTS FRONT OFFICE STAFF

GARY SAUNDERS, Assistant GM

Gary is in his second year with the Tourists. A native of Reston, Virginia, Saunders is a graduate of Virginia Tech with a Bachelors Degree in Communications. He worked in the Radio, Print and Advertising fields before embarking on his baseball career in 1992 with the Cardinals organization. Gary and his wife, Eileen, reside in Asheville with their Labrador Retriever, Sundance. Saunders enjoys Golf, Blue Note Jazz, and New Orleans Cuisine. He has authored a guide entitled "Careers in Baseball."

JANE LENTZ, Concessions Manager

Jane is now in her third season running the Tourists' concessions division, At Bo Food Services. A native North Carolinian, Ms. Lentz is a graduate of UNC-Asheville with a degree in Psychology. During the off season, Jane can be found working in the Tourists' front office. Her attention to detail and desire to constantly improve the ballpark menu are quite an asset to the organization. Jane lives in West Asheville with her Scottish Terrier, McDuff. She enjoys reading and the music of Stevie Ray Vaughan.

EILEEN SAUNDERS, Director of Merchandising

Eileen joins her husband, Gary, on the Tourists staff after six years in retail management with Belk and the Limited. Mrs. Saunders is a graduate of Western Maryland College and she hails from Baltimore, MD. Eileen handles advance ticket sales, processes all souvenir orders, and manages the Tourists Stadium Store. In her spare time, she likes mountain hiking, sailing, reggae music and warm weather. Eileen is an avid fan of "The Ren and Stimpy Show."

R. J. MARTINO, Account Representative

R. J. is one of the new faces at McCormick Field this season. He spent the 1993 season in Hagerstown, Maryland, as an intern for the Suns. Martino is a graduate of Cortland State University in Central New York with a degree in Physical Education. He is originally from Schenectady, New York. R. J. and his fiancee, Cathy, are planning a September 10th wedding. Martino enjoys shooting hoops, rugby, playing with his dog, Paddington, and eating Italian Food.

(PHOTOS PROVIDED BY GLAMOUR SHOTS)

A sales deal with Glamour Shots included makeovers and photos for the front-office staff. Tammy Faye Bakker did not do their makeup. I swear.

RON McKEE   GM
ASHEVILLE

The boss man, Ron McKee, aka the Dictator. "Don't tell me about the labor pains, just show me the baby."

Hanging with the devotees of the Pinch Hitters Club and Ted E. Tourist. Ron McKee sits far left, Gary Saunders in the center. That's about as cozy as they ever got.

Me on a rare day off, thinking that I look like Commodore Vanderbilt steaming upriver to the Biltmore Estate. Eileen Saunders isn't buying it.

Me with Officer Van Smith, the nicest tough guy you'll ever meet. This was likely right after he had just politely warned me to behave myself at the upcoming prom or I might never be seen again.

My baseball card, coming off the bench after the real Ted E. Tourist performer slept through photo day. The plastic giant head fit me almost as badly as it smelled on the inside.

FLEER
PRO CARDS

Ted E. Tourist
Asheville Tourists • Mascot

Chilling with the great Carlton Adcock as we are likely using this golf cart to smuggle unused concessions home to cook on our infamous exploding secondhand gas grill.

Me and Ted E. Tourist, wearing his oft-forgotten blue Hawaiian shirt, which was used before his new, custom red "popcorn" attire arrived from a creepy print shop in nearby sulfur-infused Canton, North Carolina.

Meticulously going over concessions inventory with Beer Stand Pam. Okay, that's a lie. We're probably looking at the visiting team's roster to see if we should get any autographs.

Donning my notorious blue nipple-ripping work shirt during a visit from college roommate David French. My smile hides the fact that I'm probably bleeding through my undershirt.

Receiving a fax and trying hard not to look like I'm receiving rotisserie baseball stats, so Ron won't yell at me about wasting paper.

GAME 11

vs. BIRMINGHAM BARONS
TUE., APRIL 26, 1994
7:15 PM

PRIME BOX $6.50

H   L   6
SEC.   ROW   SEAT

Ticket stub from the night I saw Michael Jordan get a hit, steal a base, and send the entire city of Greenville, South Carolina, into total and complete minor-league-baseball pandemonium.

The snow cone stand, aka the Kid Crack Wholesale Mart. You could never have enough bottles of blue juice, which was one part blue powder and eleventy bazillion parts sugar.

Swish raking out the final touches before the Tourists take the field. That radio on his hip is likely crackling with Ron McKee's voice, criticizing Steve's work from high atop Ron's Vatican Porch.

Hanging with the devotees of the Pinch Hitters Club. That's me, far left, Gary next to Ted, Ron behind Gary's fist, and Carlton behind Ted's paw.

I love using Marty & McGee TV to support minor-league baseball... and to show off my too-large MiLB cap collection!

My baseball play-by-play dream never happened, but I finally wore down enough people to be on TV. Here's Marty Smith and me at the 2022 College Football Playoff championship.

THE BLUES BROTHERS, MACAULAY CULKIN, AND THE CIRCUIT RIDER

S pring was giving way to summer. The azalea and dogwood blooms that painted Asheville and the mountains around it with so much color had fallen. The early June heat started carrying steam from the rivers and creeks that flow throughout the city up into the ballpark to be wrung out of our shirts in the form of sweat.

After two months of play, the Tourists weren't great, but they weren't bad, either. They entered mid-May sitting squarely on the .500 mark, an equal number of wins and losses, while sitting an on-the-fence fourth in the seven-team Sally League North Division.

The season was officially in rise-and-grind mode. The team needed a spark. The front office needed sleep. And our part-timers needed a start-of-summer talking-to. Even the bears.

"Hey, listen, Jack, we've been getting a couple of complaints."

Gary Saunders had on his signature disarming smile. The man he was talking to did not, dressed neck to toe in a bear costume. Not head to toe, because the head was sitting on the ground next to the man who was getting the talking-to. It was so weird, Ted E. Tourist's massive plastic noggin, decapitated and sitting on the floor, looking so smiley and happy while his body, with the very normal-sized human head of Jack the local actor, looked so unhappy.

The issue was that Ted E. Tourist was getting a little handsy. Or claw-sy. I didn't know what you called it—I just knew that as the season had entered summer, we'd received a couple of complaints. Ted's routine for home games was simple. He roamed the stands, waving and sauntering jollily as he handed out sponsor-supplied snacks and posed for photos with the kids and their families.

The first time we received a grievance from a mom that Ted E. might have possibly copped a feel while posing for one of those photos, we shrugged it off. I knew firsthand that the costume was more than a little cumbersome to manage. You slid your hands into these stretchy gloves, the palms of giant foam paws. Those paws had these short, thin vinyl tentacle-ish appendages that were supposed to represent Ted's claws. It would be super easy for those "claws" to tickle someone without Ted knowing it. But then there was another separate complaint brought to the customer service window. It wasn't about tickling. It was a grab. We liked Jack. So, Gary felt like a polite warning about being inappropriate would be appropriate.

Jack the actor's response did him no favors. "Listen, when I take on the persona of Ted, Ted takes over. So I can't be held responsible for what Ted does."

There was a pause, waiting on a laugh. He had to be joking, right? But the self-professed Method actor/mascot studies student just stared back, unwavering in his defense of the craft. "Well, okay, do us a favor and tell Ted that if he does it again, you're both out."

If Jack had really wanted to find guidance on how to resolve his characterization conundrum, he wouldn't have had to look far for a performance coach. All summer long, if one had thoroughly eyeballed the seats of McCormick Field, they would have spotted a movie theater marquee's worth of Hollywood veterans.

Asheville is a beautiful city, so it had enjoyed being the setting for a steady stream of film productions over the years. The summer of '94 happened to land right smack in the middle of the area's biggest moviemaking boom. There were eleven feature films shot in and around the town during the '90s, from the train crash scene in Harrison Ford's *The Fugitive* to the mountain backdrop for Tom Hanks (and his brother/body double, Jim Hanks) during the running montage in *Forrest Gump*. It felt like every Asheville restaurant had a framed photo of Daniel Day-Lewis and Madeline Stowe dining in their establishment, taken when the pair resided in a downtown hotel during the 1991 filming of *The Last of the Mohicans*. If not those two, then there was a pic of another duo, James Garner and Jack Lemmon, who marched through the streets of Asheville in a scene when they (as former POTUSs) accidentally crash a gay pride parade in *My Fellow Americans*. Kevin Costner, Jodie Foster, Ben Stiller, Michael Caine, Jim Belushi— they all had spent time in Asheville during the first half of the decade making movies, and many of them had spent at least a few innings at McCormick Field.

Kurt Russell played four seasons of minor-league ball as a second baseman and made it as high as the Class AA El Paso Sun Kings before a base runner blasted through him at second, tore his rotator cuff, and essentially ended his big-league dreams. In 1988, Russell was in Asheville to shoot *Winter People* with Kelly McGillis of *Top Gun* fame and was spotted hiding beneath a ball cap in the old wooden McCormick Field grandstand. "I loved that place," he recalled to me years later when I had the chance to chat with him during a movie press junket to promote his 2014 documentary film *The Battered Bastards of Baseball*. That film was about his last team, the Portland Mavericks, a Northwest League franchise owned and operated by his father, Bing. "I loved ballparks that reminded me of the places I played and the places my dad would take us for games. We would watch baseball wherever we could. I loved going to big major-league games, but there's just something about the connection between the fans and the players at a minor-league game. I've been on both sides of that, and I truly love it."

Bing and Kurt Russell both enjoyed incredibly prolific acting careers. Bing was a mainstay of Western TV shows. But their most memorable project together was the 1979 TV movie *Elvis*. Kurt played the title role while Bing, naturally, played his father, Vernon Presley.

Speaking of the King of Rock 'n' Roll, the first of our Hollywood visitors that season had spent her entire life connected to Elvis, though at the time I didn't know it. In the summer of '94, Shelley Fabares was known for her role on the top-ten-rated TV show *Coach*, costarring alongside Craig T. Nelson. When she came to see us, it was only a few days after she had received her second consecutive Emmy nomination for Outstanding Supporting Actress in a Comedy Series. She was at McCormick Field as the spokesperson for the National Alzheimer's Foundation, throwing out the ceremonial first pitch as human jukebox Gary Saunders expertly serenaded her over the PA system with "Johnny Angel," her number-one hit from 1962. Until that moment, I had no idea she was the one who'd made that record. I also didn't realize that she had starred as Elvis's love interest in three films over three years: *Girl Happy, Spinout,* and *Clambake.* I knew those movies. My mother loved those movies. But I hadn't realized that the King's main squeeze in all three was . . . the girlfriend from *Coach*?!

I was assigned to help Shelley Fabares navigate the crowd that day. As soon as she took her seat behind home plate, a line of fans began to form. There were middle-aged women as far as the eye could see, all with stuff in hand in the hopes that she would autograph it for them. Some of them had old records of

"Johnny Angel," and many had eight-by-ten glossy photos of her in various movie roles. There was even a guy with a football jersey from the Minnesota State Screaming Eagles, the fictional football team from her TV show. But the most frequent items brought to the seat of Shelley Fabares were VHS copies of *Clambake*. A few people held her hands and wept, some as they told her that they missed Elvis, others as they shared stories of their family's struggle with Alzheimer's. They all knew she had lost her mother to the evil disease two years earlier, and they knew that she too missed the King.

For nine innings, I watched Shelley Fabares put on a clinic of how to handle emotional, Elvis-crazed fans with style and grace. I was so smitten. Like, had to consciously work to stop myself from creepily staring at her from three feet away. When it was time for her to leave, she posed for a photo with us, gave me a hug, and said, "Ryan, thank you so much for your help today." She said my name! I thought my knees would buckle. I blurted out, "Can I ask you a question?!" My voice cracked like I was twelve years old again. "What was it like to kiss Elvis?"

"You know, Ryan, I always want to downplay it. We were never romantic in real life, just on-screen. But I'm not going to lie to you. It was pretty amazing."

So was meeting Shelley Fabares.

While she was front and center during her McCormick Field visit, our other actor visitors chose the Kurt Russell pulled-ball-cap, low-profile strategy for their Asheville Tourists experience. Had the paparazzi had their lenses open during a handful of lazy midsummer evenings, they would have spotted John Larroquette, Edward Herrmann, and Chelcie Ross, knocking down a fifty-cent frankfurter on a Tuesday night (Elm Hill Hot Dog Night!) or some large cold ones on Thirsty Thursday. Well, two of them were sipping cold ones. Not Larroquette. The owner of a shelf full of Emmys for his work on the eighties sitcom *Night Court* was at the height of his career, starring in his own self-titled TV comedy that was based largely on his own personal struggle with substance abuse. So, I took it upon myself to slide up to their seats and tell them that if they needed anything at all to let us know, and to warn sleazy lawyer Dan from *Night Court* that it was Thirsty Thursday, so there would be a lot of drinking going on around him and I felt he needed to know because, you know, temptation and all that. Larroquette smiled and said, "Thanks, kid. I'll be sure to inform my sponsor." It wasn't mean. It was funny. But it also let me know that I should probably mind my own business. He hadn't had a drink in twelve years.

At that stage of his four-decade acting career, Edward Herrmann was probably best known for playing Daddy Warbucks in *Annie,* and Goldie Hawn's hapless husband in *Overboard,* but to me, he was most recognizable as the nerdy chief vampire from *The Lost Boys*. As for Chelcie Ross, for sports junkies like me, Carlton, and Swish, he was and always would be the jerk who tried to railroad Gene Hackman in *Hoosiers,* Notre Dame head coach Dan Devine in *Rudy,* and above all, aging, Crisco-slathering, and churchgoing pitcher Eddie Harris in *Major League*. We quoted Eddie Harris so many times that summer. I still do. "Bartender, Jobu needs a refill!" "You trying to say Jesus Christ can't hit a curveball?"

Several years later, I interviewed Herrmann as he promoted a NASCAR race at the Las Vegas Motor Speedway. For years, he was the star of an omnipresent TV ad campaign for Dodge, and when the automaker went stock-car racing, they brought their spokesman to the racetrack to chat with the media and perhaps sell a few Intrepids. We talked about McCormick Field and his considerable chameleon skills in the cheap seats. "It helps to not be famous," he joked. I was anxious to ask him one question, specifically. I wondered if he had channeled his inner McCormick Field the following year, 1995, while shooting the HBO film *The Soul of the Game?* It was about the integration of Major League Baseball, specifically the bold decisions and strategies of Brooklyn Dodgers president Branch Rickey, the man who scouted the Negro Leagues searching for the perfect player to handle the impossibly difficult task of breaking baseball's color barrier. That player was, of course, Jackie Robinson. In the film, Herrmann played Rickey. When I asked what I'd wanted to ask, Herrmann crossed his brow in curiosity. He said that he had enjoyed McCormick Field tremendously but apologized because he didn't understand my question.

I explained to him that for a couple of decades in the mid-twentieth century, Branch Rickey had been a regular at McCormick Field. It was Rickey, then the boss of the St. Louis Cardinals, who devised the first true "farm system," where a major-league club contracted a series of minor-league franchises to help develop players and move them up a formal ladder of progression that would ultimately lead to MLB. Before that, the minors were a spaghetti pile of leagues and teams with roaming free agent players, all hoping to catch the eye of a scout as they jumped from team to team, none of which had any formal ties to the majors. Among Rickey's first and longest-tenured farm system partners was the Tourists, beginning in 1935 with the Cardinals and lasting until he left the Dodgers in 1951. As a result, Rickey was in Asheville a lot, often with his barnstorming big leaguers for exhibition games. The Gashouse Gang and Dem Bums all played ball at McCormick under the watchful eye of the Methodist baseball man in his fedora and dark-framed glasses.

I told Herrmann that when I had watched him in *The Soul of the Game,* perfectly portraying Rickey as he sat in ballpark grandstands watching Jackie Robinson make history, I couldn't help but think of when I'd spotted him sitting in the McCormick Field bleachers, looking out over the same field where Rickey had once watched Robinson patrol second base. Edward Herrmann got misty-eyed as he thanked me for the history lesson.

So, why were these three guys in Asheville? They were costars of the latest movie to be shot in and around town. Anyone who'd watched a Channel 13 newscast or picked up a newspaper that summer knew exactly what that film was and who was its headliner.

"RICHIE RICH" STAR SPOTTED SHOPPING
AT LOCAL WAL-MART
Asheville Citizen-Times, Tuesday, May 10, 1994

Macaulay Culkin, star of "Home Alone" was seen at the Wal-Mart Tunnel Road garden center Sunday loading a flat of annuals into a Jeep. Culkin, 13, is in town for the filming of the movie, "Richie Rich," on the Biltmore Estate.

That's right. All due respect to anyone playing baseball at our place, or racing bikes in the Tour du Pont, or to anyone else who might have thought they were even a little bit famous, they all were overshadowed throughout that spring and summer by Macaulay Culkin. Everyone in the city claimed to have spotted the blond kid with the famous screaming face, but only a handful of people had actually seen him. It wasn't for lack of effort. Asheville's collective eyes were peeled day and night. Not a home game happened when a fan didn't ask one of us if "the *Home Alone* kid" had been to a game yet. He hadn't. He was quite literally one of the biggest stars in the world. Maybe the biggest. So no, Culkin wasn't standing in line at the first baseline concession window with Big Mike and John Larroquette to buy a fifty-cent Elm Hill Hot Dog. And while I don't like to question fellow journalists, do we really believe that the star of the number-three box office film of all time, behind only *Star Wars* and *E.T.,* was down at the Tunnel Road Wal-Mart picking up some petunias? My bet is that he was either on set, hiding out, or hiding out on set.

That set was the Biltmore Estate, America's largest private-owned residence, a 178,926-square-foot Gilded Age mansion built by the Vanderbilt family in the late nineteenth century. The home and its two hundred square miles of land, located two miles south of the ballpark, were the perfect location for the home of Richie Rich, the comic book character so ridiculously wealthy that his middle initial is a "$."

Edward Herrmann was playing Richie's father, Mr. Rich. Larroquette was playing greedy traitor CFO of Rich Industries, Laurence Van Dough. Chelcie Ross was in the role of Ferguson, the security chief who—SPOILER ALERT—is in cahoots with Van Dough to steal the Rich family's fortune! The movie was fully cast, and that cast, to be honest, was way more impressive than the script they were reading.

However, one role remained to be filled. They needed a baseball player.

The *Richie Rich* production team had already reached out to Ron inquiring about renting some baseball gear, specifically a pitching screen, the L-shaped net that the Tourists used during batting practice, so that the pitcher grooving fastballs to Richie wouldn't accidentally catch a Macaulay Culkin line drive with their eyeballs. They had agreed to give Ron $300 to rent the screen.

But now they were calling in search of a human, someone to stand behind that screen. They explained that there was a scene in the film where Richie employed the help of the New York Yankees, including Hall of Famer Reggie Jackson, to help him practice in his front yard, aka the acres-large lawn directly in front of the 780-foot-tall front entrance of the house, with a massive marble water fountain in the middle of it all. The filmmakers needed a pitcher to throw that batting practice to Macaulay Culkin's titular character. When the casting agent called our front office, she explained that they were seeking authenticity, a real professional baseball player who could make the audience believe that he was a member of the world's most famous professional sports team. So, if possible, could we please send three or four Asheville Tourists pitchers to the production hotel the following day, to audition in front of the director so perhaps he could pick someone to be in the film? Ron told her that he was on the case. She could count on us. There would most definitely be a handful of professional baseball pitchers there on time tomorrow morning. She was so excited as she hung up.

It's a shame he had to lie to her.

The real Asheville Tourists were on the road and weren't scheduled to return for another six days. Ron shared his dilemma with us and said that he was going to call over to UNC Asheville and recruit some college pitchers to send to the filmmakers. We told him that was a great idea. Heck, we even volunteered to go over there with them to make sure it all went smoothly.

As soon as Ron left the room, R. J. Martino looked at us and said, "We are totally going to show up and try out for that damn movie." We figured that if we brought our gloves and wore the gear, we could pass for Yankees, right? We could at least pass for Tourists, right? And we could definitely pass for UNC Asheville Bulldogs . . . right?!

The next day, we indeed showed up. Me, Carlton, Lee, Steve, Gary, and R.J. We were geared up and already acting even before the audition began. I stuck a wad of sunflower seeds in my cheek to look like a real ballplayer. Jack the actor would have called it a creative decision. Director Donald Petrie met us behind the Holiday Inn golf resort where the crew was staying, and we paced off a sixty-foot-six-inch pitching lane on a cart path just outside his hotel room. As the filmmaker who had helmed *Mystic Pizza* and *Grumpy Old Men* looked on, we rotated duties. One of us would throw a couple of pitches to another who was crouched down to play catcher while a third stood in with a batting stance. Petrie, who at that point had directed twenty-seven films and TV episodes and even acted in another thirty-plus projects, was super nice, but he clearly knew immediately that I was a phony. I was

five-ten and weighed 135 pounds. Not exactly ready-made for taking the mound against Mark McGwire, let alone Richie Rich. The
only pitch I threw was a good one. It had pop. But it was also a
little inside and nearly hit batter Swish in the crotch. "I felt that!"
Petrie said, covering his own family jewels with both hands before
saying, "Next!"

We all performed admirably. Call it the adrenaline of live performance. But the moment that the director had seen R.J., he was
the obvious choice. Heck, he even had on a New York Yankees
cap! Once he threw a smooth strike right over the portion of side-
walk that was home plate, the competition was over. R. J. Martino
was going to be a movie star. Or at least he was going to have a
brief role in a film that, when it hit theaters that Christmas, Joe
Leydon of *The Houston Post* would write in his review: "Decently
crafted but oddly charmless."

As we walked around the side of the hotel to leave, off in the
distance we saw a blond kid sitting alone on a bench in the sunshine. He looked a little sad. We were convinced then and I remain
convinced that it was Culkin. What we know now is that he was
indeed having a difficult time. *Richie Rich* was his eighth starring
role in four years. He was thirteen years old and burned out. It
turned out to be the last movie he would make for nearly a decade,
and not long after his time in Asheville he sued his parents for
emancipation.

Then again, maybe it wasn't him. Maybe he was over at the
Wal-Mart buying begonias.

A few days later, R.J. most definitely saw Culkin. He pitched to
him, sort of, during a perfect late spring afternoon at the Biltmore
Estate. R.J. was fired up to meet Reggie Jackson, though No. 44
was in full Mr. October mode and didn't seem to want to impress
anyone other than the kid movie star. As he left the ballpark for
the set, R.J. was stopped by Ron and handed two dozen baseballs.
"Get Reggie to sign these. We'll sell them in the store." It took

some doing and Reggie wasn't super thrilled about it, but before R.J.'s time on set was wrapped, he got the balls autographed. See? I wasn't lying when I told you that R.J. was a great salesman.

You can see R.J.'s performance today, three minutes into the film. It's a beautiful tilt up from his right hand gripping the baseball to his determined face looking in for a sign. Then, wearing No. 42 the year before Mariano Rivera started donning those digits for the actual Yankees, R.J. fires off a perfectly executed pitch in front of the Biltmore, as well as a Rich family maid, chef, and butler. After a batting tip from Reggie, Richie drives a long ball into the fountain, and the chef falls in while trying to track down the big fly. It's on YouTube. Go look at it now. See? I also wasn't lying when I told you that R.J. was a good-looking dude.

When he returned to the ballpark that afternoon, we peppered him with questions about the experience. When we asked him how much he'd be paid for his nonspeaking role, he proudly told us $100. A laugh blasted out of Ron's office. "A hundred bucks! They paid me three hundred bucks to use the screen! That screen made way more money off *Richie Rich* than R.J.!" Years later, as soon as I asked R.J. about his fifteen seconds of fame, he said that's how Ron always introduced him to people, by telling them that the L-screen got a much higher acting paycheck than he did.

"He sold all those autographed Reggie baseballs, too," R.J. explained to me, adding that he didn't even get one of those balls. "So, between the screen and the autographs, Ron probably netted at least three times what I made. I should have hired him as my talent agent."

Ron would have known how to negotiate on behalf of talent because he dealt with talent agents all the time during decades of booking in-game entertainment acts. That season we had a pair of Class AAA mascots stop by: the duo of "Famous Chicken Lite" Billy Bird of the Louisville Redbirds and Homer the Dragon from the nearby Charlotte Knights. We also had Ronald McDonald (okay, it was just a dude from the local McDonald's in a clown suit handing out coupons) and Rick Dunham, an Elvis impersonator who went by "Elvis Himselvis" and, honestly, might have given our best national anthem performance of the season, though I doubt he ever kissed Shelley Fabares.

Those were the officially announced entertainers, as they appeared in the game programs and pocket schedules that were printed before the season started. Others were booked as the summer went along, such as Shelley Fabares, offered up by the National Alzheimer's Foundation, and Captain Dynamite, who I'm pretty positive was just driving by Asheville on his way elsewhere and stopped by with his Coffin of Death because he'd known Ron for years and said, "Y'all need me?" There were also the surprise baseball celebrities, coaches on the visiting teams who agreed to let us make a big deal of them. Bill Buckner was a roving hitting instructor for the Toronto Blue Jays and came to town with the Hagerstown Suns. He also signed a few balls for us to sell. I volunteered to get him to do it, because as a lifelong Red Sox fan, I wanted to tell him that I had never blamed him for losing the 1986 World Series. "Who do you blame?" he asked me. I told him it was the bullpen's fault. He just winked and walked away.

There was also a rotation of local regulars. We had "Magic Mondays" when local wizard Bill Grimsley would perform "roaming magic" in the grandstands, blowing minds with card tricks, mystical rubber bands, juggling bowling pins, and asking everyone to help by saying the magic words. "What are the magic words? 'Officer, my speedometer is broken.'" We also had Colonel Robert Morgan, who lived nearby, and was the pilot of the World War II bomber immortalized in the 1990 film *Memphis Belle*. You want to get the home crowd fired up for the Memorial Day weekend game? Trot Colonel Morgan out to the mound.

We also had free haircut days, when local barbershops and beauty parlors would set up salon chairs atop the home dugout and give free trims to lucky sports fans during the hour that led up to game time. One evening we noticed that an unusually large number of Tourists ballplayers were hanging out in the dugout during a free haircut night, way earlier than we'd normally see them. They were sitting on the first step and all staring up toward the barber chairs, gawking like they were looking at a lunar eclipse. That's when we realized that the all-female team of cosmetologists, a group we'd never booked before from this new, young, cool, hipster salon, were all wearing very short skirts . . . and zero underwear.

There was also the Circuit Rider, our only game day guest who entered the stadium riding a horse. The Circuit Rider was 175 years old. Okay, he wasn't. But he looked like it. The Reverend Robert E. Harris was a local Baptist preacher who believed that he didn't need a pulpit or a steeple to spread the gospel, preferring to stay on the move like the circuit-riding pastors of years gone by, mounted atop his trusty steed, named the Two-Eyed Redeemer. Harris always wore black, from his cowboy hat and frock coat to his colonel tie. The Circuit Rider wrote a Christian column in the *Citizen-Times,* preached in open fields and prison yards, and also held a weekly Sunday morning service in the same shopping center parking lot where Macaulay Culkin allegedly purchased his pansies. Then, the good reverend would gallop over to McCormick Field in time for Sunday's traditional two p.m. first pitch. He would enter through the service gate where James the Mountain Man killed snakes, guiding the Two-Eyed Redeemer down the first baseline while Gary played the pastor's entrance music, Gene Autry's "Back in the Saddle Again." Late-night television viewers knew that tune well, because just before Channel 13 played the national anthem and shut down their transmitter for the night, it would air a short made-for-TV devotional from the Circuit Rider. After sharing a similar testimony with those who had decided to visit McCormick Field on the Sabbath, the Circuit Rider would lead the attendees in a word of prayer in his deep but soothing, almost still voice. Then he would give the Two-Eyed Redeemer a tug on the reins and exit the way he had arrived, this time to Ernest Tubb singing "Let's Say Goodbye Like We Said Hello."

Ron never paid the Circuit Rider. Reverend Harris just showed up. In fact, no one ever paid the Circuit Rider. Harris never married and still lived in the tiny mountain house where he was born and raised. When I asked him how much money a horse-riding pastor made, he joked, "I try not to charge too much for saving souls. Last year I think I made about two hundred and fifty dollars."

Not even enough to rent a pitching screen from Ron.

Meanwhile, our favorite act of the summer showcases had to be the Blues Brothers. Not the real Blues Brothers. This was a "tribute," the Blues Brothers Act of La Crosse. They also entered the stadium down the first baseline, not via a horse, but via horsepower, in a 1974 Dodge Monaco, complete with a giant speaker strapped to the roof blasting "Soul Man," "Everybody Needs Somebody to Love," and all the songs made famous by the original Jake and Elwood Blues, John Belushi and Dan Aykroyd.

This Jake and Elwood were Bill LaRue and Bob Masewicz, a pair of Wisconsin buddies who had been on the road performing as Joliet, Illinois's, favorite fugitives since 1983. It was during a beer-fueled night at a local bar, while watching a lip-sync competition, that Bill and Bob thought, *Hell, we can do that!* and took the stage, performing a couple of songs from the 1980 box office smash. Their act caught the eye of the local minor-league basketball team, the La Crosse Catbirds of the Continental Basketball Association. That performance piqued the interest of the NBA, and teams started calling Bill and Bob to perform at halftime. When the Denver Nuggets asked Bill how much they charged, he told them $500. The caller from Denver said, "Dude, if you're going to book NBA gigs, you have to start charging at least a thousand bucks." Soon they were regulars at places like Chicago

Stadium. During Michael Jordan's rookie season, His Airness wasn't featured on the game ticket when Bill and Bob showed up. They were. Soon they were booking sixty gigs a year at basketball and hockey games. When they received a cease-and-desist letter from the Belushi estate, they hired an entertainment attorney who found them legal protection under the "Big E" clause used by Elvis impersonators. As long as they identified as an "act" or "tribute" and didn't make a movie or record an album, they were protected.

The original man behind (and inside) the Famous San Diego Chicken, Ted Giannoulas, became their mentor, and suggested that they attend baseball's Winter Meetings. They rolled into Louisville and parked their Bluesmobile right smack in the middle of the trade show, blasting "Rubber Biscuit" and handing out business cards alongside Morganna and Max Patkin.

On Saturday night, May 28, 1994, my job was to visit the little room off the clubhouse where Bill and Bob were getting into costume, delivering—as their contract rider required—four towels, "a sandwich, pizza or something like it to eat," some diet sodas, waters, a bag of ice, two "cheap T-shirts," ten to twenty bags of peanuts for something called "The Peanut Skit" as well as five hot dogs, a box of popcorn, and a drink for "The Hot Dog Skit," whatever that was. They had a third member of the team who acted as the sound technician and shared driving duties, which they all three did in shifts.

I asked them how many dates they had worked that week. They said six. I asked them how many dates they would work this year. They said 160. I had seen their contract. I knew that we were paying them $2,000 for the show. I also knew that they hadn't required a hotel room because they had blown into Asheville from Hickory that afternoon and were leaving immediately after they were done with us to work a day game in Knoxville thirteen hours later. They traveled in the same car they used for their performances, and each guy slept when he wasn't driving. This was easy math. In the movie, the original Blues Brothers sought $5,000 to save St. Helen of the Blessed Shroud Orphanage. The Blues Brothers Act of LaCrosse could have saved about two and a half orphanages every week.

Bill Murray, a minority owner in multiple minor-league teams over the years, pulled them aside after a show to say that he loved it because "I can tell that you really love these characters." Dan Aykroyd even voiced a commercial for them to promote an appearance in New England. They toured Europe with an all-star college basketball team and spent multiple winters in Honolulu on the dime of the Hawaiian Winter Baseball League. It was just a tad bit warmer on the beach at Waikiki than it was back home in La Crosse.

"We had just done a show in Miami, the Miami Miracle, and the team owner, Mike Veeck, was talking with us," LaRue told me when I tracked him down in 2022. "He said, 'How much am I paying you guys tonight?' We told him two grand. He started laughing and said, 'What a great damn country we live in!' This was the guy who was behind the infamous Disco Demolition night with the Chicago White Sox, he'd seen everything, and even he was like, 'I can't believe you guys are getting paid to dress up like Jake and Elwood and dance around and that's actually your job.'"

Bill did that job for another couple of seasons, leaving the road to raise his kids in 1996. Bob stayed out there with a new dance partner all the way until 2007.

"In 1994 in Asheville, you met us right in the sweet spot," Masewicz said to me nearly thirty years later. "People came out to the ballpark to see us. To see Morganna. To see Max Patkin. To see the Famous Chicken. Today, there is so much entertainment everywhere, I think ballpark acts are just in the background, something fun to see. But back then, we were the draw. It was so fun, it was crazy."

I remember standing in the stairwell, watching Bill and Bob,

Jake and Elwood, dancing atop the dugout and leading a sell-out crowd in "Minnie the Moocher," their echoes of the lyrics in return echoing off the mountainside.

"Hidey Hidey Hidey Hi . . ." *Hidey Hidey Hidey Hi*

"Hodey Odey Odey Oh . . ." *Hodey Odey Odey Oh*

Oh, it was more than crazy, and it was way more than fun. It was magic.

AT-BAT FOOD SERVICES

As we hammered through June and the season neared its halfway point, the Asheville Tourists were suddenly as hot as the air temps. The team had rallied from its terrible start and its stall at .500 to reach a record of twenty-six wins and twenty-three losses, sitting only four games out of first place in the Sally League's North Division, trailing the Hickory Crawdads, Hagerstown Suns, and Greensboro Bats. Jason Smith, who had moved from catcher to first base, was crushing the ball with a league-leading thirteen homers. Jamey Wright was 4-2, giving up more runs than he wanted to, but quickly becoming known as a ground ball creator of the highest order.

For us, the real story about the arrival of summer was that school was out and business around the ballpark had moved into overdrive. No corner of McCormick Field felt that impact more than concessions, and it just so happened that as the season's second stanza began, my job changed. We three interns rotated gigs, and I swapped out with Carlton, trading in my nipple-ripping golf shirts for a soft blue T-shirt featuring the screen-printed logo of At-Bat Food Services, the concessions division of the Asheville Tourists Baseball Club.

My hands spent the spring covered in paper cuts, copy machine toner, and infield dirt. I smelled like fresh-cut grass. Now those hands would be slathered in ketchup, grape flavoring, and nacho cheese. I was going to smell like hot dog water.

That reminds me. I promised I would tell you a better story about Babe Ruth in Asheville than the "Damned delightful place!" tale, and now is the time to share it.

It was Tuesday, April 7, 1925, and the Bambino was with his New York Yankees teammates as they barnstormed their way from spring training in Florida back to the Bronx, playing exhibition games versus the Brooklyn Dodgers all over the southeast, from Savannah to Atlanta to Chattanooga to Knoxville. Asheville was up next, where eight thousand fans were waiting, packed into still-new McCormick Field and in the streets and hillsides around it. As the train snaked its way through the Smoky Mountains from Tennessee into North Carolina, Ruth started feeling queasy. He'd complained about stomach pains in Knoxville, and the weaving of the locomotive was making it worse. He had turned thirty in February and by all accounts spent his entire off-season celebrating. He gained so much weight that winter that he voluntarily checked himself into a health spa in Hot Springs, Arkansas, to try to shed some of his nearly 270 pounds. To make matters worse, he'd battled the flu throughout his time in Florida and had bummed out his fans in Chattanooga and Knoxville when he chose to sit out batting practice, though he did jack in-game homers out of the ballparks at each stop.

When the train pulled into the station in downtown Asheville, Ruth was greeted by fans and news photographers, in front of whom he promptly fainted. The *Asheville Citizen* wrote that "he swooned" and fell on top of a couple of teammates, whose bodies unwittingly broke his fall and prevented him from cracking his skull on the marble train platform. Still unconscious, the Babe was carried by those teammates to a taxi that rushed him off to the nearby Battery Park Hotel. Horrified onlookers chased after the cab, and when the planet's biggest sports star (figuratively and literally) was taken to his room, dozens of fans held vigil outside the hotel doors while at least that many newspaper scribes and photographers, many traveling with the Yankees back to New York, staked out the scene.

Across town, the Babe-less Yanks beat the Dodgers 16–8, and both teams boarded the train bound for a few more games and then on to New York for the season. The bedridden Bambino stayed behind, still at the hotel and tended to by a local physician, Dr. Charles Jordan. As word spread that Ruth hadn't played in the game and no one had seen him leave town with the team, there was much speculation as to why Ruth had fallen so ill. It didn't help that every story written by the *Citizen* put the team's official description in skeptical quotes as "Flu." It also didn't help when that paper ran a photo of Ruth in bed, wearing a size 42 nightgown because that was the only garment the hotel could find that would fit him, and even that took some work. He was a size 48, so they cut a slit in the back of the shirt and threw away the pants. You couldn't tell in the black-and-white photo, but the pajama top was pink. However, you could absolutely tell from the photo that Ruth was super pissed that a photographer had somehow gotten into his room.

He finally left Asheville two days later with the intent of traveling straight back to New York, but thanks to a couple of missed connections, the train he was supposed to be on when it chugged into Washington, DC, arrived with no Babe on board. So, to those who were waiting to see him, there was only one logical explanation: Babe Ruth had died in Asheville.

That's what was written in the *London Evening News* on April 9, 1925, and the world ran with it. The rumors were further fueled when Ruth finally did arrive in New York. Another stumble, this time in his cabin restroom, had knocked him out cold once again, so he had to be carried off that train and loaded into an ambulance. Another baseball team, the Boston Braves, coincidentally happened to be traveling through Penn Station and saw the home run king being unloaded, his limp body wrapped in blankets and carried by medics. As their train pulled away, they too believed that the Colossus of Clout had shuffled off this mortal coil during his stay in the Land of the Sky, his massive body being delivered to the Big Apple from Asheville.

What we know now is that Ruth was at the very least suffering from a serious stomach abscess that required abdominal surgery. He missed more than fifty games that season. But at the time, the public diagnosis was much more judgmental. That too started in Asheville, where Dr. Jordan told reporters: "All I can say is that unless somebody is appointed to act as guardian over him at the dining table, he won't be a baseball player very long."

Stories ran rampant about Ruth going whole hog on a pile of frankfurters and a keg of beer on the train ride from Knoxville to Asheville. New York newspaperman W. O. McGeehan poured a bucket of hot sauce on those claims of railroad gluttony, famously describing Ruth's predicament as "the bellyache heard round the world." Yes, ladies and gentlemen, for a moment, everyone firmly believed that Earth's greatest athlete had killed himself in Asheville, only blocks from McCormick Field, because he had eaten too many hot dogs.

Jane Lentz, the beautifully sarcastic boss of At-Bat Food Services and one of my very favorite people, scoffed at that urban legend. "You see, I know that's not possible."

Jane and I were standing in the kitchen area of the ballpark's main concession stand, just a little less than ninety-nine years after the Babe's bout with a bum tummy. As we watched fans order food, I had been proudly recalling the Ruth bellyache story, having just read about it in Bob Terrell's book *McCormick Field: Field of Reality*. The more I talked, the more Jane shook her head. "Nah.

If killing yourself by eating too many hot dogs was possible, I would have already seen a bunch of people out here do it, especially tonight. I mean, look at this guy."

Yep. It was fifty-cent Elm Hill Hot Dog Night. And the man she motioned toward was departing the counter with an armload of wieners. To be clear, Elm Hill Hot Dogs are delicious. But you shouldn't eat nine of them at once. "That idiot. He'll be back later," Jane predicted (more about Jane and her love for "idiots" later). "Asking if we sell Pepto-Bismol."

Every gig in Minor League Baseball is exhausting. Every night after a home game meant crashing hard into the pillow at our retirement community apartment. Carlton used to make fun of me because I would shave in the bed. Way too tired to get up in the morning, I'd just lie there with my Norelco electric razor humming against my neck, my head still on that pillow, and my eyes still closed. But during the seven weeks leading into June, Carlton had come back to our apartment experiencing an entirely different plane of exhaustion. He smelled like stale beer and looked like he'd been run over by a mustard delivery truck. "McGee, my boy," he said to me when we arrived at the park for my first day on concessions intern duty, "buckle up, son."

The office of At-Bat Food Services was located within the bowels of the ballpark, through a blue door tucked in between the main row of concessions sales windows, the air thick with the pregame smell of cleaning chemicals and the in-game aroma of all sorts of food that was way too tasty to be good for you. Because McCormick Field was carved into the mountain, the playing field and seating bowl were at a different elevation than the concession area. At-Bat and its various stands of consumable commerce were located behind and beneath the grandstand, a quick trot down a flight of stairs that emptied into a concrete courtyard. That courtyard was lined with a half-dozen concession stands, manned by as many as fifty-five game day employees. It was a well-oiled machine, with several of us well covered in oil.

Greeting fans just inside the front gate was the snow cone stand. Okay, we were supposed to call it shaved ice, officially Hawaiian Shaved Ice, but everyone called it the snow cone stand. We should have called it the Kid Crack stand. That might seem like a strong comparison, but just wait until I explain to you how we made those suckers. The next window was, per the ballpark map, the secondary concession stand, but this was where most people got their goods. Hot dogs, Polish sausage dogs, nachos, Nachos Supreme!, which, like BirdZerk!, always came with an exclamation point. I suppose it was a warning of how you'd feel after ordering the nacho option that came with extra cheese, chili, salsa, and peppers. As in, two innings later, feeling a twinge in your gut and saying, "That was delicious . . . but wait . . . !!!!"

Around the bend, deep beneath the park and all connected by the catacomb hallway off Jane's office, were the Dairy Queen soft serve ice cream stand and a window offering Little Caesar's Pizza. Remember my short stint as Wingate University radio play-by-play guy? The center on the women's basketball team, Amber Burgess, did significant time in that window as our pizza salesperson. That was big. I'll tell you why later.

And then there was the grill. That place was a damn kiln, a little cinder-block room that was nothing but cast-iron grates as far as the eye could see, all glowing red. Dante may well have prophesied this exact location when he wrote *Inferno*. I have always theorized that because the grill was located at the deepest point of the ballpark structure, that furnace was connected directly to the hot magma center of planet Earth.

The two kids who manned the grill station each night were a couple of high school students and best friends, Robbie and Ryan, one standing six and a half feet tall and the other looking about half that size. I called them the Grill Boys, and they cranked out burgers and grilled chicken sandwiches (cheese was twenty-five cents extra) all while keeping the French fry oil bath sizzling at temperatures that the Vanderbilt family's construction crew could have used to melt and shape the steel for the Biltmore Estate. I always loved to listen to patrons who placed their order with the Grill Boys as if they were dining on Wagyu filet mignon at Ruth's Chris. "I'd like my burger medium rare, crispy on the outside to hold in the juices. Also, please hold off on the cheese until the very end so that it melts just right. And toast the bun if you don't mind." I heard that very request one night, placed by a gentleman who looked like the same kind of stuffy professorial type of character Edward Herrmann often portrayed on screen. (The real Herrmann's order was always "Dog, please," and he was done.) Whatever, dude. No one was placing custom orders with the Grill Boys, just as no one was ever going to be at any risk of contracting salmonella. That's because everything served up by the Grill Boys came well-done. That included the Grill Boys themselves, who ended every night by cleaning their instruments of incineration and then emerging from their food furnace soaked in sweat, stained by soot, and singed from hands to eyebrows. The big one wore glasses, and most nights he'd step out into the cool evening air, and when he took his spectacles off, he looked like a raccoon. I loved the Grill Boys.

My favorite aspect of working in concessions was the feeling I received every night. The customers were always happy. Big families every night, buying food, eating food, always smiling. And why not? We offered twenty-five individual menu items, and the most expensive of those was a thirty-two-ounce "bucket" of beer that cost a whopping three bucks. A family of four could attend an Asheville Tourists game, sitting in reserved box seats, each buying a hot dog, large popcorn, and a sixteen-ounce soft drink in a special-edition souvenir cup, and it would cost a grand total of

$40. Scale that down to general admission seats and a small drink and popcorn, and it would set you back all of twenty-six bucks. Yes, twenty-six dollars. To watch baseball and eat good food with your family while sitting in the perfect minor-league ballpark on a short-sleeve summer night watching future big leaguers mash homers as the Blues Brothers danced around between innings and Captain Dynamite blew himself up at second base.

God Bless America.

My first day as a full-time food employee, my greeter to the gig was not Jane. When I popped through that blue door that led to her office, I was met by Julio the Cat. He had been down in a dark corner of the hallway, and just as I'd seen him, he'd pounced into that corner, like he was attacking something. Then Julio the Cat strolled right by me with a field mouse hanging from his teeth. I swear to y'all I saw him nod at me. He might have even winked. All to say, "You worry about the food, bro. I'll keep the varmints out of here for you."

I stepped into Jane's office, which reminded me more than a little of Tony Torchia's. It was basically a closet, but it was much more lived in than the manager's digs that rotated through new tenants each season. This space here, this was Jane's. My ears took in the sound of the 1989 Rolling Stones album *Steel Wheels*. My eyes took in the décor of a lot of old-school Tourists signage from over the years. Then there were the containers. Bottles of oil. Empty gallon milk jugs (I'd learn soon what those were for). Giant cans of ketchup and chili and "nacho cheese product." Grady Gardner had his stacks of bags. Jane had her stacks of cans.

The workspace of Jane reflected Jane the person. It was super eclectic but also super organized. Mostly, working in concessions was super fun, but I realized very quickly that you had to earn that fun. How? By winning her trust, and that was done by working your butt off, being low maintenance, and, well, just not being an idiot. Jane hated idiots, almost as much as she loved to point out idiots. See: Too Many Hot Dogs Guy. We could have run the entire power grid of Buncombe County off the energy that came from her eye rolls when she watched patrons stand in line for ten minutes, with nothing to look at but the giant menu boards that hung over the counters. Remember, this is 1994. No smartphone screens. Still, when they worked their way to the front of the line and were asked, "What can we get you?" they would stare blankly, having no idea what they wanted. "Um . . ." And then would order the one item we didn't offer.

"Do y'all have orange soda?"

"No, sorry."

"What do you have?"

"We have Pepsi, Diet Pepsi, Mountain Dew, Seven-Up, Country Time Lemonade, and Hawaiian Punch."

"Do you have iced tea?"

"No."

"Okay, cool, then I'll just take a Dr Pepper."

Jane would say nothing. She would walk under the menu sign—the one that listed six drink options, none of which were orange soda, iced tea, or Dr Pepper—and then look up at it, hoping that maybe folks would follow her lead and catch on. Most did. But I realized very early into the job that at least one person in every line was never going to get it. Ever. I still catch them in the lines that I stand in at ballparks and stadiums all over the United States. I still implement Jane's menu stare. They still don't catch on.

That first day for me in concessions, just in case I thought maybe she'd be different down here in her element than she had been upstairs in the office amid the bosses, she quickly let me know that Jane was always Jane. She once again looked up from her ledger, over her glasses, and said to me, flatly, "What do you want?" As the weeks went on, she would continue to ask me that whenever I walked into her office. I started replying, "Dr Pepper." She would immediately shoot back, "Well, we don't have any Dr Pepper. Read the menu, dummy."

Let me tell you about this ledger, or spreadsheet, or whatever you want to call it, that she was always poring over. Jane had the only computer in the ballpark. We didn't use one to sell tickets or merchandise or to run the scoreboard or play music from the press box. Carolyn didn't use a computer to keep the books. The sales guys weren't allowed to use one to keep track of sales. Jane used a PC, but it wasn't exactly HAL 9000. It was basically a word processor that did nothing more than print out her own calculations via the *RENHR RENHR RENHR* sound of a dot matrix printer.

I am sure that in modern billion-dollar professional sports, those who run the concessions for Jerry Jones and the Dallas Cowboys at the "Jerry Dome" AT&T Stadium or for the Steinbrenner family at what I still call New Yankee Stadium, they probably make their decisions on purchasing, stocking, and selling via some artificial intelligence–powered algorithm that was written by the same nerds who came with WAR and QBR as modern sports statistics. I have been a sportswriter my whole adult life, and I still have no idea how WAR and QBR work. But all those nerd-powered analytics conjured up by my ESPN Stats & Information coworkers pale in comparison to Jane placing orders and telling us how much of what to thaw out and cook, based purely on the algorithm of her eyes, head, and instinct. Watching her was like watching Russell Crowe in *A Beautiful Mind*.

She would look at the schedule on a Wednesday in May and see that for the game that night, played against the Macon Braves, we had an announced promotion of a T-shirt giveaway for the first five hundred kids through the gate, that the choir from Asheville First Baptist Church would be singing the national anthem, and that the weather forecast was for a temperature of eighty-one degrees and a slight chance of rain. She would sit there, process it, and then say, "Okay, you need to mix an extra bottle of blueberry flavor for the snow cone stand, thaw out an extra box of chicken breasts, make sure the Dairy Queen machine is filled up. But don't really worry about running out of beer, we'll be fine there tonight."

Translation: Five hundred kids will be here for free T-shirts, and kids are obsessed with blue snow cones. They don't even ask for the real flavor, they just order "blue." We needed extra chicken to grill because all those kids would have moms with them, and moms typically ordered chicken sandwiches instead of hamburgers. The Macon Braves being in town would bring in a lot of Atlanta Braves fans, and in the Dairy Queen stand we had little plastic ice cream bowls that looked like Braves ball caps, and they'd buy them up. And finally, Asheville First Baptist Church had a gigantic choir, and they would be bringing their families, and Baptists don't drink beer, at least not in public where everyone else can see them doing it.

See? Genius.

The biggest task of the concessions intern was setting up the stands for each game. It was a long checklist. There was a lot of heating up of stuff. Chili, "cheddar cheese product" (by the way, I don't know what exactly was in the "product" because I was afraid to look, I just knew it tasted great), and hot dogs. So many hot dogs.

The first time Jane explained how to make the snow cone flavoring, I thought she was messing with me. She got out one of those empty gallon milk jugs and slammed it down on the counter. Then she took a four-pound bag of sugar and really slammed it down on the counter. Then she handed me the tiniest little paper packet of flavoring, all of .13 ounces of powder, identical to a single-serving Kool-Aid drink-mix packet from the grocery store. "Those two things, the sugar and the powder, go into that jug with the water." I was flummoxed. It made no physical sense. It was the concessions kitchen equivalent to the old saying, "ten pounds of crap in a five-pound bag." This was four pounds of sugar in a one-gallon jug.

And here's why I told you earlier that this stuff was crack for kids. You would pour the entire bag of sugar into that milk container, all nine cups of it, so much sugar that it filled that jug to the halfway point all on its own. Next came the puny puff of flavoring, be it cherry, grape, piña colada, or the coveted blue—we had twenty different flavors to add into each individual milk jug. Then you would run the kitchen faucet until the water became too hot to touch with bare hands, the same scalding temperature that we used to clean utensils, where the thermometer hovered barely one notch below boiling. You would fill that jug with water, cap it, and start shaking the hell out of it. You shook it and shook it until the mound of sugar began to vanish, bit by bit, chunk by chunk, until it had dissolved completely into the water that had now also taken on the artificial hue of the flavor packet. We used those jugs to fill the kaleidoscope of pourer-topped nozzle bottles that were lined up on shelves at the back of the snow cone stand, with big bold labels that could be seen by the kid customers.

The snow cone stand girls, Jennifer and Chastity, would take giant cylinders of ice and place them on a centrifuge machine that spun those blocks at a high rate of speed to shave off the "snow" with a blade. We'd frozen those cylinders by filling recycled chili containers with water and leaving them in the freezers overnight. If you hadn't washed them out well enough, that ice would have a little brown tone to it. And if those blocks hadn't frozen all the way between games, then halfway through the shaving process cold water would explode out of the center of the ice block like a grenade, creating an empty ice shell that we called a "Shriner's Cap."

Dang, now that I type all this out, I don't think I realized how traumatic making snow cones had been for me.

Anyway, one scoop of that shaved ice went into a paper cone, a portion about half the size of a baseball. Then that scoop received several squirts of flavoring, probably an ounce of liquid. A gallon is 128 fluid ounces. We had nine cups of sugar in that gallon. I am no chemist, but that's a lot of sugar per squirt. At only $1.50 a pop, we had a lot of supercharged, blue-toothed kids running around McCormick Field who had knocked down at least a couple of snow cones.

By the way, quick economic sidebar here. Do you realize now why snow cones were such a priority? They were the second-biggest cash racket in the ballpark. We had maybe a nickel into each $1.50 sell. So, now you are asking, hey, dude, what could possibly have better margins than a paper cone with sugar ice in it? The answer is what we set up directly in front of the snow cone stand. The Speed Pitch was an aluminum frame, covered in a flimsy net, with a vinyl backdrop that featured the outline of a batter and a strike zone. There was a bucket of James the Mountain Man's worst ball retrievals and a radar gun that had been purchased used from an old baseball scout who said it was no longer reliable enough for him to accurately evaluate pitchers. For one dollar someone got three throws. The goal was to find one machismo sucker, preferably a "If I hadn't hurt my arm back in '87 we totally would have won State" type, who could put up a decent (however inaccurate) MPH number early in the night. Then that Uncle Rico would inevitably stand there all game, keeping an eye on all the would-be takers of his self-coronated "Biggest Arm in the Ballpark" crown. Anytime someone topped him, he would immediately plunk over another buck and keep throwing until he was back atop the leaderboard. The one in his mind.

A buck. For three throws of old baseballs. For nine innings. Free. Freaking. Money.

We never warned anyone that they might be throwing their arms out, like I had done when Carlton and I were in our one-day preseason training boot camp. But we would warn people at the snow cone stand. We would see exhausted parents in the line in the late innings of a game, at like 9:30 p.m., about to buy their babies a couple of booster rocket blues, and we'd quietly whisper, "Hey, you might not want to do this." They'd always say, "Okay, we'll get them some ice cream instead."

Ah yes, the ice cream. The most surprisingly complicated relationship that I had with any corner of McCormick Field was with the Dairy Queen stand. I love Dairy Queen. I love Oreo Blizzards. I spent my entire childhood, and if we're being honest, my entire adulthood with an inability to drive by a Dairy Queen without asking everyone else in the car if, hey, y'all, should we take a break and get a dipped cone?

But even with that love in my heart and stomach, the most difficult concession setup process at the ballpark was getting the Dairy Queen soft-serve machine ready to go. What consumers see is a nice, clean, chrome machine. When one pulls down on the handle, it produces a steady flow of gorgeously stacked slow-motion ice cream magic. But if I ever meet the engineer who devised the process of how that machine is filled with the original product that becomes the actual product, it is likely to become a violent exchange.

The ice cream mix—which transforms into the delicacy that is Dairy Queen soft serve—is an incredibly sweet, white milky cream, delivered to the ballpark in a rubber bladder. The sack has a screw-cap nozzle on one corner. To connect the bag full of liquid to the ice cream machine, one has to climb a ladder carrying the not-light bag on his shoulder, holding it steady with one arm while using the other hand to unscrew the cap on the corner of the bag and then twist the now-exposed nozzle until it snaps into place in a hole located on the top of the machine. Then you have to take one more step up on the ladder and boost the bag with enough altitude and energy that the milk stuff begins pouring down into the tank below.

If you would like to experience this process firsthand, but don't want to actually apply for a job at Dairy Queen, get yourself a thirteen-gallon Hefty bag, like you'd use for a kitchen-size trash can, and fill it with water. Then tie off one end, hoist it up onto your shoulder, carry it like a firefighter up a three-step shop ladder, and try to set it on the top of your refrigerator.

Sounds great, right?

I am sure there is a way to do all this without feeling like you have just herniated a disc in your lower back, just as I'm certain there is a method that wouldn't spill at least some of that white sugar paint all over yourself. But over the course of more than a month working in concessions, I never figured those out. I am told now that I was doing it all wrong. The bag was supposed to stay in the box that it came in? I don't know, and I clearly didn't know then. But that's how I did it.

The big winner in this scenario was Julio the Cat. People always wondered what it was that ultimately created the bond between me and my new feline friend. Well, the fact that I would let him come into the Dairy Queen booth to clean up my daily spillage certainly didn't hurt. I also used to keep one of those little plastic Atlanta Braves baseball cap ice cream bowls in a secret hiding place and would set it out for him during games so he could lap it up. It's the only time I've seen a cat wag its tail out of happiness like it was a dog. Looking back now, I wasn't so much Julio the Cat's friend as I was his pusher.

I always made a bit of a mess in the Dairy Queen room, but I had only one true disaster. I've never told anyone about it until now, except for Jane, and I waited twenty-five years to do that, when we went to dinner to talk about this book. Now I will tell you. As a man grows older, I suppose he no longer worries so much about his pride.

It was a routine home game afternoon, and the only people in concessions at that time of day were Jane and myself. She was in her office on the phone with a vendor, and I motioned that I was going to head down the hall and set up the Dairy Queen machine. For whatever reason, I decided that this would be the day I was going to try to make the setup process more efficient. The most awkward part of the procedure was always unscrewing the nozzle cap while standing on top of the little ladder. So, I determined it would be a good idea to give that cap a half turn to loosen it before starting my ascent. The idea being that I could make it easier to take the cap completely off a few moments later, when I was holding the body bag, er, milk bag on my shoulder.

What I had not counted on was what happened next. As I gave the bag the big shove to launch it atop the metal box, the loosened cap smacked up against the corner of the machine. The impact snapped that cap off like a soda can pop tab. Because the heavy, limp bag was being compressed by my lifting efforts, my shoulder pressurized the ice cream mix, and it started spraying from the nozzle like air from a set of bagpipes. Years later, I was sitting on an airplane and looking out onto the tarmac as the airport emergency crews hosed down a small plane with an engine fire, smothering it with an overkill amount of white compression foam. It's the only scene I've ever witnessed that even came close to what happened in the Dairy Queen stand that afternoon.

Initially, the cream spray leak was all headed in the same direction, a white fountain that splashed against the wall behind the machine. If I'd left it alone, I would have wasted a whole bag of ice cream mix, but the mess would have stayed relatively contained to that corner as it harmlessly washed down the wall and into the drain in the center of the floor. But in my panic, I instinctively reached up and grabbed the end of the nozzle like I was going to somehow stop this Candy Land geyser with my palm. Instead, I succeeded in creating a downspout that was now covering my legs, feet, the steps of the ladder, and the ceramic floor underneath. For about two whole seconds, whatever laws of physics were holding me and the ladder and the bag in one place held true. Then it all cut loose at the exact same time.

The feet of the ladder started sliding just as the bottoms of my sneakers stopped gripping. In a moment that channeled the greatest Hollywood stuntman, I went ass over ice cream cone. When I let go of the bag and reached up to grab something, anything, to slow my fall, all my hand could find was the knob of the ice cream machine dispenser handle, which was round and super smooth. Still, my grip caught. I couldn't believe it. I hung there for a split second, proud of my self-rescue. Then the lever started moving downward, and my hand—coated in a half gallon of wet mix— went *SLIP!* I dropped hard a couple of feet to the floor. My butt landed with a smack squarely in the center of a pond of ice cream mix, causing a splash that covered the rest of me. My rear end continued to slide in the liquid, and I landed flat on my back with another splash. When I tried to sit up, I succeeded only in further self-saturation. I was like a milk-soaked turtle stuck on its back. So, I just lay there. I was embarrassed, but when my brain did a quick limbs diagnostics test, I realized that I wasn't hurt. Not physically anyway. That's when I heard the pop. It sounded like a suction cup being forcefully pulled off a flat surface. It was the bladder, having been held up there by the nozzle, a sticky surface, magic, whatever, coming unstuck off the top of the machine. It landed directly on my head, where it poured the remainder of its contents onto my face with a *glug, glug, glug.*

In the stillness of my humiliation, I could hear Jane's voice down the hallway. She was still on the phone. She didn't know! I jumped up, slipped again, my feet running in place like they were on ice, but caught myself by grabbing ahold of the concession stand counter. I walked to the door, bowlegged to stay upright on the soaked floor, and peeked out to see if anyone else was around. They weren't. I whisper-shouted, "Julio, get your ass in here!" He jogged in, and I shut the door and locked it. "Have at it, cat, but be quiet."

I connected a hose, and while he licked, I sprayed and squee-geed as silently as I could, washing the milk mix off the wall, the machine, and the floor. Then I turned that hose on myself. Convinced I had rinsed off all the now-coagulating gunk, I once again glanced out the door, and when the coast was clear, I tiptoe-sprinted out into the concourse and hung a hard left into the home clubhouse. Amazingly, no one was there. I pulled off all my wet clothes, threw them into the dryer, and turned the settings to the highest-possible level of heat. This wouldn't take long. I couldn't believe it. I was pulling this off! No one would ever know! I ran through the team shower, washed the cream out of my hair, and quickly returned to the laundry area. All the towels were either in the dirty clothes hamper or wet in the washer, so I just stood there, impatiently staring at the dryer while my body air-dried.

"Glasses, you okay?"

I turned around and covered up. It was Jack Lamabe. My glasses were the only thing I had on. After a lifetime of seeing naked dudes in clubhouses, Tomatoes could sense that this time was per-haps a little different.

"Hey, Jack. I'm okay. I had a big Dairy Queen accident. Don't tell anyone."

"All right. Glad you're okay. But you need to know this looks really f—ked up. See you after the game."

Jack Lamabe always saw us after the game, because a stop by his locker was always on the in-game to-do list for the concessions intern. Only, this task was never written down on any list, because we weren't supposed to be doing it. I am speaking of his nightly beer delivery. A six-pack of Miller Light, packed in ice, sitting in his locker, and waiting on him after the game. After every game. Wonder why his face was always so red?

These days, Asheville is proudly known as Beer City, a title it first earned in a national competition in 2009 and has successfully defended nearly every year since. More than one hundred different beers are brewed in town, and tourists with a lowercase *t* now travel to Asheville specifically to cash in their vacation days so they can try as many of those beers as possible. The city's hop into hops began that same summer, 1994, when a retired nuclear waste engineer named Oscar Wong moved to Asheville from Charlotte and opened the Highland Brewing Company in the basement of a local taproom. We'd heard about the new outfit but thought little of it because, well, it was 1994, man. Back then a "microbrew" was something that hippies cooked in their garages next to their VW vans. If you had dropped the term "craft beer," people would have thought you were talking about cheese with beer in it—you know, "Kraft beer."

Now McCormick Field prides itself on the variety of its beer selection. They bring in celebrity brewers, those who have followed in Wong's footsteps, and rotate local tastes through the ballpark taps, including a skybox-ish beer lounge that now occupies what used to be the front-office lobby. Fans stand on the Vatican Porch and sip locally concocted IPAs and pale ales. Hipsters and millennials look down their noses at anyone who orders up a domestic big-brand can of suds.

But in '94, that is exactly what the people wanted. That's why we served a grand total of six brands of brewskis. Your first five choices were Budweiser, Bud Light, Miller Lite, Miller Genuine Draft, and Coors Light. The only reason Coors Light had been added to the list was because the Colorado Rockies, partially owned by the Coors Brewing Company, had insisted on it. The most exotic beer on tap was the sixth one, Killian's Red, an Irish "original recipe" that was also distributed by Coors. People bought Killian's only when we'd run out of everything else.

All due respect to the other flavors, if we had just served Budweiser and Bud Light, everything would have felt no different.

That's what the good people of Asheville wanted to drink, the pilsner with the Clydesdales and the frog ads and Spuds MacKenzie and Harry Caray. The sponsor on Kenny Schrader's NASCAR Winston Cup stock car and Kenny Bernstein's 300-mph NHRA Top Fuel dragster and the posters of the girls in the bikinis that looked like a Budweiser bottle label . . . you know, the by-God King of Beers! That's all Tourists fans really wanted. Heck, even the guy who delivered the beer to the ballpark was known only as the Bud Man, even if he was delivering one of those other brands. The Bud Man would roll his semi up to the front gate once a week, hit the horn, and announce, "The Bud Man is here!" as he rolled the first of many hand trucks stacked with kegs into the ballpark. For every keg of one of those other brands, there were six of Budweiser.

I knew that ratio firsthand and all too well. So did Carlton and Swish. Especially every Thirsty Thursday. Our first hand and second hand and every finger on both those hands knew it, too. Because every Thursday home game we were slinging and sliding kegs around in the beer cooler like we were contestants on *The World's Strongest Man* on ESPN at three a.m. My issue was that I wasn't even the strongest man in my apartment, let alone the front office, or anywhere else in the ballpark.

On Thirsty Thursdays, fans could purchase a beer for a buck. Any beer. It was the most bizarre ballpark experience you could hope to see, because the game would almost always be a sellout or close to it, but almost none of those people ever watched that game. The seating bowl up top would be largely empty and downright quiet, like a serene Sunday day game. Meanwhile, the courtyard down below was standing room only and so loud with conversation that only occasionally might you accidentally hear sounds of the game or Sam Zurich's baritone announcements from upstairs. The line at the concession stands was never-ending. Fans were limited to two beers per purchase, so that's how they bought them. They would buy their two beers, then return to the back of the line. They'd two-fist their drinks as they socialized with their friends who stood with them. They were in no hurry as that line loitered along, timing out their drinking so that they had finished both beers just as they made it back up to the counter to order two more. Line, buy, drink, line, buy, drink . . . from the time the gates opened at six p.m. until alcohol sales ended with the final out of the seventh inning, an announcement that always elicited a mix of angry groans and panicked scrambling among the couple of thousand people who'd been camped out in the courtyard all night. We had a handful of local colleges—UNC-A, Western Carolina University, and Mars Hill College—that supplied most of our beer-guzzling customers in the spring. Groups of Western Carolina students, traveling in from Cullowhee, North Carolina, an hour away, would hire bus companies to bring them in sober for the game and haul them out drunk later that night. During the summer we had all the college students who were home from school and didn't want to hang out with their parents. We were both a cool Asheville brewery and a proven dating app long before either one of those was even a thing.

On any other game night, the concessions intern would pop into the beer cooler only a couple of times. Whichever of us was on duty would receive word from our beer stand workers—the two-woman, Atlanta Braves–obsessed machine of Linda and Pam—that they were running low on something, usually Budweiser, or that they had too much foam coming through one of the lines, usually the Coors Light. They needed us to either change out kegs or adjust one of the pressurized air tanks that were used to push the brews through the spaghetti pile of clear tubes that carried it to their taps on the other side of the wall.

But on Thirsty Thursday, there was no leaving that room. It was a solid cinder-block and aluminum box that was kept chilled just above freezing. Those kegs and air tanks were everywhere. Luckily for me, Carlton had already been there and come up with a system. Full kegs stayed spread out on the floor in one corner waiting to be tapped. The six kegs in use lined the wall where the hoses and taps were hung. Then the empties were stacked as high as possible in the back corners of the room. He'd even put a clipboard in there to keep track of it all. It was foolproof . . . as long as the fool in that room was physically capable of doing it. Carlton was built like a fullback. Dude was solid as a rock and strong as an ox. Swish was tall and ripped, and that gave him leverage and strength. They'd also had a much different college experience than me. Carlton had partied with his pals, and Swish had been on fraternity row, where they both had received plenty of keg-tapping practice. Me? I'd been hanging out at the Baptist Student Union. They didn't serve a lot of Killian's Red at the BSU. Also, I was built like Woody from *Toy Story*. I weighed 135 pounds. An aluminum keg full of beer weighs 165 pounds. Those dudes could throw them around like medicine balls. My technique had to be more nuanced, like a slide puzzle. So, the first thing I would do was throw a cup of hot water onto the center of the floor, just enough to get it slick and provide the lubrication I needed to slide those kegs around. I would wear a pair of old Sperry Top-Sider shoes, the preppy rubber-soled footwear originally made to keep rich people from slipping off the wet deck of their yachts. When I came striding in to work on Thursdays with those kicks on, a total mismatch with my At-Bat Food Services T-shirt and gym shorts, one of our season-ticket holders would always shout down at me in his best snobby *Caddyshack* snark, "Ahoy, polloi! Spaulding, get your foot off the boat!"

For three hours every Thursday, it was like the world's drunkest version of Donkey Kong. I had aluminum barrels coming at me all night. The radio would crackle, *click*. "Change out Bud Light!" "Getting low on MGD!" "The Budweiser is too foamy!" Unhook a tap . . . slide the empty keg to the left where it hit the other empties with a *GONG* . . . grab a full keg by the handles with both hands, bend your knees, and jerk it across the floor and against the wall with a thud . . . regrab the tap . . . slam it down hard enough to pop it into the top of the keg . . . turn your head away from that keg to avoid the requisite explosion of air, foam, and beer . . . twist the tap until it clicked into place . . . wait and see if it started flowing through the tube . . . adjust the air flow accordingly. Repeat.

Click. "That didn't work! It's still too foamy! And now we're out of Miller Lite, too!"

My sliding technique led to a lot of knuckle injuries as fingers were smashed between clacking metal containers, but it also worked. In the beginning. During the early innings, the kegs were all on the floor. But as we rolled through product, the stacking had to begin. I suppose I should have asked for help, but again, twentysomething pride and all that, so instead I chose to climb atop the first level of empty kegs, each foot atop a different barrel, reaching down to grab another, and then yanking it up off the floor to stack it on the others. What was I thinking, right? Making matters worse, once enough beer residue had been sprayed all over the place via my shoddy tap-connection capabilities, that floor got sticky, and dragging kegs across it became more difficult. Now my Top-Siders were a little too grippy. Ahoy polloi indeed.

The greatest sound one could ever hear was Jane sticking her head into the cooler and saying, "Eighth inning just started, you're done." Then she would give me the up-down look, my hair sticking up, my clothes soaked, my glasses coated in a fine sheen of American lager mist residue, and my knuckles bleeding, though I didn't realize that because they were also frozen. "You look good. Wring out that shirt into a cup and we can sell another beer."

I manned that cooler for a total of three Thirsty Thursdays. Most of the drinks consumed on those nights were the one-dollar, twelve-ounce size. According to the clipboard, my personal record was fifty-two kegs changed. That's 8,580 beers sold. In three and a half hours. That was nothing. Carlton's personal best that summer was sixty-two. Jane, when asked now, recalls one night when they went through sixty-six kegs. That's the equivalent of 10,890 cans of beer.

When I would emerge from the McCormick Field beer cooler as Thirsty Thursday wound down, the scene I saw was much like I have always imagined for someone who had locked themselves into a fallout shelter at the start of a nuclear war and then finally stepped back out into the world to see what was left. I don't ever remember seeing a lot of fights or belligerence. It always felt more like an evacuation. I don't know how many cab companies there were in Asheville, at the time a town of only 148,000 people. But every single one of those cabs would be lined up at 10 Buchanan Place, waiting to transport the overserved back to their homes. By 10:30 p.m., the last of them would have finally stumbled off into the night, hardly a one having watched so much as one at-bat of baseball.

"C'mon and walk me up," Jane would say as I rubbed my eyes, adjusting to the outside light after a night under a fluorescent bulb in a cold cave. Her mental spreadsheet had been in overdrive for nine innings, plus the one-hour pregame. I handed her my sheet from the clipboard cooler, and she added it to other tallies kept in all the concession stands that night. She had collected that data as well as all the cash from all the registers and had it all zipped up in a padlocked canvas bank bag. In 1994 people tended to use mostly cash—not credit or debit cards—and there was no Apple Pay. Now she walked that bag to Carolyn, who was waiting in her office, watching *The People's Court,* and hammering on her adding machine like she was Ichabod Crane. The concern was that some sort of drunk Billy the Kid type might come popping up from behind the soft pretzel stand to hold Jane up and take that money as she made the hundred-yard walk up to the front office.

She needed an escort. I'd thought it was a bit much. Besides, after a night of slinging kegs and busted knuckles, what was I going to do? Run the assailant off with my body odor?

Later, Ron explained to me the roots of his escort patrol idea. He said that during his earliest days on the job, when the crowds were still rough, more than a couple of times a would-be John Dillinger would be hanging about concessions, casing the hot dog stands with an eye on strong-arming some poor kid who had unknowingly shown his hand by counting the postgame money out in the open. Sometimes that kid was one of Ron's kids.

"This guy had waited all night, and when he made his move for the big heist, I was standing right there waiting on him," Ron told me. "I asked him his name, and he said it was Tom, or something like that. I said, 'Tom, you ever heard of Helen's Bridge?'" Ron said he pointed toward left field and informed the man that just on the other side of that mountain was an old stone bridge from which a woman named Helen had hanged herself a hundred years ago, and now people claimed that her ghost still haunted that bridge. "Tom," Ron said he told the criminal mastermind, "if you try to take this money, then we're going to rename that bridge 'Helen and Tom's Bridge,' you understand me?"

Tom was never seen at McCormick Field again.

On the way back down to continue the postgame concessions cleanup, I stepped into the clubhouse to make sure that the coaches were okay. Really, it was just to make sure that Jack had gotten his Miller Lite. I stuck my head around the corner and asked, "You guys good?"

Tomatoes, pants around his ankles, held up a can, nodded, and gave me a thumbs-up. "All good here. Thanks. By the way, you look a helluva lot better with your clothes on."

MICHAEL, O.J., AND SORRY, MR. WOLFE, BUT YOU CAN COME HOME AGAIN

In the summer of 1994, the biggest star in baseball—be it minor league, big league, whatever league—wasn't a baseball player at all. At least he hadn't been prior to 1994, and he never was again after that season ended.

Quick reminder, the story and spectacle of Michael Jordan on the baseball diamond overshadowed everything else in the sport that season. That was especially true during the spring and early summer, those pages of the calendar when baseball had usually eased to the forefront of the American sports landscape, dominating the dog days between the end of NCAA March Madness and the start of football season. The only person who'd had the ability to slow that early summertime momentum was Jordan, as he earned three consecutive NBA championships in 1991–93. But in '94, MJ wasn't a Chicago Bulls superstar, he was a Chicago White Sox minor-league prospect. A Birmingham Baron, riding the bus in the Class AA Southern League, not on his way to face the Lakers, Knicks, or Pistons, but the Huntsville Stars, Memphis Chicks, and Orlando Suns.

Jordan baseball updates took over every space of consciousness where baseball existed, from *SportsCenter* highlights to the scoreboard section of every sports page. The people of America were sick and tired of hearing about collective bargaining and revenue sharing. Their patience had run out listening to millionaire players and billionaire team owners babbling on about salary caps and reserve clauses and blah blah blah. So, in search of baseball simplicity, they turned their attention to what had started the season as a joke but had increasingly become a source of what MLB seemed to have lost the ability to produce. Fun. What was more fun than a basketball player—*the* basketball player—walking away from a $4 million NBA salary (which, at the time, was astronomical) to take his cuts in the bus leagues?

We had indeed sold out the reserved seats for our nine home games against our league's White Sox affiliate, the Hickory Crawdads, and we'd done it nearly before the season had started. The people of Asheville still held out hope that perhaps an injury or a bad batting average would have His Airness sent down from Birmingham and he would be in a Crawdad uniform in time for our first Hickory series in mid-June, or by their last two visits, scheduled for the season's final full month in August. That never happened. Michael never played an inning for Hickory. But that didn't prevent the Crawdads' front office from including him in their game program (*Bats: Right, Throws: Right, Home: Highland Park, IL*) and dedicating a third of a page in their media guide to his lengthy bio (*"in 1975 was named 'Mr. Baseball' for North Carolina's 12-year-old boys in the Dixie Youth Association"*).

The Jordan Effect even sold merchandise in our Bear Wear store. We carried a handful of Birmingham Barons caps (the Crawdads had a wall of them), and they sold quickly. It also cost me money in that store. During my time in the work rotation as ticket intern, part of the gig was manning the cash register at the shop that was located next door to the box office. The sale counter where we sat was a glass case that had baseball cards for sale and on display. Every single day they taunted me. No, not the Tourists team sets with my Ted E. card. The voices of temptation that I heard emanated from the sealed foil packs of the official national Minor League Baseball cards, a collection of only the best and brightest big-league prospects, produced by Upper Deck. With my $100-a-week paycheck I certainly did not have the disposable income to be purchasing those cards at five bucks a pop. But staring through the glass at the shimmering gold wrappers, all I could think was, "Man, if that Jordan card is in there, then I could sell it for way more than the price of a few packs of cards!"

I think I opened five packs before I gave up . . . on the first day. I opened a few more the next day. That's when my buyer's remorse panic set in. Fun fact: Did you know that you can use an Elmer's glue stick from a ballpark ticket-office drawer to reseal golden-foil baseball card packaging? Well, you can. But only if you are really, super careful how you opened that foil in the first place, pulling apart each side of the pack like a sloth opening a bamboo stalk. I figured out how to do that around pack number five. I wound up opening and resealing about thirty packs that summer. I still don't have a Jordan card.

However, I did see Jordan play. On Tuesday, April 26, 1994, the Tourists were on their second road trip of the season, down the mountain to face the Spartanburg Phillies. I had graduated high school in nearby Greenville, South Carolina. Until I went to work for the Tourists, the ballpark where I had attended the most minor-league games was Greenville Municipal Stadium, an open-air semicircle facility draped in billboards and parking lots that was home to what was, at that point, arguably the most successful MiLB franchise of the decade. The Greenville Braves were the Southern League affiliate of the Atlanta Braves, the team that owned the hearts of the entire southeastern United States, who were on TV every single night thanks to the TBS Superstation cable juggernaut, and played their home games only a couple of hours down I-85, the same route I'd traveled in my busted

Pontiac. An overwhelming number of the players in Atlanta who had become MLB postseason regulars and went on to win the 1995 World Series had played for the team lovingly known as the G-Braves, from sluggers Javy López and Chipper Jones to pitchers Steve Avery and Mark Wohlers. The 1992 Greenville Braves are still considered one of the greatest MiLB teams ever assembled, posting a record of 100-43 and sending eleven players to The Show.

But Greenville Municipal Stadium had never seen anything like the Michael Jordan road show. Neither had I. Even now, nothing has ever come close, and as of the writing of this book, I've been to nearly 130 minor-league ballparks.

It began like this: A friend of mine called and said he had a ticket for that night's game between the G-Braves and the Barons if I wanted it. I literally ran to my car and took off down the highway to make the eighty-minute drive to Greenville. I got there forty-five minutes before the first pitch, and the place was an absolute madhouse, a science experiment in overstimulation. My seat was down the third baseline, between the Barons dugout and the visitors' clubhouse, a locker room in a building that sat all the way down that line, just left of left field. Greenville Municipal was standing room only, a capacity crowd of seven thousand people, even on a spring Tuesday school night. The noise was constant, a loud buzz that rode right on the tipping point of cracking into a roar at any moment. It was like sitting inside an idling leaf blower.

Whenever a ballplayer would turn the corner, appearing in left field, and start walking toward the dugout, that crowd would lose their collective sanity. The shouts would last a few seconds, just long enough for everyone to realize that it was the wrong Birming-ham Baron, some dude they'd never heard of, and the screams would decompose into a chorus of groans. The season was only a few weeks old, so Jordan's teammates weren't yet used to the furor that followed him wherever he went. But his manager was the unflappable Terry Francona, a former college baseball national player of the year who'd played five years in the minors and a decade in the majors. He was at the very beginning of a coaching career that would eventually lead to a couple of World Series rings with the Red Sox. Francona was not rattled by Jordan Mania. He was amazed by it. He had fun with it. When his arrival in left field had disappointed the Greenville crowd, he paused along the third baseline and took a Broadway bow, laughing.

A few minutes later, Jordan appeared. I never saw the Beatles in concert, but I have taken my daughter to see the Jonas Brothers and Harry Styles. The screams that night in Greenville, South Carolina, made those arenas full of teenage girls feel like a lullaby. This had to be what it was like when the Fab Four played Shea Stadium. It never stopped. Up the road in Asheville, we had our one writer, one visiting radio guy, and one TV camera, maybe. By my count that night, there were seven TV cameras and at least that many sportswriters and photographers on the field before the game. I even saw Peter Gammons from ESPN. When I talked to Birmingham Barons play-by-play man Curt Bloom (remember him, the only one who wrote me back from my initial one hundred letters looking for work?), he told me that *Sports Illustrated*, the *New York Times, USA Today,* and the *Chicago Tribune* were all there. In Greenville, South Carolina, for a Class AA baseball game.

What I remember most are the camera flashes. They popped like strobe lights all over the stadium whenever No. 45 came into view, whether he was warming up, patrolling the outfield, or standing on deck, and especially when he was at the plate with a bat in his hand. I honestly don't know how Jordan made any contact at all when trying to hit during night games like this one, simply because of those flashes. They were blinding. The umpire cupped his hands around his facemask so he could see the pitches coming in.

A woman next to me, dressed in a UNC Tarheels T-shirt and Chicago Bulls shorts, collapsed into her husband's arms. More accurately, his arm. He'd caught her with one hand while he used the other to hold aloft a disposable Kodak camera, frantically snapping away. I am fully certain that when he had those photos developed, they were all blurry images of the back of the head of the very large man standing in front of him wearing a No. 23 Bulls jersey.

But in his opening at-bat, amid the flashes, screams, and all, Jordan drove the first pitch he saw from starter Steve Olsen through the hole in the left side of the infield for a single. Mayhem. One guy started running up and down the aisle by our section, wildly waving his hands in the air, flapping them about over his head like Kermit the Frog. I think he might have even been speaking in tongues. If he wasn't then, he certainly was two pitches later, when Jordan broke for second. He was attempting a steal! It looked weird. After all, he is six foot six and at the time still had his super-lean, first-half-of-his-hoops-career body. So, when he took off running through an infield full of guys who stood half a foot shorter than he was and were all built of much stockier frames than his, Earth's greatest athlete looked downright gangly, like a giraffe galloping over the dirt.

He was thrown out. It wasn't close. The crowd did not care. Those South Carolinians booed as if someone had just announced that the team was changing its name to the Greenville Communists. "Damn," the guy sitting behind me in his No. 3 Dale Murphy Atlanta Braves jersey said, "I believe these people have forgotten who the home team is."

Jordan came back to the plate in the fourth and drew a walk. This time he successfully stole second. As a result, the crowd became so unhinged that a kid on our row covered his ears, started crying, and his mother had to take him out into the parking lot to calm him down.

The rest of MJ's night was not great. He badly misplayed a long fly ball in right field that got over his head, ricocheted off the wall, and resulted in a triple that led to what became the winning run. He also whiffed badly in his third at-bat, looking overmatched and more than a little twisted up as he continued to sort through the controversial weight-shifting, pendulum-ish batting style preached by White Sox hitting coach Walt Hriniak. And if the Greenville Municipal Stadium crowd had sounded disappointed when Jordan was thrown out earlier at second base, it grew to a whole new level when Jordan was stuck standing on deck in the ninth as the game's final out was recorded, denied one more at-bat. Final score: Greenville Braves 4, Birmingham Jordans 3. I've never seen a home crowd more irritated that their team won.

Michael's final line: 1-for-2, with a single, two walks, a stolen base, a caught stealing, and he also extended his hitting streak to thirteen games. His batting average after three weeks was .327. By season's end that had dropped to .202. The following March, he was not at White Sox spring training. Major League Baseball was on strike, and he was back in the NBA. In 1993, the Birmingham Barons had drawn 277,098 fans to their seventy-one home games. In 1994, with No. 45 in right field, they drew 467,867.

The morning after the game, the entire Asheville Tourists staff cornered me with questions about the Michael experience. When I described it to them the same way I just described it to you, Ron chuckled and said, "I'm not sure if we didn't dodge a bullet by not having to deal with that circus."

As it turned out, we did have a circus to deal with, Asheville style. Our version of the baseball big top was erected two months later, on June 16, 1994, coincidentally against the Michael-less Hickory Crawdads. Our superstar interloper was Darren Holmes, the reigning closer for our parent Colorado Rockies. In 1993, Holmes had recorded twenty-five saves, ranked tenth in the National League, despite doing his work in the pitcher's nightmare that is the mile-high thin air of Denver. But he'd struggled with injuries in '94, and when the Rockies asked him which of their minor-league teams he wished to work with as he rehabbed, the righty they called "Holmie" asked to go home. That was Asheville, where he was and shall forever be a baseball legend for his four-sport heroics at T.C. Roberson High, where he was offered a scholarship to pitch for the UNC Tar Heels, but instead signed with the Los Angeles Dodgers, who traded him to the Milwaukee Brewers, who lost him to the Rockies in the 1992 expansion draft.

Darren Holmes arrived in Asheville on Monday night, and according to the *Citizen-Times* and its Macaulay Culkin–esque tracking of his whereabouts, the hurler dined at Outback Steakhouse so he could see the beginning of that night's game between his Rockies and the Braves on TV and then went to his grandparents' house to watch the rest of it. "They only wanted me to throw a few innings, just to see if I was healed up correctly, and wanted to send me all the way back Colorado Springs to do it," he recalled when I tracked him down in spring 2022, waiting to start his third season as a pitching coach with the Baltimore Orioles, but like when he was a player in '94, a labor dispute was messing with his plans. "But it had always bothered me that I had never gotten to pitch at McCormick Field. I grew up going there so much. I was supposed to have pitched there during high school. We had a big tournament, and I was scheduled to pitch the first game, but then it rained all week and we never played. Now I had my chance. So I said to the Rockies, hey, we're on the East Coast right now and Asheville is close by, just let me go home and see my family and friends."

What Holmes found was that he had a lot more family and friends than he'd remembered. Funny what twenty-five big-league saves can do to a man's family tree.

On Tuesday, June 14, he showed up at McCormick Field bright, early, and stoked. I was mopping some sort of mystery stain off the concrete just outside the home clubhouse when I heard a husky mountain man's voice say, "That's gross." I looked up from my bucket of dirty water to see the unmistakable goatee of a 1990s relief pitcher. He was pointing at Julio the Cat, who was watching me mop as he ate a dead bird. "Is that your cat? He's staring at you like he's your cat."

I wanted to tell Darren Holmes that he was one of the relievers on my rotisserie baseball team (y'all call it fantasy now). I wanted to tell him that Carlton had told me a few minutes earlier that the box office phone was ringing off the hook with people wanting to know not if Michael Jordan was coming to town this week, but if "Darren Freaking Holmes, hell, man, I went to high school with him!" was coming back to pitch. I wanted to say a lot to Darren Freaking Holmes. But what I actually blurted out was, "Naw, man, that cat belongs to no one. But he's cool. His name is Julio. My name is Ryan. Your name is Darren Holmes. The Holmes, er, *home* clubhouse is through that door right there."

"Thanks. Do I give this to you?" He handed me a list of names. It was his guest-pass list. Per the rules handed out to Tourists players by Ron when they first arrived in Asheville, each member of the team was permitted to request free general admission seats for guests, as long as "this privilege not be abused . . . please limit tickets and refrain from having tickets for the same people every night." In other words, we didn't care if you left seats for your parents or your girlfriend most nights, just not all seventy-one nights. We also didn't want to see a section jammed full of a guy's fraternity brothers for an entire homestand. And we really didn't want to have to referee any fights between women who believed that the guy who had left them tickets that night did so because they were his one-and-only but had realized that they were all part of his two-and-many.

Players were told to write up their pass lists and turn them in by 5:30 p.m., a half hour before the gates opened. But the red flag always went up like a hurricane warning when a player would deviate from that simple task, instead approaching you, pulling you aside, eyes shifty, and starting off with something like, "Hey, man, how've you been? You've been working hard. How about this rain? You know, I've been meaning to ask you, why haven't we hung out more?" Literally the first time he'd asked about you all season. Early in the year, I would play along. By mid-June, after two months of slinging kegs and eating leftover concessions, I'd just cut him off and say, "Who are they, and where do they need to sit?"

That's when you'd get the whole "Well, you know, man, I'm engaged and she's great and she's going to be here for this home-stand. But I also haven't seen her since winter because she's been in school back home, and well, a guy has needs, amirite? So, well, you know the girl I've been leaving tickets for all summer, that waitress from Bennigan's who always wears the cutoff jean shorts with the shiny red tube top? Well, that's not my fiancée."

This was when you'd want to say sarcastically, "Really? I can't believe it! None of us had already figured that out!" But instead, you replied, "Wow, okay, what can I do to help?"

He would want to leave a ticket for both, but he would also want to make sure that those tickets were in different sections of the ballpark, like way down each baseline. If the guy had been nice, you made it happen and wished him luck in his real-life, double-booked, nine-inning sitcom episode. However, if that player had been a jerk to you all summer, or if you were friends with that waitress from Bennigan's and she was super sweet and genuinely thought this Tourist was going to be her ticket out of town and into a better life, well, then you totally made sure both girls were seated in the same section. Then you'd sit back and hope he would hit a homer or make a big play so they would both jump up and simultaneously scream something like, "Great job, baby!" or "That's my man!" and then proceed to throw down like the Gorgeous Ladies of Wrestling . . . and he would go from too many girlfriends to zero girlfriends.

That's why there were rules when it came to the pass list, and those rules applied to everyone, even us. Unless you were Darren Holmes. He was a big deal, and heck, he was going to be in town for only a few days at the most. Unfortunately, the rain that kept him from pitching at McCormick Field during high school followed him back to the ballpark as a big leaguer. He was slated to come out of the bullpen on Tuesday night, his first game in uniform. But the game started in a drizzle that, by the middle innings, had become a steady shower. We pulled the tarp, and the crowd of 2,714, a great showing for a monsoon, booed lustily. During the ninety-minute rain delay, I ran up to the office to grab a dry shirt. Ron was bunkered in behind his desk with the Weather Channel blaring and was on the phone with both the Asheville airport and the meteorologists at Channel 13, anyone who had eyes on any sort of forecasting data.

"There's a window coming! Everyone with a radar is telling me that there's a window coming!" he shouted to us, and then ran out onto the Vatican Porch so that he could repeat it at an even higher volume down to the Tourists bullpen, where Jack Lamabe and Darren Holmes were huddled under the corrugated-metal roof swapping stories about The Show. "Be ready, Holmes! There's a window coming!"

That window never opened. Our umpires that night, both in their second Sally League season, which is like being a fifteen-year veteran in Class A years, called it a game. The crowd bellowed as they watched Darren Holmes make the walk down the first baseline under an umbrella with Lamabe. Suddenly, the gate located at the halfway point of that stroll swung open. Ron McKee was on the move and had a head of steam. He was in his blue polyester snap-buttoned coaching shorts, red "TARP CREW" T-shirt, and white sneakers with even whiter tube socks pulled up to his knees. He had broken out into a sprint. He looked like an All-American bowling ball, and his target was the two umpires before they could make it into the relative safety of their walk-in closet of a locker room.

"There's a damn window coming!"

"Ron, look at this field. It's unplayable. There's water standing in the outfield."

"It's not unplayable! We have drains out there! That clears in thirty goddamn seconds! Y'all just want to go to the hotel!"

"We don't. We want to play ball. But we can't play ball. We'll play two tomorrow."

"Two tomorrow?! Two tomorrow?! I have three thousand people here right now to see this next pitch, but you want to go to the damn hotel?!"

Those people, soaked to the bone but very quiet, could hear every word coming out of Ron's mouth, and their booing started transitioning into cheers of support for the man who, they now were beginning to realize, was out there fighting . . . yes . . . for them! Lee Tillery said you could hear every word all the way up in the press box. Ron McKee wasn't stupid. He was a promoter. This was a performance. He knew there was no chance of the game resuming. That was never the point. The citizens of Asheville had come to see their hometown hero pitch, and that wasn't going to happen. So, Ron took up that hero mantle in the meantime. He emphatically threw both hands out in their direction.

"These people paid to see nine f—ing innings of f—ing baseball!"

"Ron . . ."

"I'm calling Kings Mountain right f—ing now!" (That's where the Sally League was headquartered, Kings Mountain, North Carolina.)

"Ron . . . you need to stop . . ."

"No, you need to stop, you stupid motherf—ers!"

Okay, so the rule here has always been clear. You can't make it personal. Everyone should know this. It was explained by Susan Sarandon in *Bull Durham*. I am the son of a career college foot-ball referee who was cussed at by everyone from Joe Paterno to an angry grandma at a red light still livid about a pass-interference flag from the night before. So, I can verify that what Sarandon's Annie Savoy explains to protégée Millie (the movie's version of our girl in the red tube top) is perfectly accurate, if not downright eloquent. Sports officials are probably not going to throw you out of a game if you F-bomb them about a stupid f'ing call that they made on the field. But as soon as "that was a stupid f—ing call" turns into "you are the stupidest f—ing person I've ever seen," then you are going to be penalized, ejected, or both. Standing in the rain in front of his living room guests, Ron McKee was mak-ing it *so* personal. Alas, he was indeed thrown out of the game. Granted, the game was already over, but just as Ron's tantrum was performance art in search of making a point, so was the umpire's dramatically oversold tossing of Ron from his own saturated ball-field, complete with a windup, hop, "You're outta here!!" and a big thumb jerked toward the showers.

A little while later, as my list of job duties demanded, I deliv-ered a box of burgers and a couple of drinks to the umpires' locker room, even though Ron had told me not to, hollering, "Let them starve!" We always think of umps as older, gray-haired, heavyset guys. But these two weren't much older than me, if they even were older than me, and both were in such great shape they looked like they could have been wearing a baseball uniform instead of a blue ump's shirt. One of them said to me, "You saw that field, there was no way they could have played, right?" When I said I didn't know, because, gee, guys, I was "just the concessions intern," they asked if I could point them in the direction of the head groundskeeper to talk about it. I told them that wasn't possible. They asked, "Why the hell not?" I said, "It's Tuesday night." When they irritatingly reacted by demanding to know what that had to do with anything, I replied, "Because Grady Gardner goes line dancing on Tuesday nights."

There were no arguments about the decision to call off the following evening's Wednesday-night matchup with Hickory. It had rained all day. So now Thursday became the double-header, beginning at 6:30 p.m. A Thirsty Thursday double-header with a packed house and the local hero on the mound? Yikes. Holmes started the first game, and it was the first time we opened a Thursday contest without an endless line of soon-to-be-drunks already stacked a dozen deep and two-fisting beers before the first pitch was thrown. Everyone was in their seats. They wanted to see Holmes. I snuck up the stairs and watched his first inning through the railing as I crouched in the stairwell. He gave up a hit early but struck out two of the three batters he faced. I missed his second inning of work, when he whiffed all three hitters on barely a dozen pitches but could hear the sellout crowd of 4,112 whooping and stomping the concrete overhead as I slid kegs around the beer cooler.

Between games I walked back upstairs to breathe some nonalcoholic air. Holmes was doing his best Shelley Fabares, sitting in the stands as a conga line of locals waited to get his autograph on various and sundry items, and to chat. The more I watched, the more I realized that the chats were way more important to them than the signatures.

> "Holmes, dude, I watch you strike out David Justice and Jeff Bagwell on TV every night and I'm like, 'Well, he couldn't strike my ass out in high school!'"

> "You remember me? I'm the guy you knocked out cold in that football game down there at Reynolds that night. I still have a scar. That was awesome."

"Hey, Darren, man, we're cousins. For real. Your mom
and my aunt are third cousins, so that makes us fourth'ns,
I think."

"That was the best part, just talking to everyone and catching up," Holmes said as he reminisced with me nearly three decades later. "Everyone was so nice, but yeah, I had no idea I had that many cousins, right? It was just great being home again. You get into the middle of a season and your team is in Denver, so far away, and it's going to be October before you see everybody again. But then, because you're hurt, you can go home again."

The significance of a famous Asheville native son using those very words, it wasn't lost on me. Not in 1994 and certainly not now. It was another native of the town, Thomas Wolfe, who wrote the novel *You Can't Go Home Again,* a posthumously published cautionary tale about a writer who moves to New York and finds literary fame and fortune after penning a book based on his childhood experiences, only to discover that the people of his real hometown recognized themselves in the thinly veiled novel and angrily refused to welcome him home. That book was based on Wolfe's own experience, when he wrote his seminal 1929 American novel *Look Homeward, Angel,* about a young man's upbringing in a small North Carolina town. Today, the home where Wolfe grew up is a museum and library of his life and work. The people of Asheville absolutely recognized themselves in his writings, pseudonyms be damned, and no, they were not happy about the manner in which they or their town were represented to the outside world through Wolfe's chosen words. As I wrote this book, I thought about that danger more than a few times, especially as I stood on the porch of Wolfe's home and could see the lights of McCormick Field in the distance. At least he was smart enough to use all fake names.

Wolfe loved McCormick Field. As a teenager he served as a

batboy for the Tourists, when they played at McCormick's predecessor, Riverside Park, a city-park ballfield that played host to
many a textile-league and semipro game during the day, followed
by many fights between the men who'd played in those games later
that night. It was at Riverside where someone first complained
that every player on the home team was from out of town, report-
edly grousing: "Hell, these guys are nothing but a bunch of tourists." They won their first-ever league championship that summer,
so the Tourists nickname stuck.

Downtown, many of those "off city" players rented rooms
inside the labyrinth of a Victorian boardinghouse known as the
"Old Kentucky Home," a hilltop structure owned by an entre-
preneurial local named Julia Wolfe. She had eight children, and
the youngest, Ben and Thomas, lived in the boardinghouse and
worked alongside their mother as she looked after their guests,
whether they be tourists or Tourists. The boys took a liking to Jack
Corbett, the team's manager/second baseman, and would accom-
pany him to Riverside Park. Corbett would warm up for games
by tossing the ball with Thomas, while Ben climbed into the outfield scoreboard and hung the numbers marking hits and runs as
the games rolled along. Nebraska Crane, the hardball hero Wolfe
conjured up for his novels, including *You Can't Go Home Again,*
was based on Corbett. Thomas Wolfe left for college in Chapel
Hill at the age of sixteen, just as Riverside Park was wiped off the
map by a flood that ravaged the entire Asheville area. He didn't
return for twenty years, when he made the visit that brought the
side-eye looks and whispers that taught him that lesson about not
coming home again. The spot where he found solace was McCormick Field, the twelve-year-old ballpark located just a few minutes' stroll down the street from his childhood home, still operated
by Julia as a boardinghouse despite the ongoing Great Depression.
As Bob Terrell had taught us during our very first day on the job,
Wolfe wrote lovingly of McCormick Field that "he liked to sit in

the stands and smell the aroma of the timber and hear the thump of the bat against the ball."

Another tenant (sort of) of Mrs. Wolfe's also found peace at McCormick Field, serenity that by all accounts he sorely needed.

F. Scott Fitzgerald, author of *The Great Gatsby,* and wife Zelda had frequented the North Carolina mountains as vacationers and had befriended Wolfe while living and drinking among the writing circles of New York. In 1935, when Zelda needed psychiatric treatment, she was admitted to a hospital outside Asheville. Mr. Fitzgerald rented two rooms at the palatial Grove Park Inn, an awe-inspiring stonework golf resort that is still the anchor of Asheville tourism today. By then he was a freefalling former hero of the same Jazz Age that had powered the prodigious parties of the Vanderbilt family's Biltmore Estate on the southern edge of town. He used one room for writing, though that wasn't going well at the time. He used the other room for drinking and seducing other men's wives. That was going a little too well. Fitzgerald would consume as many as thirty-five beers a day, claiming it was all in an effort to wean himself off gin. From his window he could spot the prettiest female guests as they stepped out of their cars, and then he would rush down to greet them in the hotel's lavish, cavernous lobby. After one too many times of having to be picked up off the floor of his bathroom . . . or the hotel swimming pool . . . or the hotel bar . . . or the lobby . . . or the parking lot . . . or the room of an angry husband, Fitzgerald was warned by the hotel that he needed to get himselvis together, and soon. When he fired a pistol through the ceiling of his room as part of what he claimed to be a suicide attempt, he was told to get his drunken, fornicating, gun-toting self out of the Grove Park Inn.

During their meetings over the years, from New York to the Blue Ridge Mountains, Fitzgerald developed close feelings for Thomas Wolfe. He'd even told Wolfe that he believed that the Ashevillian's writing style was superior to Hemingway's. So when Fitzgerald found himself needing a place to lay his beer-soaked head, he went to his friend's childhood home to rent a room from that friend's mother. As Julia Wolfe gave F. Scott Fitzgerald a tour of her boardinghouse, she caught the winded author leaning against a porch railing, queasy and trying to steady his feet. She said to him, "I never take drunks," and so she didn't take him. Fitzgerald, once again homeless in Asheville, ambled away on Market Street, turning back to scream, "Poor Tom! Poor bastard! She's a worse peasant than my mother!"

According to Bob Terrell, on at least one occasion, Fitzgerald stumbled down that same road from downtown to McCormick Field to watch the Asheville Tourists play baseball. Thank heavens Ron McKee hadn't yet invented Thirsty Thursday. That poor concessions intern could have never kept up with all the beer that Fitzgerald would have sucked down.

We have no way of knowing if F. Scott Fitzgerald and Thomas Wolfe attended a Tourists game together, but they were both in Asheville in the summer of 1936. So, I like to believe that they did, sitting shoulder to shoulder, leaned back like John Larroquette and Edward Herrmann, hiding in the high rows of the grandstand, and discussing the headlines of the day. There is also no evidence, at least none that I can find, that Carl Sandburg, three-time Pulitzer Prize recipient and the "Poet of the People," ever stretched his legs in a McCormick Field box seat. But he lived out his final twenty-two years and penned some of his most memorable works in nearby Flat Rock, North Carolina. There's no way that he didn't bring his three daughters or his two rambunctious grandchildren up the road to watch some ball and eat a hot dog, right? He couldn't have passed up the opportunity to watch Jackie Robinson push the barriers of the very fight for racial equality that Sandburg spent his entire life studying and documenting, from the Civil War through the civil rights movement, right? Anyway, that's what I always told myself when I thought about those writers and that place. Especially when Darren Holmes, the pitcher laureate of T.C. Roberson High School, used those words "you can go home again."

Holmie was back home again for one more game. On Friday, June 17, the Tourists trotted out three pitchers who combined to one-hit the Crawdads. Snake Walls went seven innings and allowed that only hit, a double in the fifth. Holmes pitched the eighth and once again looked like a man playing among boys, facing three batters, and throwing only a dozen pitches en route to a pair of strikeouts and a perfect frame of work. When our closer, Jacob Viano, closed out the game behind the Colorado Rockies closer, the 4–1 win was in the books. After making a point to shake the hand of every Tourist and then coming up to the office to shake all our hands as well, Holmes was headed to Colorado Springs for two days before rejoining the big club for the remainder of the season, with no idea how long that season would last.

"I think there is definitely a strike coming," Holmes said to me between his thanks for our handling of all the craziness that surrounded his arrival. Once again, he channeled his Thomas Wolfe. "I loved coming home again, but I would rather not come home again too soon because we aren't allowed to finish the season."

Oddly enough, this final night with the Tourists had not been as crazy as the other evenings in which Holmes had pitched. It wasn't even a sellout, with a good-but-not-great Friday-night showing of just three thousand fans. Everyone knew that Holmes was scheduled to pitch, and the weather, for once, was perfect. We even had a big promotion tied to the game, a Delta Airlines trip giveaway that would award a pair of lucky fans with two round-trip seats to any destination in the continental United States. (The couple who won had full suitcases packed in their car because they thought it was some sort of "you have to go the airport and choose right now!" promotion.)

So, what was up with the slow turnstiles? The answer was given to me at that very gate as the first of our concession stand employees showed up for work that afternoon.

"Dude, the Juice is on the loose."

Lost to us at McCormick Field amid the Holmes-at-home headlines and hoopla, one simmering news story had suddenly grown into an obsession that consumed the entire nation—the brutal murder of O. J. Simpson's ex-wife and a man with whom she was talking on the front steps of her Los Angeles home. Just as our ballpark workers began arriving around five p.m. ET on June 17, LAPD Commander David Gascon was at a podium holding a press conference and uttering the now-infamous words: "The Los Angeles Police Department right now is actively searching for Mr. Simpson. . . . He is a wanted murder suspect, and we will go find him."

At six p.m., as the front gate of the ballpark was opened and we were finishing up the final touches on the concession stands, the radio in Jane's office could be heard reverberating through the catacombs as usual. But instead of the Stones, we heard the voice of Los Angeles County District Attorney Gil Garcetti, live from three thousand miles away. "Today my office filed murder charges against O. J. Simpson for the deaths of Nicole Brown Simpson and Ronald Lyle Goldman. As of this time, approximately three p.m. Pacific, nobody knows where he is."

All night long, the one-hitter played out to a soundtrack of a Hollywood thriller, an uneasy murmur could be heard in the grandstands, generated by what was happening in real time, indeed very close to Hollywood. In Gary's press box, the little TV in the corner was tuned in to the news. Clusters of fans scattered throughout the stands weren't looking at the field at all, their faces and wide eyes lit by the flickering black-and-white screens of a couple of handheld Sony Watchmen. Those TVs had been brought in by ticketholders with the purpose of keeping an eye on Game 5 of the Michael Jordan–less NBA Finals between Hakeem Olajuwon's

Houston Rockets and Patrick Ewing's New York Knicks. Instead, they were now watching . . . well, I wasn't sure exactly what they were watching. I was changing kegs and reloading the snow cone machine. Then the radio on my hip crackled. It was Gary.

Click. "Boys, we have a car chase in Los Angeles."

Thankfully, the game was a fast one. Due to the lack of hits, it lasted only an hour and fifty-seven minutes. I've never seen a baseball team run off a field that fast when there wasn't lightning involved. Throughout the night, Tourists had been vanishing from the dugout to duck into the clubhouse and grab a peek at the TV, returning to deliver O.J. updates to their teammates. As soon as the last out was recorded, they all crowded around the clubhouse television that was mounted in a corner of the ceiling, watching live images beamed from a news helicopter of a white Ford Bronco leading a motorcade of police vehicles on an excruciatingly slow pursuit around the highways of Los Angeles. No one had any idea what was going on, neither those of us standing shoulder to shoulder around a TV in western North Carolina nor even the network reporters who were openly speculating about what we were all watching.

Everyone was completely clueless except for one man, and he was standing in Carolyn McKee's office at McCormick Field, doing a much better play-by-play of the car chase than anyone on the TV news channels.

"Okay, they are probably going to take the next exit, the one past the big McDonald's that you should see on the left. . . ."

I had escorted Jane and the bank bag for its nightly delivery to Carolyn, and she, as always, had her office television on. But instead of *Judge Judy* or Oprah, she too was tuned in to the O.J. drama. Still in his uniform and cleats, a mustached man wearing a No. 18 Hickory Crawdads uniform was watching and commentating. This dude was some sort of car chase clairvoyant. Everything that he predicted would happen next, it totally happened next.

"Normally, he would take this next right, but I bet he'll go past that and turn right at the next light instead." And then the Bronco would do just that.

"The entrance to the neighborhood is coming up, but I think all the crazy fans who have come out, they have it blocked. I bet they don't know about the back entrance to the neighborhood, so they'll go there." It happened again.

I must have been gawking at him with my mouth hanging open like I was watching a Vegas magic show, because he caught me looking at him and immediately offered up a handshake. "Hi, I'm Fred Kendall."

Carolyn was totally enchanted by the athletic man in the tight pinstriped uniform and expertly manicured Tom Selleck facial hair. She all but belched out the words, "Fred here is the manager of the Crawdads, and he stopped by to pick up some meal money and also had a question about the hotel and he is also from Los Angeles, right, Fred?" She let out a little sigh, like one of those Elvis fans after Shelley Fabares had told them what it was like to make out with the King.

Kendall was indeed a southern California native, from Torrance, and of his dozen years as a big-league catcher and infielder, ten of them had been with the San Diego Padres. But, come on, millions of people live in SoCal. How in the world was Fred Kendall going full Amazing Kreskin on us as he stood in Carolyn's office, and causing her to pause her counting of the dollar bills from the Speed Pitch?

"Look! That's my house!" he explained, leaning in to get a better look at the television as the Bronco crawled through a mass of screaming looky-loos who were standing in the middle of the street, holding conflicting signs that read "Free OJ!" and "Murderer!" All of us in the rectangular office were now staring at Kendall as he continued to monitor the TV. He shrugged and explained. "Crazy, right? Yeah, O.J. lives in my neighborhood.

Well, I suppose I should probably say that he used to live in my neighborhood."

We watched the Ford pull into the driveway of the house and then watched Al "It's A.C., dammit!" Cowlings jump out of that Bronco and start pleading with the police who had them surrounded. Fred Kendall got what he needed from Carolyn and headed for the door. "We need to get back to the hotel, and I need to call home. Nice to meet you. Hope you can make it down to Hickory next week for the All-Star Game."

THE BATTLE OF HICKORY

To call the South Atlantic League All-Star Game of 1994 "a big deal" for the town of Hickory, North Carolina, would be like referring to *Star Wars* as "a hit movie" or Brad Pitt as "a nice-looking guy." No, hosting the best and brightest of the Sally League along the banks of the Catawba River wasn't merely a big deal to the people of Hickory. It was the biggest deal. Even if the game itself ended up taking a backseat to what happened the day before.

You see, the time had finally arrived. All those chess pieces had been moved around the baseball playing board throughout the summer of 1994 to get us to this moment. This stage. This show-down. A baseball beef that they still tell stories of to this day, over beverages in the darkest corners wherever the longest of longtime Sally League front-office veterans gather, from the Winter Meetings to ballpark concourses during rain delays.

Everyone remembers it differently. That's what happens when one unexpectedly witnesses history. Individual brains process overwhelming events in dissimilar ways. This is how I remember it.

The Battle of Hickory.

The Tourists, quite frankly, needed a few days off. The month of June was halfway gone, and the promise of their early summer rally had fallen flat. The champion of the season's first half in each division was guaranteed one the league's four postseason berths. We had finished fourth in the north, two games below .500, no one on the team was hitting .300, and Jamey Wright was 4-5. Our team was generic, but our attendance was booming. Over twenty-two games we'd drawn nearly forty-two thousand fans, a whopping eleven thousand more than at the same point one year earlier, averaging 1,904 per night. That's a lot of kegs tapped and nachos slathered. We interns were tired. We needed a morale boost. So, we all crammed into my Pontiac and headed east, into the foothills of Hickory, North Carolina.

All-Star games in Minor League Baseball are typically nothing more than a midseason afterthought, something for the lower levels of the sport to do while the big leagues take their long weekend to play the Midsummer Classic. But for a full week in June 1994, Hickory, North Carolina, went big. Real big. Bigger than big. I need a bigger word than "big" to express how big it was.

There was a parade, a beauty contest, a celebrity golf tournament, and a country music show starring T. Graham Brown ("I Wish I Could Hurt That Way Again") and Mark Collie ("Even the Man in the Moon is Cryin'"). There was an Early Farm Days Engine Show over at Windmill Acres and an All-Star Bass Classic fishing tournament on Lake Hickory. There were exhibition games played by the legendary King and His Court three-man softball team and a showdown between the local semipro squad, the Lenoir Oilers, and the barnstorming all-female pro baseball team known as the Colorado Silver Bullets. Before and after all the above were dinners and parties and parties and dinners, most held at the Hickory Holiday Inn with catering provided by the Woodlands Barbecue and Picking Parlor.

It was a full week of full-on Southern culture, complete with full faces of makeup, full formal attire, and oh yeah, a little bit of baseball mixed in too.

While Asheville had been home to the Tourists and professional baseball for most of the twentieth century, down east along the Appalachian foothills the 1993 arrival of the Crawdads had been the fulfillment of decades of dreaming by the people of Hickory. Even as seemingly every North Carolina town of any size had been home to a minor-league team at some point or another, no franchise had ever taken up any permanent residence in Hickory. The town's only team, the on-and-off-again Hickory Rebels, had played their last game in 1960. The truth was that the town hadn't needed baseball, or anything else for that matter, because it had tables and chairs and chests of drawers. You see, Hickory was the proud Furniture Capital of North Carolina, perpetually covered in sawdust as the hub of the state's billion-dollar furniture manufacturing and export industry.

But the 1980s were not kind to the region, as furniture manufacturing moved almost entirely overseas. Massive factories that once cranked out recliners and dining room sets now sat empty on every street corner of Catawba County, a constant unavoidable reminder of what the area had been and what it would never be again, the hearts of the town as empty as the millions of square footage of cavernous empty redbrick buildings all around it.

That sense of loss, the stripping of a region's identity, was certainly not unique to Hickory. From Lowell, Massachusetts, to the Inland Empire of southern California, the frequent moving on to greener bottom-line pastures has left so many American communities with that same feeling of abandonment. There is truly deep psychological damage done when a place has its roots forcefully cut out from underneath it by faraway CEOs and financial forecasters. Those who once worked shifts on the factory floors suddenly realize the captains of industry they used to work for never actually cared about the towns that built their empires for them, let alone the people in those towns who did the work.

But many of those once-unmoored municipalities have discovered new identities through Minor League Baseball. There are few generators of positive civic energy that can match that of a brand-new ballpark in the center of town. That's why so many of those cities sink hopeful millions of dollars into building stadiums, collective fingers crossed that it might lure a baseball team. When it does, that ballpark becomes a true community hub. There is a renewed unity among a population that wears a shared logo on their hats and T-shirts, no matter how goofy that logo might be. Finally, there is good news to talk about at the local diner, barbershop, or in the church parking lot after Sunday worship. "Hey, I saw your daughter's Girl Scout troop sing the national anthem at the game last night!" or "Did you see our team just signed Pete Rose Jr. to play first base?"

Hickory's local business leaders, eager to reignite the area, were all in on their field of dreams. The land was donated to the city, a perfect plot that overlooked the Catawba River. A huge chunk of the $4.5 million price tag was picked up by the local Pepsi bottler, Mr. L. P. Frans, so his name went over the door of the redbrick-and-concrete, five-thousand-seat facility that rose from the green hills below the Hickory airport. At a time when new minor-league ballparks were being christened around the nation summer after summer, including our own McCormick Field, L. P. Frans was the flagship. It had a postcard sunset view every night. It had room to add amenities or seats. It had parking lots for miles. Our awe of the place was topped only by our jealousy.

The first Crawdads game was held on April 16, 1993. It was a sellout. So was nearly every game played at Frans Stadium that season. They drew a South Atlantic League record-smashing 280,000 fans, almost exactly ten times the population of the town. By the middle of the '94 season the team was already ahead of that pace in advance ticket sales, thanks to the mere possibility that Michael Jordan might spend some time in Hickory. That hope was rekindled as MJ stumbled through a brutal midseason hitting slump. The locals hoped that perhaps he would even request to play there, à la Darren Holmes, because his mother lived in nearby Charlotte and was still grieving the murder of Jordan's father. But in the end, Hickory would have to settle for selling some Air Jordan gear in the team store and including His Airness's photo and bio in the Crawdads game program and media guide.

Meanwhile, the cartoonish Hickory Crawdads logo became a nationwide sensation among sports collectors. The phone rang constantly in the team's front office with merchandise orders placed by people from around the world, eager to purchase the apparel that featured the bug-like mini-crustacean that dwells in the red clay mud of the nearby rivers. Did they even know what a crawdad was? No. They just thought it was cute, and as Minor League Baseball began to boom in the 1990s, cute was king when it came to mascots.

There was no greater evidence of that fact than what we saw upon our arrival, as the staff of the Asheville Tourists rolled into L. P. Frans Stadium the day before the playing of the thirty-fifth annual South Atlantic League All-Star Game.

We had three players on the SAL's National League All-Star roster, and manager Tony Torchia had been selected as one of the bench coaches. Relief pitcher Jacob Viano was 3-0 with fifteen saves, and he was joined by first baseman Jason Smith, who'd slugged a league-best thirteen homers, and outfielder John Giudice, who was hitting a solid .291. They had been elected to those spots by the managers of the league, and though all three tried to downplay their selection, they were visibly thrilled as we drove them to the ballpark for photo day and batting practice. Among those they would be sharing the field with were future big-league All-Stars Jermaine Dye, Magglio Ordóñez, and Richie Sexson. In all, more than half of the fifty players in Hickory that weekend would go on to play in the big leagues, some for a few days, others for a decade or more.

But on this Sunday evening in 1994, they were all still no-name kids, forced to take a backseat to the Silver Bullets vs. the Lenoir Oilers and a "Legends of Baseball" exhibition game that featured a pair of Baseball Hall of Famers in Bob Feller, who was seventy-five but still pitching, and Phil "Nucksie" Niekro, who was in town as manager of the all-female Bullets. Most of the remainder of the "Legends" were older locals who had once knocked around the minor leagues, including a few who'd played for the Hickory Rebels back in the day. There were a few other notables, including pitcher-turned-congressman Jim Bunning and Minnie Minoso, a seventeen-year big leaguer who famously played in games that spanned five different decades and even more famously uttered the words that became a staple of *Saturday Night Live:* "Baseball has been very, very good to me." Minoso was eighty-two but was still somehow the life of Hickory's All-Star Game party, sent by their parent club, the Chicago White Sox, as their "director of community relations."

We settled into the L. P. Frans grandstand to take in the events and to keep an eye on our three Tourists, making sure that they were okay and where they needed to be when they needed to be there. Everything was running right on schedule.

Then, it happened. We never saw it coming, but our minds have never stopped seeing it even now all these years later. The Great Mascot Brawl of '94, or as my friend Carlton Adcock would refer to it later that night (and thus we all have ever since), the Battle of Hickory.

When I think back on it now, it unfolds like those images we all know from London during World War II. Winston Churchill hunkered down over tables in his underground War Room, sliding and moving flags and tanks around a tabletop map of Europe, watching the battles and strategies unfold before him. This was like that, only in fur and felt and on infield grass.

As the players from each team posed for pictures by the scoreboard in center field, the mascots of the South Atlantic League began to emerge one at a time from the home dugout. The MiLB mascot revolution craze had its epicenter here in Hickory. Everyone wanted to have their kind of merchandising success, especially those of us in their league. The search for the next Crawdads had sparked an inventive spirit that permeated most of the Sally League in '94. Greensboro had ditched Hornets for Bats, rolling out the design of a guy swinging a bat who looked as close to Batman as one could get without being sued by DC Comics. The Charleston, South Carolina, Rainbows were now the Riverdogs, featuring a mutt munching on a bat . . . a baseball bat, not the superhero guy from Greensboro. And the team in Columbus, Georgia, became the RedStixx, which was supposed to be a nuanced, well-researched, much more respectful tribute to local Native American tribes after a year as the Columbus Indians, but no one got it.

As a result of all this, the lineup of characters who began to assemble around home plate for their Hickory All-Star Weekend photo op was like some sort of furry fever dream, all the best and worst parts of watching Saturday morning cartoons and taking photos with amusement park mascots visibly clashing like the colors those varied Sally League mascots wore.

The Hagerstown Sun, the chosen symbol of the Toronto Blue Jays affiliate in northern Maryland, was just a dude in a baseball uniform, but a dude with a gigantic foam smiley-faced sun covering his head and resting atop his shoulders. The Sun's oversize round face was adorned with intricate solar flares and bursts of sunshine that made him look like an overly exuberant Medusa.

The Spartanburg Philly also wore a baseball uniform, but his foam head incorporated an entire horse's neck. It looked like a dark red road cone, standing two feet tall with fake eyes glued to the top. The wearer's actual eyes could be seen squinting through mesh holes cut in the base of the neck and hidden amid the Thoroughbred's goofy felt grin, presumably so that the poor soul inside could see where to steer his top-heavy, felt-maned Eiffel Tower of a head.

Roughly half of the fourteen mascots now lining up behind home plate wore those types of costumes, a baseball uniform with some sort of head wrapped around their actual human's head. So, we'll call them the Big Heads. The Big Heads included the Augusta GreenJacket, who was really a hornet, but green, a nod to the hue of the jackets traditionally awarded to the winners of the nearby Masters golf tournament. While the Big Heads were certainly impeded by their foam noggins, the rest of their body was free and easy to move around. From their neck braces down, they were just baseball players.

That was a huge advantage of which we did not have a full appreciation. Yet.

The other half of the lineup—let's call them the Big Hands— wore costumes that required a much greater commitment to character. That started with our own Ted E. Tourist, who had his head covered as always, but also wore foam and felt ursine hands and feet. Ted was also the only mascot with a prop, his suitcase, or as we would later come to describe it in more apropos professional wrestling terms, "a foreign object."

The Big Hands included the Albany Polecat, which was a full head-to-toe skunk costume. There was also a Chuck E. Cheese rip-off named Bomber the Mouse, he of the Capital City Bombers, a Mets affiliate who drew mascot inspiration from the fact that Jimmy Doolittle's raiders practiced their World War II bombing runs in the flatlands outside Columbia, South Carolina. There was also Charleston's Charlie T. RiverDog, joined by some sort of fat red fox from Columbus, Georgia, and the mind-bendingly inexplicable "Bleacher Creature," which was just a guy inside a big furry orange blob with googly eyes, there on behalf of the Fayetteville

Generals, a team named to pay tribute to the US Army military heroes of nearby Fort Bragg.

But the most handicapped of the Big Hands was from the hometown team. He was the only mascot who had no hands at all. Or legs. Conrad the Crawdad was a six-foot-tall foam-and-spandex river crustacean that was redder than Santa Claus, with giant-pupiled doe eyes that looked like SpongeBob SquarePants when he's about to cry. The poor human being hidden inside Conrad not only had his legs tied together at the ankles by a tapered spandex tail, but his hands were stuffed into two giant foam claws with no fingers. They were the world's worst mittens. As it turned out, they were also the world's worst fists.

Historians will tell you that a common trait among so many of the greatest battles ever fought is that no one truly knows who fired the first shot, the subtle pulled trigger, or secretly thrown stone that ignited a much larger conflict. Such was the case on Sunday, June 19, 1994, and the Battle of Hickory.

What I remember is all the mascots lining up into two rows, one standing and one kneeling. It only seemed natural that the Big Heads, with more body control, would take a knee up front while the Big Hands, hampered by their covered limbs, would stand along the back row. It all seemed logical, and it all seemed to start well. But then it quickly went wrong. When the Spartanburg Philly crouched up front, his giant neck still blocked someone behind him. Exactly which Big Hand that was is a detail that has been lost to time, but whoever it was used his Big Hands to slap the Philly's Big Head out of their way.

As Jack, aka Ted E., continued to remind us, the Mascot Golden Rule is that when one is inside one's costume, one is not allowed to speak. But clearly, someone here said something to someone, and it was a safe assumption that whatever was said included a couple of curse words. The horse suddenly came up off its knee, stood, turned around to face the back row, its head tilted back so that the man inside could see out of the little eyeholes in his neck, and raised his arms into a "WTH?" position. To Carlton Adcock's credit, he saw it coming a split second before it happened.

"Boys, I think the Spartanburg Philly is about to throw down."

The red horse lunged and grabbed the chest of the Albany Polecat with both hooves, I mean, hands. His right arm came back, cocked to unload a punch, but the Hagerstown Sun grabbed the Philly's elbow before he could strike. Keep in mind, no one in this group had any peripheral vision whatsoever, so as the tension grew and the grabbing started at one far end of the lineup, most of the mascots were still standing still, lined up, and obliviously waiting on the photographer to snap the group photo.

The Philly wheeled around to take a shot at whoever was holding back his would-be punch of the Polecat. His wild left hook caught a solar flare and sent the Sun's head into a half spin, stopping perpendicular to his shoulders and rendering the Sun completely blind. Sensing trouble, the Augusta GreenJacket instinctively stood up, but when he did so, his head hit the now-loosened head of the Sun, and the resulting bang inside his own head startled him to the point that he immediately went back to the ground to protect himself, but on all fours.

Now there was a lot of noise. The shouting from the angry Spartanburg Philly mixed with the rising volume of the reacting crowd in the stands, and that noise caused some of the other mascots to consider fleeing the scene. The once-docile Big Hands from the back row were starting to move.

The first to make a break for it was the Bleacher Creature, who tried to run but instead tripped over the cowered GreenJacket and went straight to the turf. Bomber the Mouse followed the Creature, and he too fell, landing atop both the Bleacher Creature and the GreenJacket. The Sun took a swing at the Philly, whose right arm he still held, and scored a direct hit into the center of the horse's neck. Clearly, the human on the inside of the Hagerstown

Sun was white-hot with anger, but from the outside all we could see was his giant smile. In fact, as the brawl began to expand through the entire group of mascots and the furry fists started flying, you could hear muffled angry shouts and even a scream or two, but they were all smiling.

All except for Conrad the Crawdad. The host mascot had been placed in the center of the lineup, the rightful star of the hometown show, welcoming his friends to the Hickory All-Star Festival. To his right, the Spartanburg Philly was now attacking his foes like a giraffe would, throwing his neck around like a whip to try to break his still-cocked right arm free of the Sun's grip. To Conrad's left, Charlie T. RiverDog was leading a breakaway of Big Hands to the safety of the open field, followed by Ted E. Tourist, who was aimlessly swinging his suitcase behind him to protect their six o'clock from any angry pursuers. Meanwhile, the dogpile that had formed atop the on-the-ground GreenJacket was inching closer and closer to Conrad's ankles, which were still bound together at the base of his spandex tail. All the while, the mud bug's cartoon eyes expressed the same level of worry shared by the trapped person behind them.

"Conrad's going down!" a woman in a Crawdads T-shirt screamed from the grandstand.

He was indeed, rolling over the foam- and felt-covered mascot bodies that now chopped him down at the knees, a tumbleweed of Big Heads and Big Hands alike. My eternal image of Conrad the Crawdad will always be of his thick red claws flailing about as he toppled. Perhaps he was trying to regain his balance, or maybe he was attempting to get in a couple of punches. Whatever his intention was, he failed.

The playing field was suddenly filled with front-office employees from every team in the South Atlantic League, pulling their mascots off each other and up off the ground. The only real casualties were some hurt feelings and some torn fabric. In minutes, there was no evidence that what we had seen had happened at all, except for one lone furry hand lying on the grass by the pitcher's mound.

"No one was hurt," a Fayetteville Generals employee said to us as he escorted the Bleacher Creature off the field, one of his googly eyes now hanging by a thread. "Hell, inside these heads no one even came close to actually getting hit."

Later that night, R. J. Martino introduced us to a friend of his who worked for the Crawdads. We spent the night riding around town in an open-air Jeep with the Hickory staff as we hit several All-Star Festival events and eventually ended up jumping from bar to bar. The last place we hit was a classic Southern roadhouse, little more than a cinder-block box building hidden just off the main highway. As R.J. and his friend started swapping minor-league war stories, I sidled up to the bar and chatted up the owner. He told me that the place had originally been built as an illegal gambling and liquor house, a popular stopover and delivery drop-off spot for the Carolina bootleggers who ran moonshine from the nearby Appalachians down to the big city of Charlotte. He claimed that legendary 'shine runners like Junior Johnson and Willie Clay Call were once regulars, as were the revenuers who chased them. He said to me, "A place like this, you never know who you might see. Ain't that right, Minnie?"

He pointed to the older black gentleman who was quietly sipping at the bar. He was sitting with two women who wouldn't have been close to his age even if you'd added them up. It was the MLB legend himself, Minnie Minoso.

I stumbled over my words as I introduced myself. I asked him for his autograph, but all I had for him to sign was my ticket stub from that day's exhibition games at the stadium. He scrawled his name illegibly, saw that the ticket was from earlier that day, slid it back to me, and smiled.

"Hey. How about that damn mascot fight?"

INTO EACH LIFE SOME RAIN MUST FALL ... AND IT'S USUALLY ON GAME DAYS

Following the Sally League All-Star break, not to mention Mascot Game of Thrones, every minor-league team hit the reset button with a 0-0 win-loss record to start the season's second act. A chance to win the second-half division title and make it into the September playoffs. A shot at redemption. But as the ~~dog~~ Julio the Cat days of summer arrived, the Tourists slogged into the second half of the season as if they were running in mud. Because they were. They might as well have replaced their cleats with galoshes. Their fight to get above .500 was second only to their struggle to find sunshine. The team came out of the break with an eight-game road trip during which they went 2-3 and had three games rained out. When the club returned to Asheville for a lengthy two-week July 4 homestand, that precipitation followed them home. We got all nine games in, but more than half of them were either delayed by rain, shortened by rain, or had a lengthy rain delay wedged somewhere into the box score. The same weather forecast could have been CTL+C'd into every single day of July, if we'd had any computers in the office that could do such a thing. "High: 85, Low: 67, a chance of an afternoon thunderstorm," of which there always seemed to be much more than just a chance. We knew the rain was coming. Every. Single. Freaking. Day. The only questions were, how close to first pitch would the raindrops begin to fall, and once it started, how long would the shower last?

That's why the centerpiece display of Ron's office was a framed poster that hung directly behind the boss man's chair, always lurking over his shoulder like a big wet jerk. It was Charlie Brown, standing on the pitcher's mound with a tiny storm cloud sitting directly on top of his head. The words above that shower read: "Into each life some rain must fall." The cloud also doubled as a speech bubble, pouring on Charlie's depressed face as he said, "And it's usually on game days!"

Meteorology is hardly an exact science, and any good GM has a personal secret sauce for predicting weather. At the ballpark, Ron would review the forecast and add it to what he saw when he walked out onto the Vatican Porch and looked skyward. He had fifteen years of experience observing how clouds and wind and rain and hail all bounced off the McCormick Field mountainside, like a veteran Boston Red Sox outfielder knowing how balls would ricochet off the Green Monster. There were plenty of aspects of the Minor League Baseball general manager gig that I never envied. At the top of that list was and has always been this, watching weather roll in at 5:30 p.m. on a 7 p.m. game night, just as fans were lining up at the gate and the teams were setting up for batting practice, and trying to decide whether the tarp had to be pulled. If you rolled it out and it never rained, the teams lost their warm-up and you looked like a dummy. But if you didn't put it out because you didn't want to look like a dummy and then it rained, and you ended up with a ruined infield, you had no ball game and a lot of angry people.

In the summer of '94, Ron mistimed it only once . . . but it was bad. The rain came midday and snuck up on us. Ron looked over the information he had (again, a reminder, this was '94 and there were no weather radar apps) and said it was just a quick summer shower and sun was coming behind it, so we could leave the tarp in the holster. He was right about it being quick and the sunshine that followed it. But it was no shower. It was a gully washer. Within minutes, rivers of water cut deep paths through the dirt between the bases. Wading pools formed in the outfield grass, filling the depressed areas of earth where the outfielders stood and paced every night. The warning tracks became so soaked they looked like some of the nearby Smoky Mountain whitewater centers, the dark red gravel swirling around in eddies and haystacks. It lasted all of ten minutes, but the field was ruined. No sooner had the cloud moved on and the sun burst out from behind it than Grady Gardner was standing in the infield holding a rake. He was wearing heavy rubber hip waders, like he was going trout fishing. Grady scooped up a handful of glop that used to be the dirt behind second base and shouted toward the office, "Hey, Ron! Maybe we should have pulled the damn tarp out!"

A couple of hours later there were several hundred fans lined up outside the gate. It was Cellular One Baseball Giveaway Night. Where they stood, everything seemed perfect. The sun was out, the parking lot asphalt had dried, and the temperature was perfect. But inside, we were raking and shoveling and tamping, and it all should have been set to the sounds of a string section playing "Nearer, My God, to Thee" because this ship was sunk. When Ron walked out with a sign that said, "Game Canceled" and tried to explain amid a chorus of boos, I didn't see embarrassment or shame. He was authentically hurt. Not by their reaction, but because he felt like he had failed them, those folks he had invited into his living room.

"Mother Nature is a bitch," he told me later that night as we carried our tools back to the groundskeeping shed after an evening of infield reclamation. Walking back out across the field we'd just repaired, he pointed to the rolled-up tarp, still not having moved all day. "And that tarp is a son of a bitch."

If you will allow me yet another Macaulay Culkin mention, and yet another movie scene simile, during that Old Testament of a July, whenever I looked down the first baseline and saw that big, ugly twenty-foot-long aluminum tube that was wrapped with our rain tarp, it evoked memories of *Home Alone*. Culkin would go down into the basement of the house, and the big metal furnace would taunt him with maniacal laughter and start evilly screaming, "KEVVVVIN!" That's exactly what that tarp would do to me on game days, cackling like the devil as dark clouds started rolling in overhead, as if to say, "MCGEEEE! Get ready, you skinny little intern. I'll be seeing you shortly!"

The tarp was a gargantuanly symmetrical 25,600-square-foot rainproof sheet of vinyl, plus various poly-whatever water-resistant substances, that was just the right size to cover the entire infield. It stretched across from just outside each baseline in one direction and then from just outside home plate to just past the end of the infield dirt behind second base. That placement might not seem so complicated or important, but it was. If it covered too much of the grass in the outfield or in the foul territory between the baselines and the ballpark's infield walls, then you ran the risk of frying up the grass beneath it should the sun decide to suddenly break out from behind the clouds and boil up the air temperatures in the midsummer humidity. But if you didn't get it pulled out far enough or had it misplaced, by even a couple of feet, then the rain would find its way underneath that cover and turn the infield dirt beneath into a quagmire of red clay mud.

Unfurling the tarp was done in two stages. First, we would line up behind the very heavy tube and on the count of three would start rolling it with a push . . . and run . . . and push . . . and run . . . tumbling out from its resting place against the wall down the first baseline and onto the field. We'd keep rolling it, careful to steer the cylinder in as straight a line as possible until the tarp was unspooled, and the roller went off on its own out into center field like a rocket stage we no longer needed. If we'd done our job correctly, then we should have turned around to be greeted by a ninety-foot silver trail laid down in short right field, waiting alongside the edge of the dirt between first and second. If we had folded and stored the tarp correctly after its last usage (never a given), then a row of rope handles sewn into the edge of the tarp would be right there, ready for us to reach down and grab, one grip per tarp crew member. On another count of three, we would each pull on our handles and take off to our left, sprinting across the infield, again traveling in as straight a line as strength, physics, and wind gusts would allow.

If all went according to plan, it was a genuinely graceful moment to witness. That silver-and-white field cover would spread like a silk bedsheet, allowing just enough air to flow underneath it so that it would glide into place, spreading out smoothly into all the right corners until it came to rest atop the infield. Once settled onto the ground, we dragged sandbags out from Grady Gardner's shed to lay atop the edges of the tarp and weigh it down. The sound of the rain landing on the top of that field blanket had the syncopation of a drum line, *smack-smack-smackety-smack,* that water wanting so badly to get in there and ruin our infield but denied access at every corner. Hopefully.

It was difficult to gauge exactly how well we'd done as we tried to judge it while standing on the field. But the crowd, with a much better view, always let us know. If it went off perfectly and the tarp had fallen into place, here on a baseball infield, one of Earth's most obsessively geometric plots of land (*Ninety feet between bases! Sixty feet six inches to the mound, which must be ten inches high! All lines measured for straightness!*), the reaction was inspiring. A terrific tarp pull triggered oohs and aahs and a round of applause like one of us had just raked a double off the right-field wall. A terrible tarp pull drew boos and catcalls worthy of an outfielder who had just run headfirst into the wall trying to track down that same double.

"What the hell was that?!" The shouts would come down from behind the sheet of rain, fingers pointing toward folded corners or an over-rotated placement. We would shout back, "If you think you can do better, come on down and we'll put you to work!"

We were serious. We totally would. For the one ironclad rule when it comes to the Tarp Crew is that you can never have enough people on the Tarp Crew. None of the storm-fighting majesty that I just described to you about how to pull a tarp is at all possible unless you have enough tarp pullers. Shall we recall the lesson that we three interns had learned the hard way during the damp April 3 soft opening against UNC-A? We'd had too few people and thus too little speed and not enough momentum to cut through the rain and ended up dragging a clumpy, water-weighed wad of plastic across the infield, so slow and so misshapen that it bulldozed a telltale trench of embarrassment behind us.

Recruiting Tarp Crew helpers was easy. Because everyone knew that whomever we could coax out of the grandstand for the Tarp Crew would receive in return a payment in the form of a red T-shirt that said in giant white letters across the back, "TARP CREW." We had a box full of them locked away in a closet just off the umpires' locker room. At McCormick Field those shirts were like cigarettes in prison. You could get whatever you wanted if you had a Tarp Crew tee to trade for it. By summer's end I had smuggled Tarp Crew shirts into the hands of people who could get me food, movie tickets, even a cassette bootleg recording of a Bruce Springsteen concert. Sure, the shirts were super cheap, basically made from tissue paper with screen printing so thin it probably wouldn't survive the very rain that had created the need for the tarp. But the people didn't care. They really, really wanted one of those T-shirts. Dentists, truck drivers, schoolteachers, hippies, hillbillies, they all took turns pulling the tarp, and all left beaming with pride as they wore their Tarp Crew T-shirt back home, some to mansions and others to shacks. The Tarp Crew crossed all social lines. The Tarp Crew achieved parity.

Despite the effort to create and re-create uniformity in the process, every pull seemed to take on its own personality, influenced by the conditions, participants, and, I will always believe, some sort of dark mystical baseball dimension. I mean, geez, the tarp did talk smack to me, right?

More than once, one of us was swallowed up by that tarp like Pinocchio being gulped down by Monstro the whale. Once the tarp pull started, it couldn't be stopped, and everything needed to happen at the same speed. That made it imperative for anyone on the crew to keep up, no matter how fast the others were going. Matched momentum was everything. But between wet grass, boggy dirt, the transitions from one of those surfaces to the other, and bad choices in footwear—for example, some intern who totally overthought his Thirsty Thursday beer cooler duty and was wearing rubber-soled, flat-bottomed Sperry Top-Siders to dash across saturated grass—all of that meant we all suffered at least one stumble during a tarp pull over the course of the season. Imagine falling facedown and then scrambling to stand back up, only to find that you can't. Why? Because an acre-size blanket that is becoming heavier by the second has just covered you up and is still moving. Your only chance of escape is to start crawling as fast as you can toward daylight in the hopes that you can get out from underneath the tarp before it vacuum-seals itself to the ground and you end up becoming the contents of a blister in the middle of a ballfield.

I had two of those falls. I still have dreams about them. They aren't great dreams.

I also have dreams about flying. I believe that most people do. But I also think the majority of those people's late-night

REM-powered minds are pulling images from little more than their imaginations to devise what the sensation of soaring off the ground feels like. Not my mind. It knows. My brain, feet, and every bit of me in between, it all knows. Because it happened on July 9, 1994, on Expert Tire Can Cooler Night.

An "Auntie Em!" kind of storm blow into McCormick Field from the angry side of the center-field mountain, with eardrum-shocking cracks of thunder and wind gusts that ripped the left-field picnic tent from its metal moorings. We really should have surrendered and let the game go into the books, but it was a Saturday night, and we had a big crowd. We didn't want to recruit fans onto the crew because the conditions were awful and deteriorating quickly. So, we commenced to pull the tarp shorthanded. I remember during the initial rollout, Swish looked over at me, squinting even more than his Clint Eastwood eyes usually did because the water was blowing in sideways. He went full *Caddyshack:* "I'd keep playing!" Lee Tillery replied, "I don't think the heavy stuff's coming down for a while!" From farther down the roller, we could hear Carlton laughing, though we couldn't really see him through the sheets of rain. When a flash of lightning illuminated his face, he responded by shaking a fist into the air. "Rat farts!"

Once the roller was gone and the folded tarp was laid out, we each grabbed a rope handle, Gary counted, "Three . . . two . . . one," and we took off running. There were only six or seven of us, and we'd spread out too unevenly. I was right in the middle, and there were big gaps between me and the guys to my left and right. The conditions were custom-made for what happened next. A gale burst of wind came down off the mountain, bounced off the grandstand, and pushed its way under the tarp, coming in low off the ground, right through my legs.

Then those legs, they were a'dangling.

Not too long ago I took my family to San Francisco, and we sat on the shores of the Presidio and watched people in the Bay as they sailed through the air, holding on for dear life to the handles of sailboard and windsurfing wings. My daughter asked, "I wonder what that feels like?" I told her I knew. Later, I was working on a story for *ESPN The Magazine,* interviewing Felix Baumgartner, the man who sky-jumped from space, leaping off a platform from 128,000 feet above the Earth. He said to me, "It is the rarest of fraternities, the people who know what that sensation feels like." I responded, "Yeah, man, I hear you brother. It's our bond."

Have you ever strapped into the thrill ride Soarin' at Disneyland, when you buckle into a seat that leaves your legs loose and swinging as it lifts you off the ground and proceeds to toss you about as you fly over the Egyptian pyramids and the Eiffel Tower? Every time I ride it, I see the people around me gasping and holding on for dear life. Not me. Because I went soarin' for real, but my view was of McCormick Field.

It's a strange sensation when your feet leave the ground unexpectedly. But when that blast of wind went through us as we ran against it, it inflated the tarp just enough to turn it into a sail. Go back to my earlier bedsheet analogy. When you take a sheet and whip it with your hands so the air rolls beneath it and blows it out over the mattress, that's exactly what happens when wind gets under a tarp. There was me, right at the entry point of the jet stream, and when the big bedsheet arched skyward, it took me with it, jerking me up by my right hand, the one that was gripping the loop of the rope handle. By the time I realized what was happening, I was in full Mary Poppins mode, arm extended, airborne as though I was holding Mary's parrot-head umbrella, my feet and legs moving like I was still on the ground running. I was too high in the air to let go. In my mind, I achieved enough altitude to see the roof of the grandstand. From up there, I could have sworn that I saw downtown Asheville, the Biltmore House, and James the Mountain Man behind the outfield wall looking for baseballs. The people looked like ants. I was Superman.

The reality was that I probably flew about six feet off the ground and was up there for only a second at the most. That was plenty. When the air bubble rolled on through to the back of the tarp, the leading edge that I was clinging to abruptly descended. The moment my feet hit the ground, I let go of the handle and went tumbling through the wet grass. In my mind's eye, I stuck the landing, feet down and fingers touching the earth, like Captain America who had just leapt from atop a building. The reality is that I resembled a no-longer-necessary hostage who'd just been thrown out of a moving van.

I skidded to a stop just shy of the visitors' dugout. It made me think of the summers of 1957–58, when Asheville lost its baseball team and built a quarter-mile racetrack in the infield to keep the turnstiles moving and generate a little revenue. NASCAR legends such as Junior Johnson, Cotton Owens, Buck Baker, Curtis Turner, and Ralph Earnhardt, father of Dale and grandfather of Dale Jr., all raced there. In fact, McCormick Field's left-field wall is still anchored by the concrete crash fence that was built to keep those race cars inside the racetrack. One day I'd even crawled up into the kudzu behind Grady's groundskeeping shack because Ron said that chunks of the asphalt from the McCormick Field Raceway were still there, tossed away when the Tourists returned in 1959. When that tarp flung me toward the third-base dugout, it wasn't my life that flashed before my eyes, but rather the images of another crash at the same spot, on July 12, 1958, when NASCAR Hall of Famer Lee Petty, father of Richard, lost control of his '57 Oldsmobile and drove it directly into that same dugout.

After my crash I popped up off the ground, made sure everything on my body was working properly, and walked down the steps into the dugout to stop my hands from shaking and recalibrate my ground legs. Sitting there, underneath the dry lip of the concrete-slab roof, was a familiar face, Crawdads manager Fred Kendall.

"You good?"

"Yeah, Coach, I think so."

"You got some nice altitude there."

"Did I?"

"Yeah, but I've seen better. Saw a guy at Wrigley Field that was probably twice that high. He might not have come down yet."

"The Windy City," I replied.

"Yes, sir. Isn't baseball the best?"

"Damn right it is, Coach."

The season's greatest tarp pull took place on Tuesday, June 14. The same night that Darren Holmes wasn't allowed to pitch because of the weather, the umpires decided to call the game after a lengthy rain delay, and Ron had come running down the base-line to be thrown out of the game, all while wearing his own Tarp Crew T-shirt. At the start of that delay, we executed a rollout of such magnificence that witnesses wept. Okay, it was just one wit-ness who cried, but still, it was a moment.

When the rain started, we began our process of looking into the stands for help, with the usual promise of a Tarp Crew T-shirt. Usually, we'd end up with a half-dozen guys coming down, mostly dads trying to show off in front of their families or fraternity dudes trying to show off for their bros or their dates. But on this night, volunteers started flowing onto the field en masse. It looked like a coordinated military maneuver. They were even all in uniform.

You see, it was Scout Night. Any Boy or Girl Scout who showed up in their uniforms could get their entire family into the ballpark for five bucks, with half that night's proceeds pledged to support local troops. The place was packed, and when we asked for help, those troops mobilized. Instead of a handful of people grabbing handle pulls, we had two sets of hands at each station. When Gary's countdown hit "Go!" that tarp unfolded, flew, and glided. We had strength. We had speed. We had numbers. The Phil Col-lins hit "I Wish It Would Rain Down" played, and that beautiful blanket settled down into the perfect position over the infield just as Eric Clapton hit the first hard lick of his guitar solo. The crowd jumped to their feet and erupted with joy. Sam Zurich's voice boomed in over the speakers. "Asheville Tourists fans, let's hear it for the Scouts! That's what I call being prepared!"

Those kids lined up, and we handed out Tarp Crew T-shirts like we were commissioning them into adulthood. They kept saying, "Thank you." We kept saying back to them, "No, thank YOU!"

I walked through the stands, headed back to concessions, and was joined on my stroll by Patty Earwood, aka Patty in the Dairy Queen stand. She put her arm around me and wiped away a tear. "I'm sorry. I know it's silly that I got emotional, but that was one of the prettiest things I have ever seen."

I assured her that there was no reason to apologize, because she was 100 percent correct. Heck, it happened half a lifetime ago, and when I think about that perfect tarp pull today, it still makes me so giddy that I feel like I'm walking on air. And I totally know how that feels.

AS GOOD AS IT GETS . . . OR IS IT?

When you looked at one of those pocket schedules, the ones that Carlton and I had spent March driving around asking businesses to stack for us by their front registers (by the way, gun-behind-the-counter barbershop guy came to a game later that season and apologized, saying, "We don't get a lot of dudes in khaki pants in my place, so I was a little suspicious."), the blocks of dates on that calendar that represented home games were printed in red. Holy insomnia, did August have a lot of red. There were six weeks remaining in the 1994 Asheville Tourists baseball season, and we had twenty-five home games in thirty-six days.

There was a lot of change happening, and as always comes with change, tension was brewing. In the big leagues, they were celebrating former Tourists batboy Cal Ripken Jr.'s two thousandth consecutive game, all while knowing that an MLB players strike was becoming unavoidable. Their union had set a deadline of August 13 for a walkout should their demands not be met, and everyone knew they wouldn't be. Meanwhile, Michael Jordan and the Birmingham Barons were back down the road in Greenville, but this time none of us went to see him. We were too busy.

Besides, MJ was hitting .190 and striking out at a clip of once per every four at-bats. Just so you know, that's bad.

The Asheville Tourists roster was beginning to look very different. So did ours. We lost Lee Tillery midsummer when his internship sent him to another team, the Capital City Bombers in Columbia, South Carolina, nearly two and a half hours away. That was a bummer of a day.

Players were changing teams too, moving up to High Class A Visalia or even AA New Haven, nine players in all, and only two came back down to Asheville once they'd climbed up the Rockies farm system ladder. Others were cut outright. They were there one day and next day they were gone, replaced instantly like water scooped out of barrel. That meant new faces were trickling into the clubhouse. I was always jealous of the players because, well dang, they were professional baseball players! But I never envied the guys who showed up during the second half of the season. Trying to find their way into the starting lineup was tough enough. Trying to wedge their way into the social structure of a team that had largely been together since early spring? That seemed nearly impossible.

It all felt very much through-the-looking-glass. Many of the older college guys who had come to McCormick Field so confident in April were now rattled by the first real baseball performance struggles of their lives. Meanwhile, the teenagers who'd arrived so green and downright scared now carried themselves like hardball veterans. Jamey Wright's win-loss record was awful, but the kid rarely gave up big hits, developing a diverse arsenal of breaking pitches that had everyone in the Sally League settling for grounders and merely hoping those balls tiptoed through the infielders' gloves for hits. Edgard Velasquez, the eighteen-year-old Puerto Rican who'd barely spoken to anyone four months earlier, had quietly developed into a player with five-tool potential. His locker, which had started the season with a couple of photos of

Roberto Clemente taped to its shelves, was now wallpapered in images of the baseball legend, including a folder's worth of newspaper clips from the 1994 MLB All-Star Game, hosted by the Pittsburgh Pirates and an unapologetic two-day tribute to No. 21. I finally had that conversation with Velasquez about Clemente's visits to McCormick Field during the 1960s. The kid couldn't stop smiling.

Unfortunately, the effect of so much alteration in the dugout chemistry had become all too apparent on the scoreboard. As August arrived, the Tourists were a whopping eleven games out of first place and showing no signs of being a ball club that had the ability to rally.

There would be no rings won by this team this season. No championship banner unveilings. No plaques hung. And yet, there was still a month of games left to play. These are the days when one finds oneself looking inward. For players, that meant just trying to rack up as many hits or strikeouts as possible while calling their agents and asking what's next. For coaches, a noncontending August means a solid month of nonstop "Why are we all here?" mountaintop philosophizing.

"This time of year, especially when a team is falling out of contention, the individualism of baseball starts to make itself known," Tony Torchia explained to us one Sunday afternoon, standing at midfield as the first pitch grew nearer with each tick of the clock. Grady Gardner had asked us to help him get the field prepped on a quick turnaround. The night before had been an extra-innings affair. That always seemed to happen on a fireworks night, when the crowd was anxious for the game to end so that the postgame show could begin, only to be forced to sit there and watch the rockets be delayed by a tenth . . . eleventh . . . even fourteenth inning. And that extended experience was a guaranteed certainty when it led into a Sunday game.

The coach continued. "That's what makes this sport unique,

you know? It's a team game, but ultimately, we measure success by the statistics of individuals."

Grady was standing on the mound, where Torchia couldn't see him but we could. The groundskeeper was looking at us, hands raised in a "Dammit, are you gonna help me here or not?!" expression. But Tony couldn't be stopped. He had his hands on his hips, staring out into the outfield, twisting a couple of blades of grass between his fingers, and pontificating on the perils of a life lived within the unique universe of the game he loved so much. Sorry, Grady, what were we supposed to do, cut Torchia off and say, "Hey, Coach, I know you're in the middle of a therapy session right now, but Grady Gardner needs us to go get a bag of lime."

Torchia was on a roll: "Really, all you can do is listen to them, hear them out, and then try to put the best lineup you can on the field that night. And when I say best lineup, that's not just the young men who are in the best physical shape or even on a hitting streak, but the guys who are in the best mental shape, or even the guys who need to find their way back into their best mental shape. . . ."

"Yeah, Skipper, we hear you."

"This job, it can be as much psychiatrist as it is baseball coach. How many times do you think I have had to talk a player out of quitting?"

"Well, geez, we don't know, Tony . . ." (*squeezes rake, twirls rake, all in the hopes of dropping a hint*).

"So many. And some of them are guys who have been in the big leagues for years now. Imagine if they had quit? That's the real victory in this game, winning over your own limitations, your own mind. . . ."

"Hell yeah, man. Hey, um . . ."

"Sorry, guys, they probably need you to do something right now, don't they?"

The most notable new addition to the Tourists roster was a

genuinely big name in baseball circles who was bogged down in one of those big mind messes that Torchia was teaching us about. John Burke was the first draft pick of the Colorado Rockies baseball organization, ever. On paper, he was as much of a can't-miss as a ballplayer could possibly be. Burke was born and raised in the suburbs of Denver, only thirteen miles south of where the Rockies were constructing Coors Field. He was drafted out of high school by the Baltimore Orioles but chose instead to accept a scholarship to the University of Florida, 1,800 miles southeast of the Rocky Mountains. As a Gator, he became a first-team All-American in 1991, throwing a no-hitter in the NCAA Tournament and pitching in the College World Series. When the Houston Astros chose him sixth overall in the '91 MLB draft, he once again chose college over the pros. After setting a school record for most career strikeouts, the prototypically built six-four, 220-pound righty was selected in the first round of the Rockies' first draft in '92, inked with a signing bonus of $336,000. The following summer he was named to the 1993 Class A California League All-Star Team, and he'd started the '94 season with Colorado Springs, Class AAA, one rung below the big leagues. Remember that *Baseball America* top-ten Colorado Rockies prospects list, the one that had Jamey Wright ranked fourth and Snake Walls ninth? Burke was ranked first. So, why in the wide, wide world of sports was John Burke reporting to Asheville in mid-August?

"Glasses, come here, I've got a question for you!" It was Jack Lamabe. He was sitting on the bench in the right-field bullpen, watching two very tall dudes toss the ball around in the outfield a couple of hours before game time. "You see that guy out there, throwing with Jamey Wright? You know who that is?"

I did. It was John Burke. He had arrived earlier that day.

"You know what he said to me earlier? He said he couldn't see home plate. Like, it's there. I see it. Wright sees it. But Burke can't throw strikes, because to him, home plate is not there. Just dirt,

I guess. I believe him when he says he can't see it. But you see it, right? Home plate?"

I told Tomatoes that yes, I could see it. Then I asked him, what was his question for me?

"Just that. If you could see the plate. But he's your same age too, isn't he, Burke?"

I told Jack that yes, he was. Almost exactly.

"Well, if you have any advice on how I should coach someone your age who says he can't see damn home plate, let me know. Because I've been doing this for a long time, played with and coached all sort of guys. But I don't have a clue how to solve this."

Neither did I. I appreciated Jack asking me to help him unlock the collective mind of Gen X, but I was still trying to figure out how to correctly fill up the Dairy Queen machine.

All these years later, Wright recalled to me Burke's arrival in Asheville. The Tourists weren't surprised to see Wright's fellow first-rounder sent down to Class A ball in August. The shock was that he hadn't been there sooner. They had all seen the exact moment that Burke's baseball brain was broken beyond repair, in March during spring training. The instant that the yips had taken over his arm and mind. Burke surrendered a home run that Wright described as "the biggest bomb I have ever seen" to none other than the man who would go on to become baseball's all-time bombmaker, Barry Bonds of the San Francisco Giants. As I once heard in a sermon from a countryside preacher, you can't unscramble an egg. Burke's egg was most definitely scrambled that day in Arizona. So much so that when he reported to Asheville, he brought with him a Colorado Springs stat line of 8 appearances, 11 innings pitched, 72 batters faced, 6 strikeouts, 5 wild pitches, 2 batters hit by pitch, 22 walks, 16 hits, and 25 runs surrendered, 24 of them earned resulting in an earned run average of 19.64. Again, just so you know, that's bad. Like, super, super bad. Not super bad in the James Brown sense, but super bad like that one kid on your

Little League team who ends up on the mound only because there was no one else left to give the ball.

The very day I'd sat with Tomatoes and watched Burke soft-toss with Wright, Lamabe had pulled Jamey aside and quietly suggested that instead of the customary one baseball, he should take a bag of seven or eight out there with him for the game of Bonus Baby Catch, just in case. The advice was indeed astute. Sure enough, Burke started spraying throws all over the lawn.

"It was hard to watch because he's a good guy, but also because it was a reminder that all ballplayers are walking this edge all the time, especially pitchers because we are all head cases," Wright explained to me. "Jack used to drive us all a little crazy because he was so old-school. He'd had us running poles [wind sprints across the outfield between foul poles] and doing all these drills right out of 1968. But sometimes you need that. We make it all so complicated, so some old-school baseball stuff, keeping it simple, that might be just what the doctor ordered. Especially then when we are all so young and dumb. Sometimes you just need someone to talk to. Your parents are nowhere around. So, you talk to your coaches."

The chats that Wright remembers best with Lamabe, Torchia, and Bill Maguire weren't about baseball at all. They were about life. He still reflects on those lessons all the time. "I still use the chicken enchiladas recipe that Moose Maguire taught me that summer, and it's still damn good."

Whatever Tomatoes finally did say to Burke helped. He made four starts as an Asheville Tourist, surrendering only three runs, and finished his August tenure with a perfect five-inning outing before heading back up to Colorado Springs.

I also had many conversations with Lamabe, but mine were all about baseball. More specifically, baseball history. "Jack, can I now ask you a question?" I'd replied to him that day as we watched Jamey Wright chasing down yet another errant toss from Burke.

He nodded. "I was looking at all the Roberto Clemente stuff in Edgard Velasquez's locker, and it got me to thinking. Did you face Clemente much?"

He told me that not only had he squared off against the Pirate icon multiple times during his stints with four different National League opponents, they had also been teammates for a season. Lamabe's rookie year of 1962 was with Pittsburgh, the third of Clemente's dozen All-Star campaigns and the year he earned the second of his twelve Gold Gloves. "Clemente was a wonder to watch play. It sure was a lot better having him play behind me in the outfield than it was having him facing me at the plate with a bat in his hand. I've enjoyed telling his nephew about that this year."

"His nephew?"

"Velasquez. Roberto was his mother's brother. Why do you think he has all that stuff up in his locker? Come on, glasses, you didn't know that this whole time?"

No, I hadn't. Because let me say it again, we in the front office were never close with the players. We had tried early, but it never clicked. There were some moments—a couple of fun early season twenty-five-cent wing nights at Bennigan's come to mind—but there was always a barrier between them and us. And whenever the wall felt like it might open up a little, an incident would come along to remind that the boundary still existed, and it was always going to exist. Perhaps the looming threat of an MLB players strike had something to do with it, but there was no question that strains of resentment were increasingly creeping into the DNA of that divide.

For example, once every homestand Ron would give us a box of baseballs to take to the clubhouse and place on a table just inside the entrance with a pen and a request that read, "Players, please sign." It usually took a couple of games for everyone to scribble their names on the balls, but when they were done, we would use them as prizes, donate them to charity auctions, or distribute them as thank-you gifts to season-ticket holders, sponsors, or members of the Asheville Tourists Pinch Hitters Club. The rest would be sold in the Bear Wear store. I think we charged twenty bucks per baseball. I still had a ball signed by the entire 1979 Shelby Pirates, so I knew how important those balls could be to people.

One day I came in to collect those baseballs, and when I did a quick scan, I noticed that one signature was missing. It was Nate Holdren, our former Michigan Wolverine linebacker-turned-designated hitter who had gotten off to such a horrible start to the season but was now crushing homers at a rate that had him fighting for the Sally League regular-season home run crown. I approached Holdren at his locker with the box of balls and the pen and asked if he'd mind knocking out those autographs so I could take them upstairs to Ron. He stood up. All six-four, 240 pounds of him, towering over all five-ten, 135 pounds of me, and started yelling. His shoulders were bowed up. I was stunned. "You guys are selling these in the store, I saw it. You are making f—ing money off our autographs and we're getting nothing, so hell no we're not signing these anymore, not unless you want to start giving us a cut! You go tell your boss that." He knew I wasn't making any policies about selling autographed baseballs, and he knew I was hardly "management," but the divide between players and front office clearly existed. He embarrassed me in front of the team, and he did it on purpose.

Right around that same time we had the only true off-day of the entire season. On August 2, the team wasn't on the road, but there was no game scheduled. It was just blank. Ron and Carolyn left early. So did Gary and Eileen. So did Grady and Jane. So, with the grown-ups gone for the afternoon, we the interns decided to set up some impromptu batting practice. My brother Sam was in town, a tank-built former walk-on infielder with the Wake Forest Demon Deacons baseball team who has always had the ability to flat-out rake. We weren't supposed to be on the playing field if we weren't out there in some sort of official groundskeeping capacity. We certainly weren't supposed to be playing on the playing field. And we absolutely weren't supposed to be "borrowing" gear from the bat room or the clubhouse. But did we do all the above? Damn right we did. We had our own gloves and an aluminum bat, but we grabbed a bucket of James the Mountain Man–rescued baseballs from the umpires' locker room and an extra stick of lumber from the bat room. We had all we needed, which was way more than we were allowed. But as we jogged through the empty, darkened home clubhouse on our way into the dugout and onto the field, I paused at Nate Holdren's locker. His bats were right there, unmarked and unlocked. So, I grabbed one. We were also short a glove, so I grabbed his mitt too.

For a couple of impossibly glorious late afternoon hours, we finally had McCormick Field to ourselves and our baseball playing fantasies. As I patrolled the outfield like Ty Cobb, shagging flies from Swish, Carlton, R.J., and my broad-shouldered brother, I remember thinking, *Why couldn't the weather be this nice on a game day?* and then my mind immediately responding, *C'mon, man, that would be a waste. This is perfect.*

And it was. We took turns trying to blast a ball off the monster wall in right field. I think Swish finally did it, of course. Sam, using his metal bat, launched a couple of moonshots over the wall in left center. As one of those projectiles sailed over Carlton's head and into Babe Ruth's honeysuckle vines, he challenged my brother, "Let's see you do that with a wooden bat!" I was on the mound, standing behind the pitching screen from *Richie Rich,* and as my brother picked up Nate Holdren's very large wooden pendulum of a bat, I quoted another movie, *Field of Dreams,* when Kevin Costner's character is throwing batting practice to Shoeless Joe Jackson and says, "See if you can hit my curve!" He could. Brother Sam struck that baseball with such force that it departed the ballpark in dead center field while still on a rise. It nailed the Marlboro Man right in the mouth.

A few minutes later, Sam was pitching to me. I too made hard contact, though my ball traveled half the distance of his. I heard the crack of the bat. I also heard a crack *in* the bat. Nate Holdren's bat. I looked down and spotted a hairline fracture, located right along the outline of one of the rings of grain in the handle. For a fraction of a second, I felt bad about it. But I was still pissed about the autograph tirade.

When we were done, I stuck the bat and glove back in his locker and went home for the night. The next day, he was yelling at me again, me and the other guys. He'd seen the crack instantly and could tell his glove had been used as well. I let him finish. Then I just reminded him that the bat room would be open shortly and he could trade that one in for a new one. I turned heel and left. I never went back into the clubhouse again that season.

As disappointing as it was, I never fit in inside that locker room. But I did fit in perfectly in every other corner of McCormick Field. We all did. For we four—sorry, now three—interns, the whole experience felt like a more fun extension of college. As for the restraints of living off a hundred bucks a week, after the first month we never thought much about it again. For all their legendary frugalness, if Ron or Carolyn had noticed us busting our butts even more than usual, fighting through a long homestand or having to pull that dang tarp way more times than normal, they would thank us with a lined handshake, an extra $50 bill stuffed in their palms. A couple of times that summer, Ron would stand up and announce, "The Tourists are on the road and it's time for a margarita lunch!" When we walked out of the office, he would have his luminous blue aircraft carrier of a Chevy Impala parked out front with the convertible top down. We would cram into the backseat and grin with our hair whipping in the mountain breeze, headed to a Mexican restaurant that was so good we didn't care about the poor sanitation rating that hung by the front door. Ron would drive, and 1960s Carolina beach music would blast from the speakers of that Chevy as the people of Asheville would shout "Hey, Ron!" as we drove by them. On the way back to the ballpark, he'd have his left hand on the wheel, his right arm stretched over the shoulder rests of the front seats, and he'd turn back to look at the three of us, mashed shoulder to shoulder in the vinyl backseat like Manhattan subway commuters, buzzed on cheap tequila. "What did I tell you guys? You ain't getting rich, but it still beats the hell out of real work, don't it?"

We never starved, but to accomplish that took some creativity. We realized early on that even twenty-five-cent wing nights were going to be too steep for our budgets. So was dating. The one time I tried to throw caution to the winds of romance and attempted to take a girl on a lavish evening out, the two of us had just settled into our seats on the resplendent Sunset Terrace at the Grove Park Inn when the waiter handed us the menus. I hadn't even made it through the appetizers when the price list caused me to feel exactly like another former resident of that terrace, F. Scott Fitzgerald, with all the color drained out of his face and barfing over the railing before passing out and falling into the shrubbery. I didn't do that, but I did tell my date I needed to excuse myself to visit the men's room and instead ran to a bank of pay phones to call the apartment and leave an SOS message on the answering machine. An hour later, as my date polished off her $40 citrus poached shrimp, I was convinced I would be spending the night washing dishes in the Grove Park Inn kitchen. That's when the hostess stepped up to our table and said, "Mister McGee? You have a phone call at the front desk." When I got there, Carlton Adcock was standing in the lobby amid the wood carvings, stonework, and the sounds of a string quartet. He was in flip-flops, sunglasses, and a City Sport T-shirt, holding a handful of twenty-dollar bills. "Dude, what were you thinking bringing a date here?"

At least once, Carlton and I had shown up at the Grove Park and walked through that same lobby, impersonating paid guests as we headed straight to the indoor pool. We figured that if you walked with purpose and carried yourself as someone who belonged, no one would question it, even as we strode back out of that lobby an hour later, soaked to the bone as our sandals sounded like wet suction cups on the baroque stone floors. "Put it on the Underhills' tab!" Carlton shouted out the window of his pickup truck as we drove away.

When the Tourists were at home, eating was never a problem, though it took some hunger-driven inventiveness and, in some cases, more borderline criminal activity. The Grill Boys knew that if they accidentally scorched a couple of hamburgers, we would gladly eat them. If the umpires or the visiting entertainment acts hadn't touched their contractually obligated boxes of hot dogs, then we would scarf those down as well. Every game night we featured a long list of prize giveaways, everything from free buckets of balls down at the French Broad Golf Center driving range to free ice cream over at the ridiculously delicious but not cheap Biltmore Creamery. Those prizes were kept in a locked Rubbermaid tool cabinet inside the ticket booth. At the end of each homestand, any unclaimed winnings were up for grabs. What I'm telling you here is that we hit a lot of golf balls and ate a lot of ice cream.

It was the end of a homestand that was always the most perilous when it came to the prospect of feeding ourselves, as we stared into canyons of the calendar that could be as many as nine days long without any grub that could be borrowed from At-Bat Food Services. That was hard to pull off even when the team was in town, seeing as how every drink cup, frankfurter, and bag of peanuts was tracked somewhere on Jane's spreadsheets and double-checked upstairs on Carolyn's adding machine. So, when facing a lengthy Tourists road trip, we would "screw up," and when we were told to pull three boxes of hamburger patties and a box of chicken breasts out of the freezer to be thawed for the final game . . . "Oh, dang it, Jane, I totally misunderstood and thawed *four* boxes of hamburgers and *two* boxes of chicken. My bad! I guess we should take that home with us. I mean, geez Louise, we can't let it go to waste, right?" My pal Amber would also take pity on us and, "Oops . . . guys, I accidentally messed up this pizza, so I guess you need to throw it out" (read: take it home). Looking back now, I know that Jane knew exactly what we were up to, but she let us have the mental victory anyway.

Back in the retirement village apartment we weren't supposed to have a grill per the fire code, but under the cloak of darkness—and knowing that our more life-seasoned neighbors all went to bed at eight p.m.—we'd secretly carried a two-burner gas grill out onto what was a way-too-small of a ledge to describe as a balcony. It was a shelf with a railing. The very-used grill came from Carlton's father, and it worked great except that the igniter button was broken. So, when it was time to light that grill and commence to cook our contraband meats, Carlton would step through the cheap vertical blinds out onto the tiny mezzanine and warn, "Fire in the hole!" before slamming the sliding glass door shut. On the other side of that glass, he would turn on the gas, stand back, and toss lighted matches from several feet away until one of them finally fell through the grill grates at just the right spot to catch a puff of propane. Through the blinds the flash of light was indeed blinding. *WHOOOOMP!* The kind of heat-driven explosion that both the Grill Boys and Captain Dynamite would have appreciated. We did that at least a few nights a week, and during my turn in the rotation on ignition duty, I lost at least half of one eyebrow. We didn't care. It was delicious, and most crucially, the price was right.

Swish's parents owned a restaurant on the outskirts of town (of course they did), and every couple of weeks they would have us out and feed us a rack of ribs. More than a few times my pal Mike Morgan at Channel 13 had me over to his parents' house, where his mother, who was also the personal assistant to evangelist Billy Graham, made biscuits that seemed to have been delivered by Reverend Graham directly from a cloud in heaven. And remember Patty Earwood, aka Patty in the Dairy Queen stand? She kept us fed via a nightly supply of Oreo Blizzards, not unlike me keeping Julio the Cat filled with batting helmet bowls of the mix used to make those Blizzards. Patty would also invite us out to the Earwood house after home games, where she served up late-night fried chicken as we laughingly recalled that evening's events and wackos witnessed.

Our McCormick Field coworkers, most of whom we'd never met just a few months earlier, became our summer family, plain and simple. We did favors for one another, be it having a surprise cake delivered for a birthday or getting the hottest prospects from the other teams to sign a baseball for our stadium workers, as I often did for Linda and Pam, our tireless beer window workers, and almost-religious Atlanta Braves fans, whenever the Macon Braves were in town.

We had shared weird experiences. We had inside jokes. When we saw each other in the concourse, we knew immediately if someone was having a good day or bad, and if they looked like it was a bad one, we wanted to see what we could do to help fix it. That's what family does. I had one of those moments with the Earwoods. I was running the pregame check of all the concession stands, and Patty wasn't at her ice cream post like she normally was. I found her down at the snow cone stand, consoling her teenage daughter, Chastity, who worked in that shaved ice stand with her best friend, Jennifer. Everyone was super upset, openly crying. As it turned out, Chastity's prom was just days away. She had her dress bought and her plans locked in, but her date had cut and run on her. Jerk. The only solution I could come up with left my mouth before I'd even thoroughly thought it all through. "I'll take you." And I did.

To be clear, the part I hadn't thought through wasn't going to prom. I had been to a few at that point, so I knew how to do it, even if it had been a while. The issue was that I couldn't buy one dinner for one date at the Grove Park, so how the hell was I going to pay for a prom night? But when Ron learned of what I had offered up, he in turn offered to help underwrite the effort. "That family has been coming to this ballpark as long as Carolyn and I have been running the place," he said to me. "And that girl has been running around here since she could walk. We're not going to let some jackass ruin her night."

We didn't. We did it up big, even if everyone at McCormick Field gave me a lot of good-natured grief about it. Van Smith, the massive policeman who worked as our de facto head of security, tapped the handle of his sidearm and fingered his handcuffs whenever I walked by. I knew he was joking, but I also knew he kind of wasn't. His wife, Sherri, also worked at the ballpark and also made sure that I knew that her man would totally shoot me if I got out of line. They even made me go out to the railyard late one night to tell the girl's father, who supervised the overnight shift at the super-scary right-out-of-a-gangster-movie train depot, about my plan. The night of the dance, I made sure to find out exactly who that jackass was, so to make dang sure he was aware of the mistake he'd made.

The Earwood family was special to me then. They are still special to me now. I suppose that we all have those too-brief relationships, where we can't help but think back and wonder how much different it might have been if the timeline of our lives had run more parallel instead heading off into a hundred different directions like the rails in that train yard. But that doesn't make me any less thankful for the one spot where they intersected. So, I suppose this is the part where I should thank the jackass who bailed on prom for helping us form that bond.

If McCormick Field was a family and we down in the concourse were the kids, then I suppose that made the big bosses up in the front office our parents. And parents, well, they fight. The little bit of unease between Ron and Gary, what we had detected all the way back at our very first meeting with the two by the elevators at the Winter Meetings in Atlanta, had been a very slow rub on a very tight rope all summer long. There was never a question of whether the tension between GM and assistant GM was going to break. It was always only a matter of when it would finally snap.

I watched them circle each other throughout the season. Ron was so entrenched in the rudimentary ways of doing baseball business, the approach that had saved the Asheville Tourists franchise and built a new ballpark. Gary was never willing to settle for the status quo, an admirable restlessness that always had him searching for the next great idea and always coveting the tools that he believed would help him make those ideas a reality. Ron was calculators, Captain Dynamite, and cheap T-shirts sold in the souvenir stand. Gary was computers, Elvis Himselvis, and special-edition bottles of Chardonnay sold in the Bear Wear store.

Ron got mad at Gary because we were using the fax machine to receive our office rotisserie baseball league stats and standings each week, and dammit, that cost money!

Ron and Carolyn got mad at Gary and Eileen because the credit card machine that they had insisted on to help boost merchandise sales in the stadium store had also generated a trickle of service charges and, dammit, *that* cost money!

Ron got mad at Gary because he had entered the Asheville Tourists staff in a corporate raft race on the French Broad River, in a beans-and-rice cookoff at the Bele Chere Arts Festival, and in a Chamber of Commerce–sponsored golf event because, dammit, they all cost money, too!

There was a whole thing for a whole day about the cover of the game programs. On the front was the newfangled multicolored Ted E. Tourist logo. The best backdrop for that art was a very light tan, so that's what color paper stock was used. "Look at this!" Ron wailed at Gary one morning, book in hand. "Look at the Bud Light ad on the back, the can and ice aren't white! Look at the Pepsi ad inside, the player's uniform isn't white, either . . . GARY!"

They couldn't even agree on what music to play. Gary was and is one of the great audiophiles I have ever known, with a particular soft spot for the blues. He and Eileen rented a condo atop the mountain that overlooked McCormick Field, and one wall of that home was like a record store rack, covered in thousands of CDs and LPs. So, it was only natural that as the person in charge of the press box, Gary liked to stretch his musical legs in the tunes he played during pregame warm-ups or in reaction to what happened on the field. He would make mixtapes befitting certain situations, be it rain or an argument with an umpire, a grand slam, or the introduction of that night's thrower of the ceremonial first pitch. You named the moment, and Gary Saunders had a tune for it in "Gary's Big Box of Music," and it probably wasn't the tune he'd played in the same situation the night before. Muddy Waters, Stevie Ray Vaughan, some B-side movie soundtrack Elvis tune that no one had heard before but was the perfect score for a run that had just been scored. Gary had it all at the ready.

That is, if Ron let him play it. On one afternoon, a solid hour before the first pitch, Gary threw in a cassette of Bruce Springsteen tunes and did for no reason other than he knew I was working with him in the press box that day and I loved the Boss. Ron did not. Maybe two songs into the album, as fans were just beginning to file in, Ron McKee blew the press box door open, hit the eject button on the tape deck, yanked that Springsteen cassette out of it, and threw it against the cinder-block wall with such force that it shattered. "Play some damn music that baseball fans want to hear! Hell, play some damn music that anyone wants to hear!"

That summer, the big tune at every ballpark was "The Cheap Seats" from country music superstars Alabama. The band had a minority stake in a Minor League Baseball franchise in Nashville, and they wrote a song released on April 11, 1994, just in time for the start of the MiLB season.

> *We like our beer flat as can be . . .*
> *We like our dogs with MUSTARD AND REL-ISH!*

It was catchy. But by July and the ten thousandth playing of "The Cheap Seats," it was a little too catchy. Playing and hearing "MUSTARD AND REL-ISH!" had become like eating your vegetables. You knew you had to do it, but you no longer wanted to.

> *We got a great pitcher, what's-his-name . . .*
> *Well, we can't even SPELL IT.*

Ron, however, never seemed to tire of it. And if he hadn't heard it in a while, our walkie-talkies would rattle to life. "Gary, dammit, let's hear some 'Cheap Seats'!"

> *We just like to see the boys hit it deep.*
> *There's nothing like the view . . . from the CHEAP SEATS.*
> *(super-twangy guitar solo)*

Ron also really loved Gary Glitter's "Rock and Roll, Part 1." You know the one, the stadium anthem with the tribal drumbeat and the sliding guitar.

> *Nun-nun-nuuhhhh-nuh*
> *N-nuh-nuh*

And Ron *really* loved one-hit wonder Napoleon XIV's 1966 nonclassic "They're Coming to Take Me Away." Whenever an opposing pitcher was being pulled off the mound and sent to the showers, Ron would push the transmission button on his radio and say nothing more than "Gary, play it!"

> *(Clap-clap-clappity-clap)*
> *They're coming to take me away, HAHA . . .*
> *They're coming to take me away, HO HO, HEE HEE,*
> *   HA HA . . .*
> *(Clap-clap-clappity-clap)*

One night, Gary pressed play, looked at me, and said, "If I keep playing this song, they're going to have to take me away."

I couldn't walk the stands during a game without one of the members of the Pinch Hitters Club asking me to verify if all the stuff Ron was saying to them about Gary was real, because if it was . . . well . . . Ron was their man and *by gawd he's the guy that got us here doing it how it did it!* It was a real-life manifestation of the conversation I had eavesdropped on at that luncheon I crashed back at the Winter Meetings half a year earlier. What was it Mr. Bryant had said to me? *"You are catching our business at a helluva time, Ryan. It is fun. It will always be fun. We are in this business to have fun. But make no mistake about it, buddy, it is still a business."*

The ways in which the business of Minor League Baseball was done had become a fistfight wherever the games were played. From the Appleton Foxes and the Shreveport Captains to the Vancouver Canadians and the Medicine Hat Blue Jays, the entire minor-league world was in a tug-of-war. They worried about how to maintain a balance between the old ways of doing things, the very methods that had gotten them all to where they were now, and the newer, increasingly corporatized practices that might very well be their only chance of surviving in the future. When we were down in the ticket office keeping track of daily sales, all in cash, by jotting hashtags with a pencil onto a sheet of paper, Ron and

Carolyn saw a tried-and-true way of doing baseball business. Gary and Eileen saw a dinosaur walking headfirst into the tar pits.

I could always see both sides. What pained me was the tension between two men I genuinely looked up to. They had both seen something in me, Carlton, Swish, R.J., and Lee, and yet, their relationship was doomed. Everyone knew it. It was only a question of when it was going to end and how much collateral damage would be done before that time finally came. I hated it. I loved Gary and Eileen. They cooked for us. They invited us to stay in a friend's lake house and let me pilot the pontoon boat all weekend. Gary gave me a copy of his book *Careers in Professional Baseball,* which I really could have used before tripping my way through the Winter Meetings. I even babysat their dog, Sundance.

I also loved Ron and Carolyn. They never failed to ask me how I was doing. When my parents visited, they treated Mom and Dad like royalty. Ron and I even had a season-long inside joke about our names. When spoken in the deep-throated dialect of western North Carolina, "Ron McKee" and "Ryan McGee" sound nearly identical. That led to a lot of phone call confusion. I fielded a lot of calls from sales clients and vendors who had asked for Ron McKee and instead got Ryan McGee. In return, Ron McKee accidentally met my brother and my college roommates over the phone because they'd asked for Ryan McGee and got Ron McKee. And did I mention those $50 handshakes?

So, when one would complain about the other right after they'd left the room, be it Ron talking about Gary or Gary talking about Ron, it genuinely hurt my heart.

For me personally, the biggest loss in their fight was my dream of being the radio voice of the Asheville Tourists. Ron had always been reluctant to jump into sportscasting because, well, *dammit, it cost money!* Gary had expressed concern to me early in the season about the challenge of broadcasting in the mountains. Asheville was a city ringed by three-thousand-foot ridges, so large chunks of the potential audience would always miss out because the hills and valleys of Appalachia were like walls that blocked radio signals from any transmission tower trying to push out a signal.

But in early June, I had taken a meeting with a man who had a solution to those problems. My father, a career college administrator and fundraiser, had a longtime working relationship and friendship with a pillar of the Asheville business community, Mr. Glenn Wilcox Sr. I had known him since I was six years old. He'd made millions in the travel industry and invested a large chunk of that success into a network of AM radio stations around western North Carolina. Mr. Wilcox loved baseball, almost as much as he loved money. So, when he had me up to his office, high atop downtown, he introduced me to the man who ran his radio stations, and they showed me a plan they had drawn up to broadcast Tourists home baseball games via a series of radio towers and stations that would reach from the foothills all the way to Tennessee. They would sell some of the ad inventory but would leave a sizable portion of that sales pie to our front office to do with what they pleased. Mr. Wilcox wanted me to take it to Ron immediately so that we could have our new Asheville Tourists Radio Network up and running by the season's second half.

"I will," I told him, trying hard to keep my throat from warbling nervously. "But I want to be the play-by-play announcer."

"Oh, don't worry," Mr. Wilcox said to me. "I was counting on that."

So, I took a second meeting, this time with Ron and Gary in Ron's office. I've never been more confident. I felt like Michael Jordan was back on the basketball court and I had the easiest job in the world, tossing His Airness an alley-oop pass and then standing back to watch him dunk it. Instead, I got Patrick Ewing blocking my shot into the upper deck. I honestly can't remember the details of how or why my radio proposal was thrown into the shredder. I just remember feeling like my spirit was leaving my body to float up into the back of Ron's office, next to Charlie Brown and his warning "Into each life some rain must fall . . ." Someone said something about timing. Someone said something about never having done this before. Someone said something about . . . I don't know, at some point the conversation became a broken record. Like Alabama's "Cheap Seats." So, like that song, and like so many of the conversations I had with Ron and Gary when they were together and started disagreeing again, it turned into background noise. I just tuned it out, waited for it to end, and went back to doing whatever my assignment was that day. Whatever it was, it was not going to be me on the radio.

For more than a month, no one spoke of it again. It was so strange. It was as if the meeting had never happened. I called Mr. Wilcox and told him our plan had essentially been tossed into the ballpark dumpster. He said to keep my chin up. "Ron can be a tough nut to crack, but he can be cracked. Anyone can if you keep applying a little bit of pressure."

Then, as the first of our four big August homestands ended, Ron called me into his office. He told me that he hadn't forgotten about the radio proposal, and he still wasn't convinced. But he also said that he wanted to talk about it some more, during the off-season. I cocked my head and crossed my brow. The internship was scheduled to end as soon as the season did, over Labor Day weekend.

"Carolyn and I have really enjoyed having you here this season. We all have. So, we want to figure out a way to keep you around. Not sure how yet. I have a feeling someone is probably going to be leaving," he said with a point of his eyes toward the door, down the hall and in the direction of Gary's office. "Maybe this winter we can talk about this radio thing. I'm not saying we're going to do it. We probably aren't. But if you are going to work for me full-time, you are going to have to learn how to sell people on doing stuff they don't want to do. So, think about how you want to sell me on us doing radio, but that is some shit that I really don't want to do."

I shook Ron McKee's hand, and he told me not to tell anyone about our conversation. "Hell, I should keep you around just because you have cut my phone calls in half this season, people asking for Ron McKee and then hanging up because they got Ryan McGee."

Then he reached down to the floor next to his desk, picked up a box, and slammed it down onto his desk. It was a dozen baseballs.

"Take these down to the clubhouse and get the team to sign them. If anyone down there gives you any more lip, tell them to come up here and they can try yelling at me."

He jerked open the desk drawer that we'd always heard about but had yet to see its contents. I leaned over. There it was. The gun. And yes, it was sitting next to a bottle of amber liquid, and they were both atop a magazine. I believe the publication was titled *Leg Show*.

"THE BIG CLUB IS SENDING YOU UP"

Julio the Cat died on Wednesday, August 17, 1994. I was not there. It was early in the morning, and the first staffer to arrive at the office, as was the case most days, was R. J. Martino. He was at the back door, on the top step, and was unlocking the office when he heard a familiar meowing that turned out to be Julio's last words. An hour later, when Carlton and I arrived at work, R.J. was waiting for me. He somberly informed me that he had greeted the familiar orange feline with a pleasant "Good morning, Julio, what's up?" The cat then let out a loud *GACK!* and lurched. R.J. said that Julio the Cat pulled up into what looked like a pouncing position, froze in place, and then just flopped over onto the ground, bereft of life. "I'm so sorry, McGee. It was so sudden. I think it must have been a heart attack or something."

Oh, there was no doubt in my mind that it was a heart attack, most likely brought on by a steady diet of bowls filled with a sugar-and-milk-ice-cream-mix concoction. Sorry, Julio.

By the time we'd gotten there, Julio's body had already been taken away by Animal Control. So, I went down to the Dairy Queen stand, pulled his batting helmet milk bowl from its secret hiding place, and buried it under a far corner of the McCormick

Field infield dirt, where in April, we'd first seen him and his two dozen feral friends gleefully rolling around in Speedy Dry.

I remember that exact date of Julio the Cat's departure from this world because of what happened later that afternoon. The announcement came from Carolyn, shouted from the office doorway out into the ballpark, where I was cleaning up the press box from the previous day's game. "Ryan McGee, you have a phone call!"

I hollered back. "Are you sure it's for Ryan McGee and not Ron McKee?"

She laughed and assured me that the call was indeed for me. I took it in the press box. "Hi, Ryan, it's Al Jaffe at ESPN. We would like to offer you a job as a temporary production assistant. It's a six-month contract, after which if you've done a good enough job, we will hire you full-time. Congratulations." I turned and looked at the Asheville Tourists schedule calendar that was pinned to the bulletin board on the press box wall and let out a snicker. On August 19, 1993, Al Jaffe had told me that if I hadn't heard from him within one year of that day, ESPN was never going to call. Now here he was, on the phone offering me a job. It had been 363 days.

I thanked him. Then I asked if I could have some time to think about it. He said no. I begged. I explained that I had a job. I said I couldn't just quit on them without at least talking to them first. What I didn't tell Mr. Jaffe was that only seven days earlier the general manager of a Minor League Baseball team had told me that he wanted to hire me full-time, with a chance—however slim it might be—of becoming a radio play-by-play man. Jaffe told me that he could give me until the end of the next day, that a little project called ESPN2 was growing faster than anticipated and they were in dire need of help. He said that if he hadn't heard from me by then, he would move on to the next person on his list. This was assuming that someone over the last year could have possibly had an answer to his hockey questions so much worse than mine that they were somehow ranked even lower than I had been.

When I hung up the phone, I slumped down into a press box chair and stared out into McCormick Field. It wasn't silent like it had been the first morning that Carlton and I had arrived for work. Now it was filled with the morning sounds of a minor-league ballpark getting ready for its fifty-seventh home game of the season. The rope on the outfield flagpole made a gentle metal slapping noise as it blew in the breeze, the flags flying because when R. J. Martino got to the office each morning, he always made sure the colors were up. Down the third baseline, I could hear just a little bit of Brooks & Dunn's "Boot Scootin' Boogie" playing from the groundskeeping shed and the Robin Hood smack of Grady Gardner's arrows thwapping into a target. Below me, I heard the Rolling Stones' newest album, *Voodoo Lounge,* snaking its way up through the concourse from Jane's office, now decorated with a poster I had drawn up for her of that album cover, proclaiming, "Welcome to Jane's Voodoo Lounge." In the box seats below, I could see Gary working his sales magic on a potential client, smiling, and pointing toward the billboards on the thirty-six-foot right-field monster wall as he was no doubt describing how amazing their corporate logo would look up there on a game night like tonight. In the distance, I could also see Eileen, carrying a box of new Bear Wear merch down the stairs to be displayed in her store. I heard the air brakes signifying the Bud Man's arrival to deliver a truckload of kegs before the next night, a Thirsty Thursday. The pop of a catcher's mitt came from down in the bullpen as Tomatoes Lamabe worked out the newest pitcher promoted from rookie ball, whose eyes could hopefully see home plate. Finally, I heard Ron McKee, laughing, as he stood on the Vatican Porch, joking with Carolyn about who-knew-what.

"Yo, McGee, we're getting lunch. You want anything?"

I looked up to see Carlton and Swish standing in the door of

the press box. I told them about the phone call. They both immediately started smiling and offered congratulations. Swish shook
my hand, and Carlton clapped and shouted out into the ballpark,
"MCGEE!" and gave me one of Earth's greatest sounds, the signature Carlton Adcock laugh.

I spent that afternoon talking to people about my decision, and
when I say people, I mean everyone, from Gary and R.J. to Jane
and Eileen to the game night employees. From the Earwood family and the Hooters manager ticket tearer to Linda and Pam at the
beer stand. I talked to Van and Sherri. If Julio the Cat had still
been alive, I would have talked to him about it too. To me, there
was still a decision to be made. What if I moved to Bristol, Connecticut, and that six-month trial period at ESPN went as badly
as my job interview had? That would put me back into the unem-
ployment line and well after the 1995 minor-league season had
already started, meaning it would be way too late to land a baseball
job. Ron was already offering me a baseball job. And man, I still
loved McCormick Field SO much. That night at the retirement
village it was like I was back in Atlanta, pacing the floor of my
cousin's guest room as I debated whether to take a $100-a-week
internship with the Asheville Tourists or hold out for that nonpay-
ing radio gig with the New Britain Red Sox and their blind color
commentator. I called my parents. I called my brother. I called my
college roommates. I didn't sleep a wink.

The next morning, when we rolled into the office, Ron was
standing on the Vatican Porch. He pointed at me. "I hear you have
talked to everyone in this ballpark about some ESPN job offer you
got, except for me. I also hear that you have to decide about this
today. And you look like shit, so I'm guessing this isn't going so
great. Let's talk."

We went into his office, and he shut the door behind us. I sat
down, took a deep breath, and braced my vocal cords to begin

reciting the same pros-and-cons list that I had given everyone else the night before. Mid-inhalation, Ron McKee stopped me.

"Ryan, why the hell are we even discussing this right now? You're taking that job. It's freaking ESPN." He pointed to his little office TV. It was of course the one time it wasn't tuned in to the Weather Channel. It was showing a *SportsCenter* special about the now-five-day-old Major League Baseball players strike. I explained the six-month trial period. He didn't care. "If you go up there and screw up or if they don't see a reason to keep you around, then you call me immediately. Even if I don't have something for you here, we'll find something with a team somewhere. I've been doing this for a while. I know some people."

Finally, I breathed.

"You got the guy's number at ESPN?" Ron held out his hand. I handed him the sheet of paper from the press box that I'd scribbled it onto, and he started dialing. When the ringtone started, he handed me the handset. I told Al Jaffe I was taking the job. He said he needed me there in one week. When I hung up, Ron stood up. He shook my hand. "Congratulations. We're all really proud of you. Just make sure you don't screw it up."

There was a beat of silence. He let go of my hand, and his smile vanished. "Now get your ass out of here. We still have a game tonight and you're really going to need this last hundred bucks. Living in Connecticut is expensive as hell."

We had a double-header that night. A freaking Thirsty Thursday double-header. The Tourists lost both games to the Charleston RiverDogs, by a combined score of 12–2, falling to a second-half record of 19-30, an unsurmountable eighteen and a half games behind first-place Hickory. But John Burke looked good in his first Asheville outing, and Edgard Velasquez smacked his tenth homer of the season.

As the second game wound down, Gary's voice crackled over

the walkie-talkies and said that I was needed in the grandstand. I figured an overserved Thirsty Thursday patron must have thrown up or a gang of kids tweaked up on blue snow cones had attacked someone. I popped up out of the stairwell into the main walkway. As soon as I did, Sam Zurich's voice boomed over the speakers and filled every rafter of McCormick Field. "Baseball fans, we are saying goodbye tonight to one of our own. Ryan McGee, the handsome gentleman you see standing there behind home plate, is leaving tomorrow to start a new job at ESPN. Thank you, Ryan, and good luck! Let's give him an Asheville Tourists send-off!"

The crowd stood and applauded. Attendance was officially listed as 2,880, but it was Thursday, so the number in the seating bowl was probably closer to five hundred. Still, it was amazing. As my eyes welled up, something grabbed my wrist and pulled my arm aloft, like a boxing referee signaling the winner of a bout. It was Ted E. Tourist. Jack, about whom we'd not received a groping complaint in months, broke his own rule and from inside the giant plastic head, I heard the actor saying to me, "A standing ovation! Congratulations!"

Right on cue, the song started playing. *"We like our beer flat as can be . . ."* It was Alabama. *"We like our dogs with MUSTARD AND REL-ISH!"* I looked up to the press box. *"We got a great pitcher, what's-his-name . . ."* Gary Saunders was smiling at me, nodding as he fake-grooved to the tune. Then he bit down on his lower lip with his teeth and started way overdancing to the summer's way overplayed baseball song. *"Well, we can't even spell it!"*

Okay, I lied to you earlier. I did make one more swing through the clubhouse that summer. And I did it on that last night. I wanted to say goodbye to trainer Marc Gustafson, the Tomato, Moose, and the skipper. Torchia motioned for me to come into his teensy office and stood as he set his phone down onto his desk. "I heard about the new job. Congratulations. I managed the Bristol Red Sox, just around the corner from ESPN, and also New

Britain, not too far away. You will like it. Pack a winter coat. Get some chains for the tires on that little car of yours. Go get some pizza in New Haven. Good luck."

Tony Torchia shook my hand, winked, and then sat back down at his desk as he put the phone back to his ear and started reading from his notebook into an answering machine two time zones away. "Sorry about the interruption. But as I was saying, I thought Burke really showed great command tonight, particularly with his first-pitch fastball. . . ."

One week later, I was in Connecticut. I'd spent my first day at ESPN in training. During my new employee's tour of the building, we walked through the *SportsCenter* newsroom, where Keith Olbermann and Dan Patrick were brainstorming with producers about how to fill another late August show with no Major League Baseball highlights. We visited the screening room, where rows of televisions that normally would have been looking in on MLB games from around the nation were instead showing the O. J. Simpson pretrial in Los Angeles and highlights of Michael Jordan's Birmingham Barons. "We're going to start broadcasting minor-league games to replace the big-league games we're losing to the strike," my tour guide explained, excitedly. "We've even gotten the rights to that Alabama song to use for the opening of the telecasts. You like that song?"

The next night my Pontiac Grand Am pulled into the parking lot of Beehive Field, the 4,700-seat chain-link-fence-dominated ballpark that was home to the New Britain Red Sox of the Class AA Eastern League. Jim Lucas's last words to me at the Winter Meetings were to let him know if I was ever in the area, and perhaps he'd even let me sit with him in the broadcast booth for an inning. So, I did. When I called him, he said to come on out that night as the Brit Sox were hosting the Binghamton Mets. When I entered the press box, it took me back to Monroe, North Carolina, calling high school football games with the Foxx on WIXE in

Dixie. I realized that we were in a converted football stadium. The press box was long and made of wood paneling that came right out of your grandparents' living room; it was a single-wide mobile home in the sky.

Jim greeted me with the politeness that I had seen in Atlanta. Then he introduced me to Don Wardlow, who sat there with his books of braille baseball statistics, and at his feet, there he was, Gizmo the seeing-eye dog. Earlier that summer they'd made history when they called an inning and a half of an MLB game, a June 24 matchup between the Cubs and Marlins.

Then Jim did something extraordinary and completely unexpected. He said, "Here, do an inning!" and before I could react, he had already pulled out his chair and was pushing me into his seat. Don welcomed the audience back from the commercial break and verbally reset the game situation, that Binghamton was at the plate in the top of the fourth inning. Then he introduced me as the play-by-play voice of the New Britain Red Sox for the next inning. The Mets scored a couple of runs. There was a long double off the wall. Every batter who came to the plate, I was mesmerized by Wardlow, who would stuff both hands into the binders of printed pages, swipe his fingers left and right, and then immediately start listing each batter's strengths and weaknesses, how they had performed earlier in the night, and even what their favorite movies were. I was so fascinated by Don that I completely forgot to keep score, Lucas having to grab the scorebook and pencil from in front of me to fill it out.

"Ryan McGee, our guest sportscaster, you strike me as the kind of guy who likes to quote movies all the time. Am I getting that right about you?" I thought to myself, *Oh, Don Wardlow, you have no idea. Just wait until a couple of decades from now when you read my book about all this.*

My six outs on the mic went by so fast. Then Jim Lucas took his place back in his seat, and they let me hang out and watch them work for a couple more innings. It was truly amazing to witness their mind-meld friendship producing a flawless baseball broadcast.

I spent the remainder of the game sitting in the aluminum bleachers of Beehive Field. That's when I realized I was never going to be able to watch a Minor League Baseball game the same way ever again. I caught myself eyeing the box seat patrons and wondering if the New Britain Red Sox had their own version of the Pinch Hitters Club or if they had ever considered employing box seat waitresses. I realized that it was a Thursday night and way too calm, so I wondered why they didn't call Ron and get permission to make it a Thirsty Thursday. I had a hot dog, a box of popcorn, and a blue snow cone, and rated them all as if I was Bobby Flay judging a chef's work on a reality cooking show. I laughed to myself, wondering what Big Mike was eating that night at McCormick Field.

I looked out across the parking lot and saw a construction site. New Britain was getting a new ballpark right next door to this one. With the new digs was coming a new name. The New Britain Red Sox would become the Hardware City Rock Cats, a nod to the town's longtime role as a tool manufacturer, along with a cartoon mascot feline that wore an Elvis pompadour with a leather jacket and sunglasses, ferociously stroking a guitar like The Who's Pete Townsend, all while giving a heavy-metal hand signal. If that reads like they were trying too hard, then I have written a very accurate description of the Hardware City Rock Cat.

Today, both Beehive Field and New Britain Stadium are still there, just up the road from ESPN headquarters, but both are largely empty. The local Minor League Baseball franchise is now downtown, the Hartford Yard Goats, playing in beautiful Dunkin' Donuts Park, built in 2016. But they were no longer members of the Eastern League. No one was. Now they played in the antiseptically renamed "Double-A East." All of the old league names were gone, even the Sally League, after surviving resurrections and revivals dating back to 1904. California League, International League, Texas League, some with origins that reached back to the 1880s, were torn apart and repurposed under the personality-stripped banners of "High-A" and "US-Based Rookie." It all went over like a wet loaf of bread and was thankfully corrected following the 2022 MiLB season. But saving league names wasn't enough to save the forty teams that vanished in 2021, cut from farm systems because they had been deemed unnecessary. By whom? By Major League Baseball, who formally took control of MiLB when the longtime business agreement between the two organizations expired at the end of the 2020 season, the same year when zero minor-league games were played because of the COVID-19 pandemic. For an industry that depends on front-gate cash flow, it was crippling. MLB swept in to take advantage and did so with a stunning lack of empathy or understanding.

Places like Burlington, Iowa, which had been home to a big-league-affiliated team since the Bees franchise was founded in 1889 and had played professional baseball at Community Field since 1947, lost their baseball team in December 2020. Now the Bees are a summer collegiate team. It's baseball, but it isn't the same. Similar stories are told in places like Burlington, Vermont, where Centennial Field, the 120-year-old home of the Vermont Lake Monsters, was deemed too old for MLB's tastes. Lancaster, California, home of the JetHawks and longtime popular entertainment spot for the thousands of military families in the area, was said to be in a high-desert location that made it too difficult for MLB scouts to accurately evaluate talent, so the team was axed. Staten Island, Lexington, Kentucky, Lowell, Massachusetts, and Hagerstown, Maryland, dozens of teams all wiped off the MiLB map. One must wonder and can safely assume that no one at Major League Baseball ever descended from their skyscraper offices in Rockefeller Center and traveled out to see what those teams, ballparks, and the experiences they combined to create on a midsummer Saturday night meant to those communities.

What's more, those same suits are now demanding that many of the teams who did survive the purge have to make sweeping capital improvements to their ballparks, and they must pay for said improvements with nary a dollar of help from Major League Baseball itself. In 2021, the Asheville Tourists front office was handed a list of mandatory facility changes from MLB that totaled more than $22 million. In 1992, McCormick Field was reconstructed from the ground up for $3 million. Even when adjusted for inflation, that price tag comes out to one-fourth of what is being demanded of them today. Not to tear down and start over, but to cross off a tediously endless checklist of tasks such as widening doors and replacing showers. A list drawn up by MLB's labor attorneys. Yes, the same good-natured, stadium cup–half-empty folks who brought you the 1994 players strike that canceled the World Series and, as this book was being written, the owners lockout that had delayed the start of the 2022 MLB season.

In late fall 2022, as this book was headed to print, team president Brian DeWine made a public plea for help, warning that if city and county leaders didn't pledge future financial aid before the start of the 2023 baseball season—the very week this book was scheduled for release—then the upcoming summer might very well be the last for the Asheville Tourists.

Imagine someone with an actual beating heart, who claims to love baseball, looking at a spreadsheet on a computer at a Fifth Avenue Starbucks and deciding that the national pastime in the very places where it truly touches the hearts of that nation might be better off without McCormick Field. Without the next Ron McKee or Gary Saunders. Without James the Mountain Man braving snakebites to retrieve baseballs. Without the Circuit Rider and the Two-Eyed Redeemer galloping in to save souls before a Sunday-afternoon matinee. Without jazz saxophone national anthems, panty-less miniskirt haircuts atop the home team dugout, and mascot fights. Without a McCormick Field sunset, settling in over the ballpark as fireworks explode overhead and—sure, why not?—Alabama's "Cheap Seats" reverberating off the trees, the forest, and the honeysuckle vines that line the magnificent little bandbox carved into a nook of the Blue Ridge Mountains.

That's the imagery I carry in my head. It's what I see in my mind's eye the very instant someone mentions the Asheville Tourists or McCormick Field. It has been that way every single day of my life since the summer of 1994, and it will be that way until I depart this Earth to be rejoined with Julio the Cat.

"My, my, what a ballpark! What a beautiful place to play. Delightful. Damned delightful place!"

As I drove out of the Beehive Field parking lot in New Britain, headed to my new home to start my new job, I thought of Babe Ruth's words. I already missed McCormick Field terribly. But then I remembered that on that very night, my baseball dream had finally come true. I had done an inning of professional radio play-by-play. I reached down to the dashboard and turned the radio knob. There it was. The New Britain Red Sox postgame show, the very program I once had interviewed to host. The guy who got the job instead of me was recapping the game, a big late-season win for the home team. I realized he was talking about my inning! He said, "Binghamton got onto the scoreboard in the top of the fourth, and here's how it sounded. Describing the action is a special guest of Jim and Don, Ryan McGee. . . ."

It was the long double off the wall. I pulled my Pontiac over to the side of the road and leaned into the speaker in the driver's-side door so that I could hear it more clearly. I wished I hadn't.

My call, it was terrible.

WHERE ARE THEY NOW?

On Saturday, September 25, 2021, the patrons of McCormick Field took their seats. This time there was no ball game. Instead, a podium had been placed by home plate and a blue Chevy Impala convertible was parked on the infield grass. It was a memorial service for Ron McKee, who had passed away four days earlier at the age of seventy-five. I tried so hard to attend, but work had sent me to Columbia, South Carolina, that morning, and there was no way I could get from there up the mountain to Asheville in time for the midafternoon ceremony. Jane was there. So was R.J. They were joined by a couple of hundred other people, including general managers and front-office executives from countless MiLB teams around the nation. Nearly every person in attendance had worked at the ballpark in some capacity, proud citizens of what was most definitely a dictatorship and not a democracy. But it was also a family tree.

Most of the stories that were told that day were like that dictatorship line, everyone recalling Ron's revolving door of very direct truths. *"Don't tell me about the labor pains, just show me the baby."*

Ron and Woody Kern owned the Asheville Tourists until 2005, when they sold the franchise for $6 million to Palace Sports &

Entertainment, owners of the just-crowned NHL Stanley Cup champion Tampa Bay Lightning, the Detroit Pistons, and a handful of arenas and amphitheaters. PS&E sank a lot of money into McCormick Field but kept the charm of the ballpark largely intact. They sold the franchise to the DeWine family of Ohio in 2010, who immediately implemented an image rebrand, sending Ted E. Tourist into semi-retirement when they designed a new mascot and logo of a Tourist with a bag over his shoulder and ready to travel, but with a lunar head. They called him Mr. Moon, a nod to the old Asheville Moonshiners name that predated the use of Tourists.

Today's general manager had been an intern just two seasons after I was. Larry Hawkins loves the Asheville Tourists, McCormick Field, and the McKee family. When I dropped by the ballpark for a visit and some book research in late August 2021, it was Larry who informed me that Ron's health had been failing. We called Carolyn to see if we might stop by and visit, but when she hesitated, I figured that meant Ron wasn't up for company. I convinced myself that was okay, because I would be coming back through town in October to cover a football game in Knoxville. I was anxious to share the first draft of this book with him, though I knew reading it would come with an afternoon of very loud suggestions and corrections. October turned out to be too late. Not sure if I'll ever forgive myself for that.

Gary Saunders did indeed leave the Asheville Tourists after the 1994 season. Gary and Ron never mended fences, and their rift played no small part in Gary being forced to find work in independent-league baseball as Ron's lengthy list of loyalists kept their distance from Gary in the years that followed his time in Asheville. He did, however, become GM of multiple teams, including the Myrtle Beach Pelicans of the Class A Carolina League. Always a tremendous writer, his memoir *Runaway Train* about his time as GM of the Meridian Brakemen is an unvarnished and downright stress-inducing look at the challenges of navigating independent, non-MLB-affiliated Minor League Baseball, where the front office doesn't just manage the ballpark, but also has to find and sign players for their rosters. After a dozen years in the Ole Miss athletic department, Gary semi-retired to Florida, where Eileen sells real estate. It should also surprise no one that Gary found his way into another press box, on the microphone as the Sam Zurich and DJ for the Pittsburgh Pirates spring training and minor-league complex in Bradenton, Florida, home of the Marauders.

R.J. stayed with the Tourists for several seasons and has had a tremendous career in sports business, from the Charlotte Knights and Tampa Bay Lightning to the Florida Panthers and the University of Miami. We reconnected in 2020, when he oversaw local sales and operations for Miami's hosting of the 2021 College Football Playoff National Championship game. But that game ended up being the only college football national title game I have missed since 2011. Thanks, COVID. When my daughter was little, she watched *Richie Rich* entirely too many times. Three minutes into each viewing she never failed to scream, "It's Dad's friend!"

When I asked R.J. for his greatest Ron McKee lesson, he said it came from what had bugged him most about his first weeks with the Tourists. It was always a little awkward that R.J. had his desk sitting in the front-office lobby, and sure, it was because there wasn't an open office to put him in, but he says now that he realizes there was also a method to Ron's madness. The boss liked to eavesdrop on rookie salesperson R.J.'s sales calls. "I would be on the phone with someone, trying to convince them that buying an eighth of a page ad in our game program was the greatest purchase of their lives, and in the middle of it, Ron would start yelling from his office," R.J. recalled. "He would say, 'Don't do that over the phone! Schedule an appointment! Go see them in person!' That was, what, thirty years ago? And that's still how I prefer to do deals now. That's the Ron McKee in me."

Jane, now Jane Nanney Exner, is still in Asheville, still raising her beloved Scottish terriers, still rocking out to the Stones, still frustrated by idiots, and still making me laugh. The next time I saw her after I left the ballpark in '94 was four years later, when she surprised me by coming all the way to Charlotte for my wedding. She stayed employed with Ron and Carolyn the longest before eventually moving on to various jobs around the county, wherever they needed someone to get their numbers in order and, yes, to get some idiots in order. She is my go-to whenever I am wondering what happened to all the folks who worked at the ballpark that summer. Jane has kept track of them all. Thanks to Facebook, I've kept tabs on a lot of them as well, especially the Earwoods. Chastity has a beautiful family of four. One day I was sitting in the crowd of a PTA meeting at my daughter's elementary school in Charlotte when I spotted a woman with her family walking in the door. "Dang," I told my wife, "that looks just like Jennifer from the snow cone stand!" And it was. She lives about a mile away from where I am writing this sentence in my home office.

Carlton Adcock and I never go more than a few months without texting. And just like it was back in the day, the topics of conversation are random, but usually related to sports. He married way up and moved to Boston, where he has become an amazing father to a pair of precocious girls. He and Stephen Whitt have stayed in touch all these years, getting together for NASCAR races in Bristol, Tennessee, and football games back on campus at the University of Tennessee. Nearly two decades later I was finally able to hook up with them on the eve of a NASCAR event I was covering at Bristol Motor Speedway. We met at Carlton's parents' house, and his father prepared us perfect steaks, cooked on a grill with a working igniter button. We all looked older. Swish looked exactly the same. Hell, I think he was actually better looking than he was in '94, and of course he was. Lee Tillery has had a fantastic career in parks and recreation management. He is currently overseeing operations in High Point, North Carolina, where among his end-less list of duties is working with the High Point Rockers, an inde-pendent minor-league team that plays in a sparkling city-owned ballpark. Their president is Pete Fisch, who was a youngster on the staff of the 1994 Hickory Crawdads. All I had to do was ask Fisch one question about the '94 Sally League All-Star weekend and he became instantly exhausted.

Both Tillery and Fisch ended up working with Mark Seaman. Remember him? I always felt terrible about taking that last intern-ship spot with the Tourists, but it was Mark who went on to have the most distinguished MiLB career of us all, and it's not even close. He became GM of both the Knoxville Smokies and Hickory Crawdads and is now an executive with the city of Hickory.

Tony Torchia managed two more minor-league teams, the Brevard County Manatees and the Mid-Missouri Mavericks, in 2002–03. In between Asheville and those gigs, he served as a hit-ting coach throughout Class AAA ball, in Las Vegas, Colorado Springs, and New Orleans, still always one step below the big leagues. He also spent time working with MLB's international ini-tiative and still worked as a substitute teacher back home in South Florida during the off-season. Always teaching.

Moose McGuire returned to Asheville in '95, where at the age of thirty-one he coached the Tourists to a 76-63 record before mov-ing on to two seasons in High Class A Salem, Virginia, before leav-ing the bench to become one of college baseball's most respected umpires. His pitching coach in '95 was Jack Lamabe, who died on December 21, 2007, back in Baton Rouge, where he had once coached the LSU baseball team. The very next year I wrote a book about college baseball, and LSU was a huge part of that story. I found myself in Baton Rouge working on it, wishing I could call the Tomato. Again, I was too late.

A total of thirty-nine players wore the uniform of the Asheville Tourists in 1994, and only five of them made it to The Show, four if you remove rehabbing Darren Holmes from the equation. John Burke made it to the Colorado Rockies in '96 and made twenty-eight appearances over two seasons with a record of 4-6. Then his baseball career was over. Edgard Velasquez changed his name to Edgard Clemente in '98 and later that year made his MLB debut with the Rockies. Over parts of the next three seasons, two with Colorado and one with the Anaheim Angels, he hit eight homers and drove in thirty-two runs. John Thomson, the Mississippian who'd handed out batting helmets to protect us from Captain Dynamite's body parts, pitched in the big leagues for ten seasons with five different teams, most notably as a 14-8 starter with the 2004 NL East–winning Atlanta Braves.

It's been fun over the years tracking the other guys. Keith Grunewald became a player agent, applying the lessons he learned as a two-time MLB draft pick and five years in the minors to guide those on that same baseball ladder. I was covering an event in Tampa and thought I recognized a sheriff's deputy, standing watch with his K-9 unit, and I had. It was Jacob Viano. As I have covered college baseball over the years, I have seen names such as Doug "Snake" Walls and Nate Holdren pop up as high school coaches and youth hitting instructors. Once, during my early work travels with ESPN, I had an issue with a rental car in Connecticut, and when the manager came out to apologize and fix the situation, it was John "Juice" Giudice, who went on to a career in medical sales. Trainer Marc Gustafson moved up through the ranks quickly and has been in the front office of the Colorado Rockies for more than a quarter of a century, most recently as senior director of amateur scouting operations.

As for the Bonus Baby, Jamey Wright made his major-league debut with the Colorado Rockies on July 3, 1996. He went on to pitch in nineteen (!!) big-league seasons, spending time on the rosters of ten different teams. Nearly all those years were spent in middle relief, as a reliable ground ball producer, and most of those seasons began as a nonroster invitee to spring training, meaning he had to earn his way into the big-league clubhouse by Opening Day. He pulled that off twelve times. Now he channels his inner Tomato as a special minor-league pitching instructor with the Los Angeles Dodgers.

"That was a special group in Asheville," he recalled to me from his home in Dallas, where he was about to go full dad mode and spend an afternoon driving kids to various sports practices. "A big chunk of us ended up together in [Class AA] New Haven the next year too. Here's all you need to know about those guys. It's been more than twenty-five years, and there's still a group text I have with a bunch of them. That just doesn't happen with guys who were in the minors together."

Jamey Wright paused. Then he added one last thought before jumping into the truck. "I've really enjoyed talking to you, McGee. We should have talked more that summer. Seems like we would have gotten along."

As I write these final words of this book, I do so at a desk that is covered in game programs, ticket stubs, and photos from the summer of 1994. My Ted E. Tourist baseball card is framed on the wall. A baseball signed by the team, the one that Ron told me to take for myself, is in an acrylic holder on my bookshelf. Most of the names on that ball are faded, but I can still read Tony Torchia and Jamey Wright. Nate Holdren's cracked bat is leaning against my office chair.

They all bring back memories. They all make me smile. I hope that my sharing of those memories has also made you smile.

Long live Julio the Cat.

ACKNOWLEDGMENTS

Anyone who has ever attempted to write a book will immediately express to you how difficult that task can be, and they are speaking the truth. However, in this case, I honestly cannot remember ever sitting down at the keyboard and not smiling the entire time that my fingers were banging away. That's how much I loved the summer of 1994 and the people who experienced that season with me.

It is why the most enjoyable aspect of this project was reuniting with a lot of those people, be it in person, on the phone, or online. Rapid-fire texts with Carlton Adcock. Dinner with Jane Nanney Exner. Climbing into the kudzu behind the McCormick Field outfield wall with current Tourists president Larry Hawkins. Reading Gary Saunders's fantastic manuscript about his time with the Meridian Brakemen. Laughing in the grandstand of the former home of the Winston-Salem Warthogs, now the ballpark of the Wake Forest University Demon Deacons, as I exchanged memories with Lee Tillery. Firing off random two a.m. Facebook messages to the likes of Amber Burgess and R. J. Martino to ask, "Hey, I know it was like thirty years ago, but you sold pizzas in concessions, right?" and "Wasn't your desk in the lobby?" Phone conversations with former Tourists ballplayers, all of whom shared awesome stories that made me wish we'd had a closer relationship back in '94 (they said Nate Holdren is a good guy who'd had a bad day with me and the signed baseballs) and also shared some information that made me kinda glad that we didn't hang out (they also said that Holdren had a habit of expectorating tobacco juice all over whatever ground he was standing on, even if it was carpeted).

There were also the talks with those who are no longer with us, the memories of conversations that I've kept in my mind all these years. The chattering of Ron McKee, the baritone boom of Sam Zurich, and the narrator's tone of Bob Terrell, as clear to me now as if they were back in the McCormick Field press box together. Thankfully, Terrell's words still live on in the archives of the *Asheville Citizen-Times,* files that proved invaluable as I tried to sharpen up my fuzzy memories of Tourists games gone by. Bob's work also lined my library. His books on McCormick Field, *The Old Ball Yard,* and *Field of Reality* sit on a shelf alongside the works of former Tourists PR man Bill Ballew, who took the torch from Terrell in the twenty-first century and carried on the important task of preserving McCormick's legacy via a series of books and stories.

Many thanks to the incomparable Jane Dystel and the entire team at Dystel, Goderich & Bourret. When we very first chatted several years ago, she asked me, "What's the book you've always wanted to write?" This was the answer, and she made it happen.

Also, thank you to my new friends at Doubleday. Jason Kaufman's guidance and enthusiasm are a writer's dream. Ana Espinoza did an amazing job of keeping the damage done by my deadline-stretching skills and short attention span down to a minimum. Production editor Nora Reichard successfully navigated and course-corrected my Southern-isms and self-taught punctuation skills. And thank you to those who deal with me on a daily basis, my friends and colleagues at ESPN who gave me the green-light and the time to pursue a passion project.

I sleep with my other editor, the unfortunate Mrs. Erica McGee, who had already heard so many of these stories over and over after so many years of marriage, and then was subjected to my recalling them all again, in print. All of this while she was working on a massive writing project of her own. Daughter Tara is the soon-to-be college student whom we took to McCormick Field as a little girl simply so that I could spend nine innings pointing and saying, "That's where your dad flew in the air on the tarp!"

Speaking of dads, our family's love of baseball is begat directly from his blood. Pops and I still sit together at minor-league baseball games, spending at least a few summer evenings watching our beloved Charlotte Knights. Yes, we still critique the quality of the hot dogs and the creativity of the promotions, guests, and giveaways.

But the greatest thanks go to those who make all that happen. The folks who clock in at minor-league ballparks every single night. I finished this book as the 2022 MiLB season was coming to a close and my "Ballparks Visited" list that I keep on my laptop was at 129. I book my work travel around games. I've hit every corner of the nation, from the New Hampshire Fisher Cats and Daytona Tortugas to the Eugene Emeralds and El Paso Chihuahuas. I've eaten a batting helmet full of nachos via the Tulsa Drillers, gnawed on a corn cob from the Cedar Rapids Kernels, and scarfed down a plate of honey-covered biscuits from, naturally, the Montgomery Biscuits. Over the last two years I've worn more than a hundred different minor-league ball caps on our *Marty & McGee* TV show. Why? Because I love it.

But my love for the game takes a backseat to my respect for those who work in the game. None of them are getting rich. None of them are getting any sleep. None of them are getting any recognition or attention. They are totally cool with that. They do it because they love it, even when the baseball powers that be seemingly work so hard to make life harder for them.

That's why we should all love them back. And it's why I hope my collection of stories from my brief time among them does them proud.

ILLUSTRATION CREDITS

Page 3, bottom left: Courtesy of Gary Saunders
Page 5, center right: Courtesy of Gary Saunders
Page 8, center right: Courtesy of Gary Saunders
Page 8, bottom right: Courtesy of ESPN Images
All other images courtesy of Ryan McGee

ABOUT THE AUTHOR

Ryan McGee is a senior writer for ESPN and cohost of *Marty & McGee* on ESPN Radio. He has won five Sports Emmys, including two for his scriptwriting and feature work on *College Gameday*. McGee has authored several books, including cowriting the *New York Times* bestseller *My Race to the Finish* with NASCAR superstar Dale Earnhardt Jr. He also works as a field reporter for ESPN's *SportsCenter* and feature reporter for *E:60*. McGee lives in North Carolina with his family.